Also Available From

Achieving a Healthy V ... Action Plan for Families

Allergies and As......... what Every Parent Needs to Know

Autism Spectrum Disorder: What Every Parent Needs to Know

Baby and Toddler Basics: Expert Answers to Parents' Top 150 Questions

The Big Book of Symptoms: A–Z Guide to Your Child's Health

Building Resilience in Children and Teens: Giving Kids Roots and Wings

Caring for Your Adopted Child: An Essential Guide for Parents

Caring for Your Baby and Young Child: Birth to Age 5*

Dad to Dad: Parenting Like a Pro

Food Fights: Winning the Nutritional Challenges of Parenthood Armed
With Insight, Humor, and a Bottle of Ketchup

Guide to Toilet Training*

Heading Home With Your Newborn: From Birth to Reality

Mama Doc Medicine: Finding Calm and Confidence in Parenting, Child Health,
and Work-Life Balance

My Child Is Sick! Expert Advice for Managing Common Illnesses and Injuries

Nutrition: What Every Parent Needs to Know

Parenting Through Puberty: Mood Swings, Acne, and Growing Pains

The Picky Eater Project: 6 Weeks to Happier, Healthier Family Mealtimes

Raising an Organized Child: 5 Steps to Boost Independence, Ease Frustration,
and Promote Confidence

Raising Kids to Thrive: Balancing Love With Expectations and Protection With Trust

Retro Baby: Cut Back on All the Gear and Boost Your Baby's Development
With More Than 100 Time-tested Activities

Retro Toddler: More Than 100 Old-School Activities to Boost Development

Sleep: What Every Parent Needs to Know

Waking Up Dry: A Guide to Help Children Overcome Bedwetting

Your Baby's First Year*

*This book is also available in Spanish.

**For additional parenting resources, visit the HealthyChildren bookstore at
https://shop.aap.org/for-parents.**

What Every Parent Needs to Know

ADHD

3rd Edition

Mark L. Wolraich, MD, FAAP

Joseph F. Hagan Jr, MD, FAAP

American Academy of Pediatrics

DEDICATED TO THE HEALTH OF ALL CHILDREN®

American Academy of Pediatrics Publishing Staff

Mary Lou White, *Chief Product and Services Officer/SVP, Membership, Marketing, and Publishing*

Mark Grimes, *Vice President, Publishing*

Holly Kaminski, *Editor, Consumer Publishing*

Shannan Martin, *Production Manager, Consumer Publications*

Jason Crase, *Manager, Editorial Services*

Sara Hoerdeman, *Marketing Manager, Consumer Products*

Published by the American Academy of Pediatrics

345 Park Blvd

Itasca, IL 60143

Telephone: 630/626-6000

Facsimile: 847/434-8000

www.aap.org

The American Academy of Pediatrics is an organization of 67,000 primary care pediatricians, pediatric medical subspecialists, and pediatric surgical specialists dedicated to the health, safety, and well-being of infants, children, adolescents, and young adults.

The information contained in this publication should not be used as a substitute for the medical care and advice of your pediatrician. There may be variations in treatment that your pediatrician may recommend based on individual facts and circumstances.

Statements and opinions expressed are those of the authors and not necessarily those of the American Academy of Pediatrics.

Any websites, brand names, products, or manufacturers are mentioned for informational and identification purposes only and do not imply an endorsement by the American Academy of Pediatrics (AAP). The AAP is not responsible for the content of external resources. Information was current at the time of publication.

The persons whose photographs are depicted in this publication are professional models. They have no relation to the issues discussed. Any characters they are portraying are fictional.

The publishers have made every effort to trace the copyright holders for borrowed materials. If they have inadvertently overlooked any, they will be pleased to make the necessary arrangements at the first opportunity.

This publication has been developed by the American Academy of Pediatrics. The contributors are expert authorities in the field of pediatrics. No commercial involvement of any kind has been solicited or accepted in development of the content of this publication. Disclosures: The editors report no disclosures.

Every effort is made to keep *ADHD: What Every Parent Needs to Know* consistent with the most recent advice and information available from the American Academy of Pediatrics.

Special discounts are available for bulk purchases of this publication. Email Special Sales at aapsales@aap.org for more information.

Printed in the United States of America

9-410/0519   1 2 3 4 5 6 7 8 9 10

CB0110

ISBN: 978-1-61002-264-4

eBook: 978-1-61002-265-1

EPUB: 978-1-61002-266-8

Kindle: 978-1-61002-267-5

PDF: 978-1-61002-268-2

Cover design by Daniel Rembert

Publication design by R. Scott Rattray

Original artwork by Anthony Alex LeTourneau

Library of Congress Control Number: 2018943109

Reviewers and Contributors

Editors

Mark L. Wolraich, MD, FAAP
CMRI/Shaun Walters Professor of Pediatrics
Chief, Section on Developmental and Behavioral Pediatrics
Director, Child Study Center
University of Oklahoma Health Sciences Center
Oklahoma City, OK

Joseph F. Hagan Jr, MD, FAAP
Clinical Professor in Pediatrics
Larner College of Medicine
University of Vermont Children's Hospital
Burlington, VT

Reviewers and Contributors

American Academy of Pediatrics Subcommittee on Attention-Deficit/
Hyperactivity Disorder

We would also like to thank the contributors, technical reviewers, medical writers, and the editor in chief of the previous editions, Michael I. Reiff, MD, FAAP, for all their work on the first and second editions of this book.

To my daughter, who has worked so hard to manage her ADHD.

Mark L. Wolraich, MD, FAAP

To the wonderful patients and families who have partnered with me over the years to find their strengths to successfully manage the ADHD portion of their lives. Each of you has much to be proud of.

Joseph F. Hagan Jr, MD, FAAP

Contents

Please Note

Many kinds of health care professionals provide primary care for children and manage their attention-deficit/hyperactivity disorder. These include pediatricians, pediatric nurse practitioners, and pediatric physician assistants, as well as family medicine physicians, family nurse practitioners, physician assistants, and others. To be inclusive and specific, we will refer to your child's health professional as a *pediatric clinician*. Likewise, both women and men are pediatric clinicians, so expect alternating pronouns for us as well.

The information contained in the book is intended to complement, not substitute for, the advice of your child's pediatric clinician. Before starting any medical treatment or medical program, you should consult with your child's pediatric clinician, who can discuss your child's individual needs and counsel you about symptoms and treatment. If you have any questions about how the information in this book applies to your child, speak to your child's pediatric clinician.

A Note on Gender

A good deal of discussion went into the use of pronouns *he* and *she* in this book, particularly when describing different subtypes of attention-deficit/hyperactivity disorder (ADHD) or different problems faced by children with ADHD. Although boys and girls can have any subtype of ADHD or any of the related problems, the ratio of boys to girls diagnosed with ADHD is about 3 to 1, and the combined type of ADHD, with all 3 key elements (impulsivity, hyperactivity, and inattention), is diagnosed about 2½ times more frequently than the predominantly inattentive type. However, if all the children in a school system were evaluated, it is likely that the inattentive type would be found to be about 1½ times more common than the combined type; the inattentive type is more likely to go undiagnosed, and girls are more likely to have that subtype than boys. With this as background, we have attempted to balance the use of *he* and *she* pronouns in this book in an interchangeable way.

Introduction

You have probably picked up this copy of *ADHD: What Every Parent Needs to Know* either because your child was recently diagnosed with attention-deficit/hyperactivity disorder (ADHD) or because you wish to learn more information about how you can best help your child with his ADHD. This book is the combined work of many health care and mental health professionals with expert levels of experience in caring for children like your child. All these colleagues are convinced that children, adolescents, and adults with ADHD, as well as the families that support them, will have the most success in school and in life if they understand what ADHD is, how it is properly treated, what to expect, and how families, teachers, and pediatric clinicians can work together for the lifelong management of ADHD.

Almost all children have times when their attention or behavior veers out of control. For some children these types of behaviors are more than just an occasional problem. Children with ADHD have behavior problems that are so frequent and significant that they interfere with their ability to function adequately on a daily basis. Attention-deficit/hyperactivity disorder is the most commonly diagnosed developmental-behavioral condition in children. Approximately 6% to 9% of school-aged children are affected. It is a chronic condition whose symptoms continue in 60% to 80% of adolescents and even into adulthood. It can have effects on children's learning, ability to regulate behavior, social skills, and self-esteem.

If you are just starting out and learning about a new diagnosis of ADHD, or if you have just experienced a bump in the road or a setback in your child's treatment, turn your attention to the not-so-distant future. Someday, before very long, your child will graduate high school and go off to college or enter the workforce. In *ADHD: What Every Parent Needs to Know*, you will learn about how to build your child's ADHD support and management team so that he can enjoy his success. You will learn what ADHD is and what it is not. You will be better prepared to make treatment decisions. You will be able to choose treatments that are proven to be effective and to ignore claims for treatments that do not work. You will learn to use your own strengths as parents to build your child's confidence to support his success. Your pediatric clinician will help you understand that your child can succeed, and how you can help.

Today's print and online media bombard parents with a mind-clogging glut of advice. Media reports claim that ADHD is both overdiagnosed and underdiagnosed! Many argue ADHD is overtreated, but careful studies show that it is often undertreated. Claims for medications can range from "groundbreaking" to "dangerous." How can a responsible parent sort through this quagmire of contradictory information?

In this book you will learn when to suspect ADHD and how it must be carefully diagnosed. Careful and accurate diagnosis is the most important first step in helping your child.

Once your child is diagnosed with ADHD, now what? How can you and your child's pediatric clinician, teachers, and others help your child address his problems and begin to experience success? It can happen! You will learn treatment options and be guided in how to choose wisely for your child. And since not every child's treatment is immediately successful, you will learn to be an advocate for your child, and you will be alerted to other problems that might complicate your child's ADHD.

Discussions of evidence will be commonly found in this book. With so many contradicting opinions about the best treatment for ADHD, it is helpful to learn how to identify true evidence about treatments and to carefully analyze claims of effectiveness. You will want to become skilled at deciding what to consider and what to ignore. You will learn how to assess these claims about various treatments. There are alternative and complementary treatments for ADHD you may wish to consider, as there is evidence that they are effective in certain ways. There are also such treatments where the evidence shows that they do not work—or are even possibly harmful!

What will the future bring for your child's teen years and beyond? Your success in helping your child with ADHD will grow from your understanding of this condition. You will find that some things come easy for you child and other things are hard. You will learn to help your child manage his ADHD by finding his strengths and helping him apply these strengths to build his confidence. He will soon manage his studies and develop strong lifelong skills that will serve him in this effort. And he will do so with your help and guidance.

CHAPTER 1

What Is ADHD?

Andrew Scott had always been an active child. From the time he learned to walk his parents noticed he was "into everything." Andrew's preschool teachers frequently commented on how active he was, and his kindergarten teacher observed that he was "quite a handful." First grade passed without any major problems, though his level of activity seemed to overwhelm some of the other children during playtime. In third grade, however, Andrew began to fall behind in math and reading. His teacher said he was too restless. During class he bothered the children around him. He seemed unable to focus on a learning activity for longer than a few minutes. On the playground he was "over-physical" with his peers, invading their space and then overreacting when they pushed him away.

Around the middle of the year, Andrew's teacher met with his parents. His teacher told them that Andrew's problems paying attention, his high activity level, and troubles with schoolwork may indicate the presence of attention-deficit/hyperactivity disorder (ADHD). She explained that ADHD often goes undetected until children enter school and academics and social relationships begin to be affected.

Despite the teacher's positive attitude, Andrew's parents were stunned by her recommendation that their son be evaluated for the causes of this behavior. They had always been challenged by their active child, but they had never considered his behavior out of the ordinary for a healthy young boy. As Andrew's father often pointed out, Andrew was "just like me when I was in school"—eager, excited, and always on the go. While both parents agreed that Andrew could use some extra help with his social skills and reading, they did not see how these behaviors could be thought of as a medical condition. "I think his teacher just can't handle him in class," Andrew's mother told her husband later when they were back at home. "She has a discipline problem and she calls it ADHD. I think it's the school that should be evaluated."

The Keller family was experiencing similar confusion. Their 12-year-old daughter, Emma, was also having problems. However, she was on the quiet and somewhat anxious side. Since early childhood, she had been a "dreamer" whose thoughts tended to drift easily. She often forgot things she had recently learned or been told and spent much of her time alone. In recent years, her "randomness" and lack of organization had begun to seriously affect her school performance, social life, and family relationships. She was having trouble completing tasks and was messy and careless about her schoolwork. Her parents noted that she was often forgetful or spacey. At times it seemed as if her mind was elsewhere and that she was not listening. Still, Emma's parents felt that her behavior was typical of many girls her age and was nothing that a little maturation and help with organization could not cure. Was it really necessary, they asked Emma's pediatrician, to consider this a medical issue or to start an evaluation?

As different as Andrew's and Emma's situations seem to be, both are typical for children with ADHD. Attention-deficit/hyperactivity disorder limits children's ability to filter out unimportant input, focus, organize, prioritize, delay gratification, think before they act, or perform other activities called *executive functions* that most of us perform automatically. In children such as Andrew, with *hyperactive-impulsive* elements to his ADHD, the disorder presents itself as his not being able to control impulses or regulate activity levels, even when he knows how he is expected to behave. In those with *inattentive-type* ADHD, including Emma, not being able to filter information means that someone walking by the classroom can claim as much attention as the teacher's lecture, and that a date with a friend can be forgotten in a flood of unsorted information.

These behaviors—short attention span, forgetfulness, not being able to sit still, unusually high activity level, and a tendency to act before thinking—are common in children. Families are often surprised when their child is referred for an evaluation. Adding to their confusion is the fact that these behaviors are present but to a lesser degree in all children and adolescents, although those with ADHD exhibit more extreme and immature forms of these behaviors. Many school systems will not allow teachers to describe their concerns as "perhaps ADHD" because they feel this is a diagnosis to be made by a physician or a psychologist. Instead they will describe the behaviors that a child is showing that are interfering with his learning.

These behaviors interfere in significant ways with children's day-to-day functioning, and they do not outgrow them at the same pace that other children do. Because other disorders, such as learning disabilities, oppositional defiant disorder, autism spectrum disorder, obsessive-compulsive disorder, anxiety, and depression can resemble ADHD (and, in fact, often accompany it), it can be difficult to tell whether a child has another condition, ADHD, or both. Finally, the fact that ADHD is diagnosed through careful observations of inattentive, hyperactive, and impulsive behaviors across the major settings of a child's life—rather than with laboratory tests used to diagnose such disorders as type 1 diabetes—leads some adults and the popular press to question whether ADHD exists at all.

Yet a large body of convincing evidence suggests that ADHD is a biological, brain-based condition. The scientific research on ADHD is more thorough and compelling than for most behavioral and mental health disorders, and even many medical conditions. Even so, among many parents, it remains controversial and misunderstood. As early as 1998 the National Institutes of Health, responding to public concern and debate about ADHD diagnosis and treatment, assembled a group of experts for a consensus conference on ADHD. These experts published their conclusions stating that ADHD is indeed a medical disorder.

Attention-deficit/hyperactivity disorder is among the most prevalent chronic childhood disorders, second only to asthma. National survey data from 2016 show 9.4% of US children have been diagnosed with ADHD. The Centers for Disease Control and Prevention has reported that about 4.5 million children (ages 3–17 years) in the United States have ADHD, and the condition currently accounts for as many as 30% to 50% of child referrals to mental health services. Many people believe that the prevalence of ADHD has increased significantly in recent decades, perhaps due to environmental factors, but there is no convincing evidence that this is the case. The number of children who have ADHD has likely remained roughly stable, but the number of children diagnosed with the condition has increased as more clinicians have become familiar with its symptoms and the problems it can cause. In addition, while it was originally thought to go away by puberty, it is now clear that many continue to have symptoms even into adulthood.

A generally reliable method for diagnosing ADHD based on the child's behavior and functioning has been established. Parents whose children have been adequately evaluated for ADHD, and who have implemented appropriate treatment as a result, frequently report that the difference before and after their child's treatment is "like night and day." While ADHD cannot be cured, children can be helped to compensate for their problems so that school performance and social relationships improve. As a result, their self-esteem increases, as do their chances for future successes.

In this book, you will learn how ADHD is defined and recognized, how it is evaluated, and how, according to the latest reliable scientific research, it can best be treated. Researchers have identified the types of behavioral, academic, and social supports most likely to be useful at school and at home. Courses and specific therapies have been developed to pass this information on to parents and teachers in the community. You will also learn about special concerns in the evaluation and treatment of preschoolers and adolescents with ADHD, and the changing effect of this chronic condition over time. This is not to say that we now know everything there is to know about the nature and proper treatment of ADHD. A number of questions remain to be answered, and there is a great deal of research still to be done. Active, ongoing studies may provide further insight into how these children can improve their experience at each stage of life. The good news is that the evaluation and treatment of ADHD is at a much more advanced stage today than ever before. Armed with the knowledge provided to you in these pages, you and your child will be able to address the challenges of ADHD with confidence and optimism.

Before learning about how ADHD is recognized, diagnosed, and treated, however, it is necessary to understand exactly what ADHD is—and what it is not. In this chapter you will learn

- How the view of ADHD has evolved over time
- How ADHD is defined today
- What scientists believe may cause ADHD
- How the condition typically alters a child's experience and what are its long-term effects

Through it all, always keep in mind that you have "a child with ADHD," rather than "an ADHD child." He is a child first and foremost, and the problems associated with ADHD can be worked on. Never lose sight of the whole picture.

Myths and Misconceptions About ADHD

Much misinformation has circulated about attention-deficit/hyperactivity disorder (ADHD) and its causes, diagnosis, and treatment over a number of decades. Following are untrue assumptions about the disorder, along with explanations aimed at clarifying the issues.

■ **"My preschooler is too young to have ADHD."** Many parents believe that ADHD is a problem of school-aged children. But, in fact, the symptoms of ADHD, and the diagnosis of the condition, can occur as early as the preschool years. At times, even doctors have difficulty differentiating typical behavior from behaviors that suggest a preschooler has ADHD. Although a young child may typically have characteristics like impulsivity or hyperactivity, these can be symptoms of ADHD as well. A pediatrician will evaluate the intensity of these behaviors in a preschooler to help in making the diagnosis. Attention-deficit/hyperactivity disorder is diagnosed when these problems get to the point where they are significantly and consistently interfering with a preschooler's life, development, self-esteem, and general functioning.

■ **"He's just lazy and unmotivated."** This assumption is a common response to the behavior exhibited by a child who is struggling with ADHD. A child who finds it nearly impossible to stay focused in class, or to complete a lengthy task such as writing a long essay, may try to save face by acting as though he does not want to do it or is too lazy to finish. This behavior may look like laziness or lack of motivation, but it stems from real difficulty in functioning. All children want to succeed and get praised for their good work. If such tasks were easy for children with ADHD to accomplish, and provided rewarding feedback, those children would seem just as "motivated" as anyone else.

■ **"He's a handful—or, she's a daydreamer—but that's normal. They just don't let kids be kids these days."** It is true that all children are impulsive, active, and inattentive at times, sometimes to the extreme. A child with ADHD, however, is more than just a "handful" for his parents and teachers or a "daydreamer" who tends to lose herself in thought. The child's hyperactivity and/or inattentiveness constitutes a real day-to-day functional disability. That is, it seriously and consistently impedes the ability to succeed at school, fit into family routines, follow household rules, maintain friendships, interact positively with family members, avoid injury, or otherwise manage in his or her environment. As you will learn in Chapter 2, this clear functional disability is what pediatricians look for when diagnosing ADHD and recommending treatment.

- **"Treatment for ADHD will cure it. The goal is to get off medication as soon as possible."** Attention-deficit/hyperactivity disorder is a chronic condition that often does not entirely go away but, instead, changes form over time. Many older adolescents and adults are able to organize their lives and use techniques that allow them to adequately compensate for their weaknesses so they are able to forego medical treatment, but many continue various forms of treatment and receive support throughout their life spans. Depending on the circumstances and demands as a person matures, this may or may not include continuing with medication or other treatments for ADHD at different times, even through adult life. The true goal is to function well at each stage of childhood and adolescence, and as an adult, rather than to stop any or all treatments as soon as possible.

- **"He focuses on his video games for hours. He can't have ADHD."** For the most part ADHD poses problems with tasks that require focused attention over long periods, not so much for activities that are highly engaging or stimulating like media and video games. School can be especially challenging for a person with ADHD because the typical classroom lecture can be relatively unstimulating in terms of visuals, sound, and physical activity. Assignments can be long and require sustained, organized thought and effort, and the daily routine can be less structured and predictable than a child with ADHD might require. Most children with ADHD are diagnosed during their school years precisely because the academic, social, and behavioral demands during these years are so difficult for them. The difficulties that such children experience may make it seem that school is the problem (and, certainly, that possibility should be considered), but it is more likely to be a result of the child's struggle to manage in this environment.

Other situations that can be problematic for children with ADHD include social interactions, with their constant, subtle exchange of emotional and social information; sports that require a high degree of focus or concentration; and extracurricular activities that require them to sit still, listen, or wait their turn for long periods.

- **"ADHD is caused by poor parental discipline."** Attention-deficit/hyperactivity disorder is not a result of poor discipline—although behaviors that stem from ADHD can challenge otherwise effective parenting styles. Inconsistent limit-setting and other ineffective parenting practices can, however, worsen its expression. In chapters 5 and 6 you will find a number of proven parenting techniques that can help children with ADHD manage their behavior.

- **"The problem is with the school program. They are not strict enough with my child."** Just like ADHD is not a result of poor discipline, it is also not caused by bad teachers or a lack of school rules. The best teachers can see when a child is struggling and will partner with parents to seek solutions for success in school.

- **"If, after a careful evaluation, a child doesn't receive the ADHD diagnosis, she doesn't need help."** Attention-deficit/hyperactivity disorder is diagnosed on a continuum, which means that a child can exhibit a number of ADHD-type behaviors yet not to the extent that she is diagnosed with ADHD. This does not mean she doesn't need help coping with her problems. The family of a child who does not meet the criteria for ADHD but has similar problems may be offered pediatric counseling, education about the range of typical developmental behaviors, home behavior management tools, school behavior management recommendations, social skills interventions, and help with managing homework involving organization and planning.

- **"Children with ADHD outgrow this condition."** Parents and many doctors once believed that as children with ADHD enter adolescence and then move into adulthood, their ADHD will no longer be an issue. But recent studies have shown that some aspects of ADHD can persist well into adult life for many of these children. Some adults can still benefit from the use of ADHD medication for the rest of their lives. Others have developed enough coping skills and improvement that medication can be discontinued. Sometimes in older teens and adults, medications may be used intermittently for situations and tasks that need fuller concentration. Medication use may often vary depending on what occupation they choose and their ability to succeed in relationships and other social activities. No matter what the circumstances of particular adults may be, however, they can make adjustments in their environment, take full advantage of their own strengths, and lead very productive adult lives, even when aspects of ADHD still persist.

How Is ADHD Defined?

On television and online, in magazines and newspapers, in social media, and in thousands of everyday conversations, there is ongoing debate around whether certain "ADHD-type" behaviors are a typical childhood experience or constitute a disorder that requires treatment. The issue of exactly where and how to draw the line between typical behavior and a clinical condition may become even clearer as increasingly sophisticated diagnostic techniques provide researchers with more information about the nature of the precise brain processes involved in children with ADHD, but the use of these tools and techniques for these purposes still lies in the future.

For more than a century physicians have been aware of children displaying the behaviors that we now call ADHD. In 1902 British pediatrician George Still first formally documented a condition in which children seemed inattentive, impulsive, and hyperactive, stating his belief that this was a result of biological makeup rather than poor parenting or other environmental factors. Research in the 1980s supported this hypothesis and led to the use of the term *attention-deficit disorder*. In 1987, in response to even more precise information provided by new studies, the term *attention-deficit/hyperactivity disorder* was introduced.

Today ADHD is defined by the American Psychiatric Association as developmentally inappropriate attention and/or hyperactivity and impulsivity so pervasive and persistent as to significantly interfere with a child's daily life. Children with ADHD have difficulty controlling their behavior in most major settings, including home and school. They may speed about in constant motion, make noise nonstop, refuse to wait their turn, and crash into everything around them. At other times they may drift as if in a daydream, failing to pay attention to or finish what they start. They may have trouble learning and remembering; they may appear disorganized. An impulsive nature may put them in actual physical danger. Because they have difficulty controlling this behavior, they may be labeled a "bad kid" or a "space cadet." These problems begin to occur relatively early in life (before age 12 years), though they sometimes are not recognized until a child is older. However, if there are absolutely no indications of ADHD before age 12 years, an alternative explanation for a child's later behaviors should be sought.

Professionals have identified clear differences between the functioning of a child without ADHD and a child with the condition. The presence of ADHD may be suspected if the

1. Inattentive, impulsive, or hyperactive behavior is not age appropriate—that is, if it is not typical of children of the same age who do not have ADHD.

2. Behavior leads to chronic problems in daily functioning. A mild tendency to daydream or an active temperament, which may cause occasional problems for a child but is not seriously disabling, is not considered evidence of ADHD.

3. Behavior is the child's usual way of acting and not a result of poor care, physical injury, abuse or neglect, disease, or other environmental influences. One way to determine whether the problem is environmental is to look at whether the problem occurs in more than one setting, such as at home and at school. If not, then an environmental cause, such as stresses at home or an inappropriate classroom placement, is more likely than ADHD to be the cause of the problem for the child.

For a child's condition to be diagnosed as ADHD, *all 3* of these conditions must be met. Attention-deficit/hyperactivity disorder can only be recognized by its symptoms and by the problems that these symptoms create for the child. This is why it is so important for parents, teachers, mental health professionals, and medical experts to work together when evaluating a child for ADHD. Each contributes his or her own observations, experience, and expertise to create a comprehensive picture of the child's social, academic, and emotional progress.

For the most part attention-deficit/hyperactivity disorder poses problems with tasks that require focused attention over long periods, not so much for activities that are highly engaging or stimulating, such as a video game.

Attention-deficit/hyperactivity disorder is divided into 3 general subtypes: *predominantly hyperactive-impulsive presentation, predominantly inattentive presentation,* and *combined presentation.* Children with predominantly hyperactive-impulsive–type ADHD may fidget or squirm in their seat, have difficulty waiting their turn, and show a tendency to be disorganized. They may act immaturely, have a poor sense of physical boundaries, and tend toward destructive behaviors and conduct problems. Children with predominantly inattentive-type ADHD, on the other hand, may seem distracted and "spacey" or "daydreamy" but not show the hyperactive component of the disorder. They may seem to process information slowly and may also have a learning disorder, anxiety, or depression. Children with combined-type ADHD typically exhibit many of the behaviors of the first 2 subtypes.

Girls and ADHD

The fact that many more boys than girls are diagnosed with attention-deficit/ hyperactivity disorder (ADHD)—at a ratio of approximately 2 to 1 or 3 to 1—has led to the mistaken belief among many parents and teachers that ADHD is a "boys' disorder" that rarely occurs in girls. More girls remain undiagnosed because they have the inattentive type of ADHD and tend to be overlooked entirely or do not attract attention until they are older. This means that girls are less likely to be referred for evaluation and to receive the help they need. Even when diagnosis and treatment have been obtained, girls with ADHD are further disadvantaged by the fact that most ADHD research to date has focused on boys. Little is known about potential differences between the genders in the development of the condition over time or response to medication and other forms of treatment. Compared with other girls, girls with ADHD experience more depression, anxiety, distress, poor teacher relationships, stress, external locus of control (the feeling that "the winds of fate" control their destiny instead of themselves), and problems in school. Compared with boys with ADHD, girls with ADHD experience more difficulties from feeling anxious, distressed, depressed, or spacey. They have less of a feeling that they can take control in solving problems that they face.

If your daughter has been referred for evaluation for ADHD, or if you suspect that she may have the condition, it is important not to discount the possibility just because she is female. Teachers may not recognize more subtle signs of inattention. They may under-refer girls for evaluation, even when their symptoms are the same as boys'. As a result, girls are less likely than boys to receive sufficient medical treatment once they have been diagnosed. Be aware that some sociocultural beliefs about girls (that they tend to daydream, that they just are not interested in academics) may mask a real problem in your child's ability to function. If your daughter is diagnosed with ADHD, ask the pediatrician to keep you updated on ongoing research about the development of ADHD in girls, the particular challenges girls with ADHD are likely to meet, and the different ways in which they may respond to various forms of treatment.

These subtypes tend to be diagnosed at different ages and stages of development. Because of the hyperactivity and impulsivity, children with predominantly hyperactive-impulsive type or combined type may be diagnosed as early as the preschool years in extreme situations. Children with predominantly inattentive type often go undetected until fourth grade or even later, when increased demands for sustained attention and more homework lead to significant problems in functioning. In the early grades children learn to read, but at around fourth grade they need to begin to read to learn. When this transition takes place, children with inattentive type typically begin to have more problems.

While the problems of hyperactivity/impulsivity and inattentiveness may seem at first to be unrelated, they both influence a child's inability to focus and function well in school, with peers, and in the family. Attention-deficit/hyperactivity disorder can be thought of as a range of "attentional disorders" with a number of possible symptoms shown at different ages and developmental stages.

What Causes ADHD?

No single cause has yet been identified for ADHD. Many risk factors have been noted, however, that affect a child's brain development and behavior, which, acting in combination, may lead to ADHD symptoms. They include genetic factors, variations in temperament (a child's individual differences in emotional reactivity, activity level, attention, and self-regulation), medical causes (especially those that affect brain development), and a host of environmental influences on the developing brain (including toxins such as lead, prenatal alcohol use, and nutritional deficiencies). Some research finds that children with ADHD may experience a delay in the typical maturing of their brain. Despite the many advances in research on the causes of ADHD, none of these findings are yet ready to help physicians make the diagnosis of ADHD.

Researchers are certain that ADHD tends to run in families. Close relatives of people with ADHD have about 5 times greater chance of having ADHD themselves, as well as a higher risk for such common accompanying disorders as anxiety, depression, learning disabilities, and conduct disorders. An identical twin is at high risk of sharing his twin's ADHD, and a sibling of a child with ADHD has about a 30% chance of having similar problems. Although no single gene has been identified for ADHD, research continues in this area. Brain imaging studies have found some differences in brain anatomy between children diagnosed with ADHD and those who have not been diagnosed, but no consistent pattern has yet emerged from these studies that would be helpful in confirming a diagnosis. The fact that children and adolescents respond so consistently to stimulant medications, and that these medications influence biochemical systems in the brain, suggests that biochemical causes may contribute to ADHD symptoms as well. This remains an area of active research. In the coming years newer brain-imaging tools and more sophisticated genetic techniques are likely to continue to shed more light on the processes underlying ADHD. Still, it is unlikely that a single cause will be identified.

ADHD Over Time

Attention-deficit/hyperactivity disorder is a complex disorder with different challenges arising at each new phase of a child's development. Children who are at risk for developing ADHD generally carry some symptoms with them as early as preschool age and continuing throughout adolescence and even into adulthood. Attention-deficit/hyperactivity disorder is sometimes diagnosed in preschoolers, who display extremely high activity levels and impulsiveness. As children grow into adolescence, their ADHD-associated behaviors may persist and become just as problematic as they were earlier in life. They may have difficulty concentrating and be disorganized and easily distracted. Problems in adolescents with ADHD symptoms are likely to be expressed in different ways than they were in early childhood. Hyperactivity, for example, frequently takes center stage in early childhood but diminishes and may no longer be a problem by late adolescence or early adulthood. Inattention and impulsivity are likely to persist and can affect an adult's educational experience, work life, and relationships. Driving can also be a challenge with an increased chanced for accidents or traffic tickets. Learning disabilities that were present during childhood also continue to exist in later years, as can any emotional, behavioral, and social problems that have not been fully resolved. (For more information about ADHD in adolescence, see Chapter 11.)

At one time or another all children and adolescents with ADHD may face some challenges relating to family relationships, status among their peers, social skills,

Often it may be difficult for your child to switch from one activity to another. Give your child advance notice before the start of new events (eg, mealtimes) to help ease transitions.

academic achievement, self-esteem, self-perception, or accidental injury. With help, however, children can learn to manage their symptoms in their early years as well as through adolescence and into adulthood. Early and accurate diagnosis is the first step toward organizing a plan that can make a difference to your child and your family.

As you begin to focus on the problems and issues that your child is facing, do not forget to appreciate and encourage his unique strengths and abilities as well, and to communicate that to your child. A child with ADHD (like all other children) not only thrives on positive reinforcement and praise but also desperately needs to know that his symptoms do not make him "bad," "undisciplined," "stupid," "unmotivated," or "lazy" as is so often implied. Educating affected children about what ADHD is—and what it is not—will help them cope with whatever discouraging comments or self-doubts come their way. The more they understand, the greater are their chances of success.

Finally, children with ADHD frequently grow up to become successful and happy adults. In the chapters that follow you will learn how to identify, treat, effectively parent, and advocate for your child in ways that will help him minimize his challenges and fulfill his enormous promise.

A Parent's Story

Missed Clues and Lost Opportunities

"I suspected from my son's preschool days that he might have ADHD—not because of his activity level but because he could never stay focused on a single activity and he tended to forget things he had just learned. To me it was obvious that he was having real problems, but his teachers did not believe me because he is also unusually bright. They assumed that his restless behavior and underachievement were a result of 'just being bored.'

"It was only in middle school, when my son began forgetting homework assignments, not taking notes, and even forgetting to take home books that he needed for homework from one day to the next, that his teachers began to think something serious might be going on. I remember one day when I was at the school for a parent-teacher conference, I saw him standing in the hall looking confused. I asked him what was wrong, and he told me he'd forgotten how to get to his next class. He did not know what to do or where to go.

"That was the day I decided to have him evaluated by his pediatrician. He was diagnosed with ADHD and is being treated now. His situation has improved, but I wish we had done this earlier before he fell so far behind. It is a huge relief to him, at least, to know that the problems he had been having at school were not his fault but were symptoms of his condition. My biggest hope for him is that he realizes the potential he had when he was born."

Roberta, Pittsburgh, PA

CHAPTER 2

Does My Child Have ADHD? Evaluation and Diagnosis

If only it were as clear-cut to diagnose attention-deficit/hyperactivity disorder (ADHD) as it is to diagnose a broken bone. Unfortunately, this is not the case. A broken bone is suspected after an injury and because of pain. A simple x-ray confirms the diagnosis. Furthermore, a broken bone just doesn't work like it did before it was fractured. As you will learn in this chapter, neither of these advantages exists in determining whether a child has ADHD.

No laboratory tests—no urine or blood tests, and no behavioral tests by themselves—can prove objectively whether ADHD is present. To complicate things further, the symptoms that characterize ADHD—inattention, hyperactivity, and impulsivity—occur in most children from time to time. Deciding whether a child's behaviors signal the presence of ADHD is, therefore, a complex process that involves comparing a child's behaviors and abilities to function with those of other children his age. To do this, pediatricians and mental health professionals must rely on information from parents, other caregivers, and a child's teachers or other school professionals through observations, interviews, and questionnaires specifically designed to evaluate behaviors seen in children and adolescents with ADHD. Interviews including both parents and the child being evaluated are also used to determine if there are other alternative causes for the behavior or to find if there are additional problems, such as anxiety. In addition, the interviews help to evaluate whether specific problems may be interfering with a child's life on a daily basis. A diagnosis based on these types of evaluation procedures can become even more challenging when, as is often the case, other problems exist, such as vision or hearing problems, emotional disorders, or learning disabilities. An evaluation may require a team of professionals with different specialties because some of the accompanying problems are more medical in nature, some are more psychological, and others are related to learning and language processes.

Several professional organizations, including the American Academy of Pediatrics (AAP), have developed guidelines in recent years that standardize the evaluation process for ADHD. As a result, diagnosis of the condition has become more consistent and accurate. In this chapter you will learn how a child is evaluated for ADHD, from the first recognition that "something may be wrong" through a methodical assessment of the specific problems that need addressing. Along the way you will find information about

- The types of behaviors that often alert adults to the possible presence of ADHD in children
- How your child's pediatric clinician will evaluate him and arrive at a diagnosis
- How your child's particular subtype of ADHD will be identified
- How clinicians will pinpoint the presence of any accompanying conditions
- How a team approach that involves you, your child, his educators, and his clinicians all working together can bring about the best diagnosis and prepare you for planning a course of treatment

Early Warning Signs: When ADHD Is First Suspected

Most experts agree that the tendency to develop ADHD is present from birth, yet ADHD behaviors are often not noticed until children enter elementary school. One reason for this delay is the fact that nearly all preschool-aged children frequently exhibit some of the core behaviors or symptoms of ADHD—inattention, impulsivity, and hyperactivity—as part of their typical development. But as other children gradually begin to grow out of such behaviors, children with ADHD do not, and those behaviors interfere with how well the child can function. This difference becomes increasingly clear as the years pass. School settings can highlight a child's problems relating to inattention, impulsivity, and hyperactivity because classroom activities demand an increased amount of focus, patience, and self-control. These types of demands are not as prevalent at home or in playgroups, so in those settings, the child may have had fewer problems.

Usually by the time a child with ADHD reaches 7 years of age, his parents have already become aware that their child's inattentiveness, level of activity, or impulsiveness is greater than is typical. Sometimes these suspicions develop later, particularly in bright children when the problems are mostly with paying attention and not hyperactivity, but it is unusual for ADHD symptoms to not have occurred before 12 years of age. So if symptoms are not observed until the teen years or later, and can't be remembered before age 12, it is likely something other than ADHD is causing the issues.

You may have noticed that your child finds it nearly impossible to focus on a workbook for even a short period, even when you are there to assist him. Or you may still feel as worn out at the end of a day with your overly active 8-year-old as you did when he was 2. Your child may ask adults questions so often that you have begun to suspect it is not "normal." Or, you may have noticed that he does not pick up on obvious social rules that his playmates are already beginning to adopt, like respecting others' personal space or letting other people have a turn to talk. It can be difficult for a parent to tell whether such behaviors are just part of the typical process of growing up ("Plenty of 6-year-olds get bored with workbooks!") or whether you are not strict enough ("Maybe I've been too inconsistent with setting limits?"). Are the behavior problems severe enough to indicate a concerning problem? Will they improve as your child matures? For a child to be diagnosed with the disorder, the AAP advises pediatric clinicians to gather information about the child's behavior in at least one other major setting besides his home—including a review of any reports provided by teachers and school professionals. By comparing the child's behavior in 2 or more settings, the pediatric clinician can begin to differentiate among such varied reasons for attentional problems as a "difficult" but typical temperament, ineffective parenting practices, inappropriate academic setting, and other challenges. The pediatric clinician can also clarify whether the child's behavior is interfering with his ability to function adequately in more than one setting—another requirement for diagnosis.

"Something's Not Right…":
What Parents Notice When ADHD Behaviors Emerge

It is sometimes hard to match the behavior we observe in our children with the formal terms used by pediatricians and other medical professionals. We rarely think of our children as having "hyperactive-impulsive problems." Instead, we think, "Why can't he ever settle down?"

To confuse matters, the terms that doctors and other clinicians use for these behaviors have changed over the years. The term *ADD* (attention-deficit disorder) was once commonly used and referred primarily to the form of attention-deficit/hyperactivity disorder (ADHD) with "inattentive-only" symptoms. These children are not overly active, and their symptoms may even go unnoticed by many adults for a while because their behavior is not disruptive. To the most common children with ADHD, the qualifying description of "with hyperactivity" had to be added to ADD. Now, all children with this condition are considered to have ADHD, but within that diagnosis there are 3 subtypes: inattentive, hyperactive-impulsive, and combined subtypes. When reviewing the list that follows of typical remarks made about children with ADHD, ask yourself how many times per day or week you say or think the same things yourself. It is true that all parents make such comments now and then, but parents of children with ADHD continue to see the same behaviors on a daily basis and for extended periods—long after other children have progressed.

Parents of Children With Predominantly Inattentive-Type ADHD Say

- "He seems like he's always daydreaming. He never answers when I talk to him. I wonder if he hears me."
- "He loses everything. I've had to buy 4 new lunch boxes since school started."
- "I'll ask him to go up to his room and get dressed, and 10 minutes later I find him playing with his toys with only his shirt on."

- "He can't remember what he learns because he misses instructions and explanations in school. Even though we work so hard on his schoolwork at night, by the next day he's forgotten everything."
- "Some teachers have called him their 'space cadet,' an underachiever, an 'airhead,' or their 'random student.'"

Parents of Children With Predominantly Hyperactive-Impulsive–Type ADHD Say

- "He never slows down. You can never get him to sit down to finish a meal or get ready for bed."
- "He interrupts constantly. You can't have a decent conversation when he's in the room."
- "He never thinks before he acts. He knows he shouldn't run across the street before stopping to look, but he does it all the time. I worry about him being safe—he just isn't."
- "He operates out of order—like, 'ready…fire…aim.'"
- "His classmates don't like him. He's always 'getting in their face.' No one invites him over to their house. He always has to be first and things always have to be his way."

First Steps Toward Evaluation

If you have begun to think that your child's poor progress at school, limited friendships, or frequent discipline problems add up to more than typical childhood behaviors, schedule an appointment with his teacher or school counselor as soon as possible. These people see your child daily in a group setting, where they can compare his behavior and ability to function to that of many other children of the same age. Teachers and counselors are trained to recognize symptoms of ADHD and similar disorders, but even with special training it can be easy to miss milder symptoms or a subtler problem. Certainly, they will be interested in your observations and concerns and will be able to give you a clearer idea of your child's experience at school, where ADHD so often manifests itself and creates problems.

Often it is the teacher or counselor who first notices that a child is failing to progress in ways that may indicate that he has ADHD or a related disorder. In these instances, it is important for the teacher to contact the child's parents without delay to discuss the issue. Although teachers may identify more than 15% of their students as showing many of the behaviors compatible with ADHD and recommend those students for an evaluation by their pediatric clinician, not all these students will actually be diagnosed with ADHD after a careful evaluation. Regardless of whether your child will end up being diagnosed with ADHD, it is important to follow up on teachers' concerns. The sooner a child with ADHD symptoms can be evaluated, diagnosed, and effectively treated, the greater his chances of succeeding in school with good self-esteem.

If you and your child's teacher or other caregiver agree that your child is clearly having problems functioning in the areas of difficult-to-manage behaviors or learning at home or at school, make an appointment with his pediatric clinician to consider beginning an evaluation. Pediatricians are used to evaluating children for developmental or behavioral problems, and because ADHD is such a common problem, they often screen for it in school-aged children during routine health visits.

Questions Your Child's Health Care Professional May Ask You About School

- "Do you have any concerns about your child's development or learning? How is your child enjoying school? What concerns do you have about his social or academic experience?"
- "Please share any concerns you may have about your child's mood or behavior, such as attention, hitting, temper, worries, not participating in play with others, irritability, mood, or activity level."

Confirming the Diagnosis and Identifying Your Child's Specific Problem Areas

Not all active children or children who don't pay attention well have ADHD. Many ADHD "symptoms" are typical behaviors in preschool-aged children. Differences in development and variations in behaviors must be carefully considered in the diagnostic evaluation. Pediatricians and other experts rely on knowledge about how ADHD-type behaviors are expressed at different ages, as described in the following boxes:

Common Symptoms of Inattention

Early Childhood (preschool and early school years)

- **Behavior within typical range:** Difficulty paying attention more than briefly to a storybook or quiet task such as coloring or drawing.
- **Behavior signaling an inattention problem:** Sometimes unable to complete games or activities without being distracted, is unable to complete a game with a child of comparable age, and only attends to any activity for a very short period before shifting attention to another object or activity. Symptoms are present to the degree that they cause some family difficulties.
- **Behavior signaling the possible presence of attention-deficit/hyperactivity disorder (ADHD), predominantly inattentive type:** The child is unable to function and play appropriately and may seem immature, does not engage in any activity long enough, is easily distracted, is unable to complete activities, has a much shorter attention span than other children the same age, often misses important aspects of an object or situation (eg, rules of games or sequences), and does not persist in various self-care tasks (dressing or washing) to the same extent as other children of comparable age. The child shows problems in many settings over a long period and is affected functionally.

Middle Childhood (later primary grades through preteen years) and Adolescence

- **Behavior within typical range:** May not persist very long with a task the child does not want to do, such as reading an assigned book or homework, or a task that requires concentration, such as cleaning something. Adolescents may be easily distracted from tasks that they do not want to perform.

- **Behavior signaling an inattention problem:** At times the child misses some instructions and explanations in school, begins a number of activities without completing them, has some difficulties completing games with other children or grown-ups, becomes distracted, and tends to give up easily. The child may not complete or succeed at new activities, has some social deficiency, and does not pick up subtle social cues from others.

- **Behavior signaling the possible presence of ADHD, predominantly inattentive type:** The child has significant school and social problems, often shifts activities, does not complete tasks, is messy, and is careless about schoolwork. The child may start tasks prematurely and without appropriate review as if he were not listening, has difficulty organizing tasks, dislikes activities that require close concentration, is easily distracted, and is often forgetful.

Adapted from Wolraich ML, Felice ME, Drotar D, eds. *The Classification of Child and Adolescent Mental Diagnoses in Primary Care: Diagnostic and Statistical Manual for Primary Care (DSM-PC) Child and Adolescent Version.* Elk Grove Village, IL: American Academy of Pediatrics; 1996.

Common Symptoms of Hyperactivity/Impulsivity

Early Childhood (preschool and early school years)

- **Behavior within typical range:** The child runs in circles, does not stop to rest, may bang into objects or people, and asks questions constantly.

- **Behavior signaling a hyperactivity/impulsivity problem:** The child frequently runs into people or knocks things down during play, gets injured frequently, and does not want to sit for stories or games.

■ **Behavior signaling the possible presence of attention-deficit/hyperactivity disorder (ADHD), hyperactive-impulsive type:** The child runs through the house, jumps and climbs excessively on furniture, will not sit still to eat or be read to, and is often getting into things that could be harmful or he was told not to touch.

Middle Childhood (later primary grades through preteen years)

■ **Behavior within typical range:** The child plays active games for long periods. The child may occasionally do things impulsively, particularly when excited.

■ **Behavior signaling a hyperactivity/impulsivity problem:** The child may butt into other children's games, interrupt frequently, and have problems completing chores.

■ **Behavior signaling the possible presence of ADHD, hyperactive-impulsive type:** The child is often talking and interrupting, cannot sit still at mealtimes, is often fidgeting when watching television, makes noise that is disruptive, and grabs toys or other objects from others.

Adolescence

■ **Behavior within typical range:** The adolescent engages in active social activities (eg, social media, dancing) for long periods and may engage in risky behaviors with peers.

■ **Behavior signaling a hyperactivity/impulsivity problem:** The adolescent engages in "fooling around" that begins to annoy others, and he fidgets in class or while watching television.

■ **Behavior signaling the possible presence of ADHD, hyperactive-impulsive type:** The adolescent is restless and fidgety while doing any and all quiet activities, interrupts and "bugs" other people, and gets into trouble frequently. Hyperactive symptoms decrease or are replaced with a sense of restlessness.

Adapted from Wolraich ML, Felice ME, Drotar D, eds. *The Classification of Child and Adolescent Mental Diagnoses in Primary Care: Diagnostic and Statistical Manual for Primary Care (DSM-PC) Child and Adolescent Version.* Elk Grove Village, IL: American Academy of Pediatrics; 1996.

To create a uniform process for diagnosing ADHD among school-aged children, the AAP has created a list of standard guidelines for pediatricians to follow in evaluating a child reported to be inattentive, hyperactive, impulsive, or struggling academically, or having behavioral problems. These guidelines are based on the latest evidence about ADHD and other problems that might be seen along with ADHD, and the diagnostic procedures most commonly used. You should expect your child's pediatric clinician to follow these recommended steps or a procedure much like them. The evaluation process will most likely require at least one long visit or 2 or 3 regular visits to the doctor, possibly longer sessions than you may be used to, and the filling out of a number of questionnaires, checklists, and other information to help evaluate your child. Your child's pediatric clinician may also ask you to forward questionnaires to his teacher or ask the teacher to write a brief statement about your child's behavior and learning in the classroom before your first visit to make the initial interview more productive.

The American Academy of Pediatrics Recommends...

Diagnostic Guidelines for ADHD

To ensure that children referred for evaluation for attention-deficit/hyperactivity disorder (ADHD) receive the most reliable, thorough, and accurate assessment possible, the American Academy of Pediatrics has developed a set of diagnostic and evaluation guidelines and recommends that pediatricians follow the steps outlined as follows. Your child's pediatrician may prefer one variation or another of a particular step (eg, talking in person or on the phone with a teacher, asking the teacher to write a brief narrative instead of or in addition to requesting written questionnaires), but, in general, each of these steps should be considered.

1. **Pediatricians should initiate an evaluation of ADHD for any child 4 to 18 years of age who has significant academic or behavioral problems and symptoms of inattention, hyperactivity, or impulsivity.** Attention-deficit/hyperactivity disorder often becomes apparent when a child enters a structured school setting, but symptoms can emerge prior to kindergarten or may not be recognized until adolescence.

2. **To make a diagnosis of ADHD, pediatricians should determine that** ***Diagnostic and Statistical Manual of Mental Disorders,*** **Fifth Edition** **(***DSM-5***), criteria have been met (including documentation of several symptoms in more than one major setting) with information obtained primarily from reports of parents or guardians and teachers.** The *DSM-5* is a manual published by the American Psychiatric Association that describes all mental health conditions in children and adults. Information obtained from parents, guardians, and caregivers should be the basis for determining if the *DSM-5* criteria are met. This most recent revision of *DSM* was released in 2013.

3. **In the evaluation of a child for ADHD, pediatricians should include assessment for other conditions that might occur along with ADHD, including emotional or behavioral (eg, anxiety, depressive, oppositional defiant, and conduct disorders), developmental (eg, learning and language disorders), and physical (eg, tics, sleep apnea) conditions.**

Your child's pediatric clinician will start by listening to your observations and experience with your child's behavior and the difficulties that you have observed him having, along with your explanations of why you think (or do not think) that they may be related to ADHD. In addition to examining written reports from teachers, school counselors, or caregivers, your pediatrician may ask you to relate what you have been told about your child's behavior in school and in his other daily settings outside the home. In many cases, parents' and teachers' opinions about a child differ significantly. This is common and not unexpected. Your child's pediatrician will be prepared for this possibility and will listen carefully to reports from each reporter. She may ask to speak with other adults in your child's life (eg, your spouse or partner, former teachers, coaches, others in your community) to gain a broader impression of the types of problems your child may be experiencing.

Do not be surprised if your child's pediatric clinician seems to rely much more on these reports than on her own observation of your child. Children with ADHD do not necessarily exhibit their typical behavior while in the doctor's office, so she will not expect to see them. (Keep in mind that ADHD, an attentional disorder, usually manifests itself in routine or monotonous situations, and visits to the doctor's office tend to be stimulating and outside of a child's usual routines.) Likewise, though she will perform a physical examination, she will not rely on this to indicate whether ADHD is present because there are no physical findings that, by themselves, verify ADHD. Instead, she will look for signs of medical conditions that can be associated with symptoms of ADHD. Your pediatrician will carefully review your child's and your family's medical history for ADHD, related disorders, and other medical conditions that can have ADHD-like symptoms. Because ADHD has been shown to run in families, the discovery that you or other relatives have experienced ADHD-specific or similar symptoms may help point the way toward an accurate diagnosis.

It will be helpful to familiarize yourself with the behaviors associated with the core symptoms of ADHD. They are broken down into 3 categories: inattention, hyperactivity, and impulsivity. You will want to share your observations of your child's specific behaviors with your pediatrician.

Children who have *inattentiveness* have trouble focusing and are easily distracted. They may lose interest in one task and become engaged in another. When observing your child, you

School settings can highlight a child's problems relating to inattention, impulsivity, and hyperactivity because classroom activities require an increased amount of focus, patience, and self-control.

should look for behaviors that signal inattention problems, which can include your child making careless mistakes on homework, not listening to specific instructions or steps told to him, and having trouble focusing and maintaining his attention. Do you notice that your child is forgetful? Does he lose track of his belongings often? Does he become easily distracted and move from one task to the next rather quickly and also fail to finish specific tasks? Lack of organization can be another identifying behavior. Does your child find it hard to keep his schoolwork organized in the right folders? Is his backpack messy and not organized? Does he have trouble getting off to school in the morning because you have to constantly remind him to take his lunch box, homework, or gym uniform to school? Do you notice that your child avoids doing things that require longer periods of attention? Does he struggle doing longer homework assignments or finishing a board game?

You will also want to observe and report behaviors associated with *hyperactivity*. Do you notice that your child is unable to sit in one place for a period of time? Does he continually get up from the kitchen table while he is doing his homework? Does he fidget or always have something in his hands that he is playing with? Is it hard for him to stay seated and focused? Is your child talking nonstop, or does it appear that he is always on the go? Does he have a hard time engaging in quiet activities like reading or doing an activity by himself?

The last symptoms that your pediatric clinician will want to know about is impulsivity. *Impulsivity* means doing things without thinking through them first. Does your child have a hard time waiting his turn? Do you notice that sometimes he may play out of turn? Does he have trouble being patient? Do you notice that your child interrupts others while they are talking or that he blurts out answers before questions are completed? Your pediatric clinician is going to want as much information about these behaviors as you can share.

You might want to keep a notebook and write down any of your observations that you find concerning so that you can share specific instances with your child's pediatric clinician. The pediatric clinician may have you and your child's teacher complete a rating scale that asks you to indicate the presence and severity of these and other behaviors.

Once your child's pediatric clinician has collected as much information about your child as you can provide and taken a family medical history, she will move on toward the first of what may be a series of structured questions, checklists, and evaluative procedures to identify your child's specific problems. She may ask your permission to have your child's teacher speak to her and complete some rating scales as well. Creating the best treatment program for your child begins with your child's pediatrician forming as complete a view of your child as possible in many life settings. Other medical or mental health professionals to whom your child's pediatrician has referred you may also administer parts of the evaluation.

The AAP advises health professionals to begin by determining whether your child's behaviors match those considered necessary for making the diagnosis of ADHD. The behaviors comprising the "diagnostic criteria" for ADHD are set out in *Diagnostic and Statistical Manual of Mental Disorders*, Fifth Edition (*DSM-5*), developed by the American Psychiatric Association. This manual is presently considered the gold standard for professionals who diagnose behavioral and emotional disorders. The *DSM-5* lists 9 behaviors that apply to each of the 2 ADHD presentation types: *predominantly inattentive* and *predominantly hyperactive-impulsive*. A child whose symptoms occur inappropriately often for at least 6 of the 9 behaviors described for each subtype may be diagnosed as having that disorder if the behaviors are interfering with his school activities or relationships with siblings, friends, you, or your spouse. A child with 6 or more behaviors in both categories is at risk for and may be eventually diagnosed as having a third type of ADHD presentation: *combined*.

Children and adolescents can only be diagnosed as having ADHD if

- Several of their symptoms were present before age 12 years.
- The symptoms have been observed in 2 or more major settings, like at home and child care or at home and school.
- The behaviors significantly impair the child's ability to function in academic or social situations.
- The symptoms cannot be accounted for by another condition, either physical or mental, such as head trauma, physical or sexual abuse, depression, substance abuse disorder, or a major psychological stress in the family or at school.
- The symptoms have been present for 6 months or longer and are more pronounced than for most children at the same developmental level.

Of course, all children exhibit many of these behaviors some of the time. Still, by considering to what extent such behaviors interfere with the child's ability to function at home, in school, and in social settings, your child's pediatrician or other health professionals can begin to arrive at a better idea of whether or not ADHD is the best explanation for the problems. As you have learned, it is necessary to differentiate behavior that is age appropriate from behavior that strongly suggests a full diagnosis of ADHD. As you and your child's pediatrician consider these detailed descriptions of different types of behavior, you can develop a better idea of whether his behaviors are typical for his age, represent problems that need to be addressed, or signal the likelihood of ADHD.

Simply knowing that your child's behaviors meet criteria for ADHD does not fully make the diagnosis or necessarily pinpoint the areas that cause him the most difficulties in his day-to-day functioning. Determining how much the behaviors cause problems that make your child fail or get in trouble in school and interfere with how he gets along at home with you and his siblings and how he gets along with friends is also important in making a diagnosis and determining how severe it is.

Using the criteria for making the diagnosis is important, but establishing the ADHD diagnosis is just the first step. A second major aim of an evaluation is to describe the problems caused by the ADHD behaviors specifically enough that they can be translated into a treatment plan. (See Chapter 3.) Your pediatrician will ask specific questions of you and your child to determine *functional impairment*—that is, the condition's effect on your child's day-to-day life. The functional impairments associated with ADHD include difficulties interacting positively with family members; keeping friendships; problems with social skills, academic achievement, and following household rules; issues of self-esteem and self-perception; and problems with accidental injuries. Your pediatric clinician recommendations for a treatment program for your child will depend to a large extent on these functional difficulties. They will become the main "targets" for treatment.

As you and your child's pediatric clinician work through these detailed descriptions of different types of behavior, your child's problem areas should become increasingly clear. Some of these may fall out of the usual difficulties expected as a result of ADHD alone. Pediatricians, parents, teachers, and other members of a child's support team must thoroughly consider other environmental, situational, and emotional factors that may be influencing or causing these behaviors.

Special Circumstances: Preschool-aged Children

We now know that the diagnostic criteria for ADHD can be applied to preschool-aged children and that these criteria can appropriately identify children with the condition. However, there are added challenges in determining the presence of key symptoms of ADHD in preschoolers. Remember the requirement that ADHD needs to be diagnosed in settings other than just at home. Preschool-aged children are not likely to have separate observers if they do not attend a preschool or child care program. Even if they do attend these programs, staff in the programs may be less experienced than grade school teachers to provide accurate observations.

Where there are concerns about the availability or quality of nonparent observations of a child's behavior, your pediatric clinician may recommend that you and your spouse or partner complete a parent training in behavior management (PTBM) program prior to confirming an ADHD diagnosis for preschool-aged children. The PTBM program should include learning to identify age-appropriate developmental expectations and specific management skills for problem behaviors.

These training programs are designed for all parents, and a child does not need a specific diagnosis to benefit from PTBM programs. They can help parents to more effectively manage their child's behavior, and even in children with ADHD the skills you learn may be sufficient for addressing your child's behavioral needs.

Your child's pediatric clinician may then obtain reports from the training program instructor about improvement in behavior attained through the program. If you are in programs where your child is directly observed, instructors can report information about the core symptoms and function of the child directly. You might also consider placement in a qualified preschool program. Qualified programs include Head Start or other public prekindergarten programs. Preschool children displaying significant emotional or behavioral concerns may also qualify for Early Childhood Special Education (ECSE) services through their local school districts, and the evaluators for these programs and/or ECSE teachers may be excellent reporters of core symptoms of ADHD.

Is It Only ADHD, a Coexisting Problem, or Both?

One of the advantages offered by thorough discussions during the evaluation, as well as diagnostic tests and rating scales that you, your child's teacher, and others complete, is that they frequently pinpoint other emotional or developmental problems that exist alongside or in place of ADHD. As many as two-thirds of children with ADHD have one or more additional or coexisting conditions. The most frequent coexisting conditions include learning disabilities, language disorders, and other behavior problems such as depression, anxiety, and oppositional or defiant behaviors.

If your child seems frequently sad or prefers to be isolated, talk with your child's pediatric clinician about possible evaluation.

Your child's pediatric clinician may be initially alerted to the possibility of some of these conditions by the reports you or other adults have provided. For example, a child described as frequently sad or irritable and who prefers isolated activities may be at risk for depression. A child who experiences frequent fears or unusual anxiety at being separated from a parent, and who has relatives with anxiety disorders, may have a similar disorder himself. Poor school performance may indicate a learning disability in addition to ADHD. Oppositional defiant disorder and conduct disorders are indicated by negative, disobedient, and oppositional behaviors toward authority figures and, less frequently, by a persistent violation of others' basic rights or of common social rules. Children who have experienced trauma or who have posttraumatic stress disorder may also have problems with attention due to their traumatic experience. They may also have had trauma and also have ADHD.

Coexisting conditions will be discussed in greater detail in Chapter 9. For now, though, it is important to consider the fact that such accompanying disorders can have a profound effect on how well your child functions behaviorally, emotionally, socially, and academically. Your child's pediatrician and others working with your child should carefully consider whether such disorders may be your child's central challenge in his ability to function in his environment. To determine this, further evaluation, including referrals to other specialists, may be necessary. These evaluations can be part of the process to arrive at the most accurate diagnosis and treatment plan for your child.

The Importance of Teamwork

Evaluating a child for ADHD and related conditions is not an overnight, cut-and-dried process, nor can it be necessarily completed by your child's pediatrician or another health professional alone. Arriving at a diagnosis of the problems or disorders causing them is an undertaking that requires accurate observation, insight, experience, and even a certain amount of educated intuition on the part of parents, teachers, and medical and mental health professionals alike. A number of conditions that lead to behaviors similar to those resulting from ADHD must be considered and either eliminated or identified. The functional, real-world effects of each disorder must be carefully considered before an effective treatment plan can be put into place.

Assessing a child for ADHD requires patience and a great deal of teamwork from all adults involved—and this is good practice for the challenges to come. If the diagnostic process for ADHD seems complex, the process of choosing and implementing treatment may be even more so. For this reason, one of your foremost goals during this period should be to create and maintain clear lines of communication among the members of your child's diagnostic team. If you disagree with a teacher's assessment of your child's school performance, air your concerns now and work toward arriving at a better mutual understanding of some kind. Make sure that your child's pediatrician's findings and conclusions are reviewed with you in detail. This can avoid misunderstandings or unnecessary concerns about diagnoses, labels, or future recommendations. Ask questions. Share your concerns. Keep teachers' reports, evaluation reports, and other materials used for diagnosis together in one file so that you can easily present and review them when necessary. The more professionals you see, the more important it is for you to have your own complete home-based medical record.

Become as expert about the condition and your child as you can and join with other parents to advocate for the needs of your child.

Diagnosis is only the first step in a long journey that you and your child are undertaking. By making sure that your child's support team agrees and that you are all focusing on the important issues, you can look forward with greater confidence to the day when your child's situation will be improved.

Q & A

Q: *I have ADHD, but because I have usually done well in school I was not diagnosed until I went to college, when my inability to keep to the task at hand began to seriously interfere with my school performance and relationships. As a child, I was quiet and shy, and because I did not have the hyperactive type of ADHD, no one noticed my condition. Now I am concerned that my daughter, who is in kindergarten, may have the same form of ADHD. But her teacher says she's doing well in school and has the usual number of friends even if she does have more trouble paying attention than most of her classmates. The teacher has discouraged me from having my daughter evaluated. Should I follow her advice?*

A: Children with inattentive-type ADHD are often first identified when the work demands of school start to accelerate—by third or fourth grade. Similar to your own experience, girls are often identified late, or not at all. You have a head start on this by already knowing a good deal about ADHD. The question now is whether your daughter's behaviors are still in the typical range for a girl in kindergarten or whether they are an early expression of ADHD. The really good news from her teacher is that she is doing well in school and with social situations. An evaluation should be considered if her behaviors start to interfere significantly with her school progress or other areas of functioning. As you suggest, ADHD does tend to run in families, so it is especially important to keep carefully tracking your daughter's progress. At this stage you might just want to bring your concerns to your child's pediatrician so that you can both keep a watchful eye on the situation and actively screen for problems at regular intervals.

Q: *My son has just been referred for assessment for ADHD. My neighbor tells me that her teenaged daughter was diagnosed with ADHD as a child and treated with stimulants for years, and then they found out that she had a learning disability instead. How can I tell if my child's problems are due to ADHD and not some other problem?*

A: Situations like this are the reason that the AAP and other professional organizations suggest that evaluations for ADHD follow a standard format and look at a broad range of areas of functioning instead of just ADHD itself. Estimates are highly variable, but a significant number of children who have been diagnosed with ADHD also have learning disabilities. Similarly, a significant number of children who have been diagnosed with learning disabilities also have ADHD. This is also true for other conditions, like oppositional defiant, conduct, anxiety, and depressive disorders. This emphasizes the importance of the AAP guideline recommendation that the evaluation of a child with ADHD should include assessment for coexisting conditions.

Q: *My son, who is in fourth grade, has just been diagnosed with ADHD. Both his teacher and doctor agree. I also agree that he is overactive and has trouble focusing. He is starting to have problems with his schoolwork and friendships even though he is a very bright and loving child. I can see that he needs some help, but I am also very concerned about his getting "labeled" and what negative effects this might have on him.*

A: You share a common concern of many parents whose child has just received the diagnosis of ADHD. In a sense, the diagnosis just tells you what you already know—that the problem behaviors you described during your child's evaluation match the diagnostic criteria for ADHD, and that they are causing your child significant problems on a daily basis. The diagnosis may be a starting point for receiving different levels of help at school. For example, the diagnosis will allow teachers to better understand and help your child.

   On the other hand, the diagnosis can be misunderstood. Teachers or other adults who interact regularly with your child but do not realize that your child has ADHD miss the opportunity to teach and be helpful. You and your child's pediatrician can also contribute a great deal to this effort with your child's own teacher in many positive ways. Community support groups like CHADD: The National Resource on ADHD can provide you with a forum for discussing this and a place to meet parents who have already had experience with many of these challenges.

CHAPTER 3

What Should We Do?
Treatment Options

"It was a shock, even after all the interviews, evaluations, and reports, when Andy was diagnosed with ADHD," writes a parent about her experience with her 8-year-old son. "On the one hand, I was so relieved to have an explanation for Andy's behavior. On the other, I was concerned that now the teachers and kids at school would 'label' him in negative ways. I was also worried about whether medications might be prescribed for him. I wondered, too, how Andy would respond to the diagnosis—would he lose even more self-confidence now that he knew he had a disorder?"

If your child has been diagnosed with attention-deficit/hyperactivity disorder (ADHD), you have probably asked similar questions and experienced some of the same concerns. You may also face a variety of responses to plans for your child's treatment—and much conflicting advice—from friends, relatives, educators, your partner, and even your child. Friends who have not been educated about ADHD may insist that your child's behavior is just the result of a discipline or parenting problem. You may feel that teachers who have witnessed the positive effect of stimulant medication in many children with ADHD are pushing you to put your child on the same type of medication. Your spouse or partner may believe that an alternative treatment is the answer, while your child may insist that she does not have a problem at all—that others' concerns about her are "their problem."

Such opinions and concerns are common and understandable given how much inaccurate information about ADHD has been spread through the media, the internet, and other channels, and it is important that it be addressed. In this chapter and the next one, you will find the responses to many of the questions that you and others are likely to have about treatment for your child. You will learn

- Which types and combinations of treatment programs have been shown to be effective for ADHD.

- How to develop a *treatment team*. This team likely will include, if possible, your child's teachers, pediatrician or other pediatric clinician, and other mental health clinicians (eg, psychologist, psychiatrist or therapist) as needed. It is likely to be a virtual team. Often, one important role for you as a parent will be to make sure that communication among team members occurs. While other team members can provide you with accurate information about your child's diagnosis and treatment, you are the expert on your child.

- How the treatment team can then help you and your child to create a management plan to address the target goals that you and your child develop with your team.

- What your child's team can provide with ongoing observation and follow-up visits that can be used to monitor your child's progress and adjust aspects of his treatment when necessary to better address his ongoing needs.

- How to help your child understand the treatment plan and become a member of the treatment team at each stage of his development.

What Should I Tell Them?

As you move from an attention-deficit/hyperactivity disorder (ADHD) diagnosis toward the creation of a treatment plan, you are likely to face a number of questions and remarks from friends, relatives, teachers, and others. Here are some responses that may help you and your child through awkward situations and answer some of your own questions.

Your child's teacher might say, "I have had several students with ADHD in my classes in the past. I recommend that your child be put on medication as soon as possible."

Response: "My child's pediatrician tells me that the most effective treatment plans need to include several things and medication may or may not be part of it. We need your help in determining if he needs any changes in his classroom activities to monitor and improve his behavior. Your feedback and observations are essential as we start the treatment process. If we make the decision to use medication as a part of the overall treatment plan, your observations and comments will be critical to monitoring and refining it."

A concerned relative could comment, "Everyone knows that ADHD is just a teacher's excuse to have kids 'medicated' so they stay quiet and the classroom is easier to manage."

Response: "ADHD has been clearly identified as a behavioral disorder. It is common, and it is treatable. Medication is just one of the ways that children can be helped to display fewer behavioral challenges and have more self-control from the teacher's perspective—but equally important is its ability to help children attend to daily tasks and, thus, function better."

That same relative could also say, "I don't care what the doctor says. There is no way you should give your child drugs."

Response: "First of all, the use of the word 'drugs' makes medications sound like they are bad or illegal and not the most appropriate choice when talking about medications for ADHD. It can lead to some parents thinking that their child is better off without taking anything. But, in fact, stimulant medications for ADHD have been shown to make an enormous positive difference in the lives of many children. The medications for ADHD are very much like prescribing inhalers for children with asthma—both can help the symptoms enough to allow him to live a typical life. Before making up our minds about treatment, we will talk to experts in the field, look at the research, read to inform ourselves, talk with other families whose children have been diagnosed with ADHD, and discuss our child's situation with him and with his doctors."

A concerned grandparent sometimes will worry, "He just seems depressed to me. How do you know it's ADHD and not some other problem?"

Response: "It's true that a number of other conditions, like anxiety problems and depression, can mimic some ADHD symptoms. The evaluation my child just completed was designed to eliminate or identify most of them. Some children may have depression or anxiety disorders along with ADHD. By treating the ADHD, it is possible to reduce the anxiety. Some of the coexisting conditions, such as depression and posttraumatic stress disorder (PTSD), may start out looking identical to ADHD and only evolve into the specific disorder. That's why we'll continue to monitor and review his symptoms throughout childhood to make sure the diagnosis and treatment are still correct, timely, and appropriate."

It is not unusual for your child to complain, "There's nothing wrong with me. It's other people who have a problem. My behavior is fine—they just can't handle it!"

Response: "I can see how hard it is on you when you feel like your teacher is always singling you out and picking on you, or when we always seem to be arguing about following rules at home. Now that we are finished with your evaluation, we can start learning more ways to turn these things around and make a happier situation at home, at school, and when you are out with your friends."

Taking Action: First Steps in Developing a Treatment Plan

Attention-deficit/hyperactivity disorder is a chronic medical condition like asthma or diabetes. Treating ADHD is more like treating asthma. With type 1 diabetes, a simple blood test will determine the diagnosis and a child will either have it or not. Children with the diagnosis of type 1 diabetes will have to control it with everyday medication and treatment.

On the other hand, like asthma, ADHD ranges in the severity of the problems it causes. It can be mild, moderate, or severe, and some children display problem behaviors similar to ADHD but not severe enough to require diagnosis or treatment. Unfortunately, there are no individual definitive diagnostic tests for ADHD, like there are for diabetes, asthma, and many other disorders, but there are some specific symptoms that help us make the diagnosis.

Of course, all children have difficulty paying attention, controlling impulses, and being fidgety some of the time. When these behaviors become a problem, it is not necessarily ADHD. Talk with your child's pediatrician. Your pediatrician can suggest a number of ways to help, including counseling about the range of typical developmental behaviors, home behavior management tools, school behavior management recommendations, social skills work, and help with managing homework flow, along with organization and planning.

If the symptoms begin to significantly interfere with your child's functioning at home and school on a daily basis, your pediatrician or clinician will work with you to create a more comprehensive and organized overall plan. That plan will include considering a diagnosis of ADHD. If ADHD is confirmed, the plan for your child may also include recommendations for medication management, behavior therapy, and other forms of treatment and support. Interventions are all coordinated through an individualized and specific treatment plan.

The core ADHD symptoms of inattention, hyperactivity, and impulsiveness are the initial noticeable symptoms which then are followed by the "functional disabilities" that often concern parents and teachers, such as schoolwork production, difficulty adhering to family rules at home, and challenges with maintaining friendships. These issues will also become the "targets" for treatment. The American Academy of Pediatrics has provided a set of guidelines to help pediatricians to develop comprehensive treatment plans for children with ADHD.

The American Academy of Pediatrics Recommends...

Treatment Guidelines for ADHD

- Attention-deficit/hyperactivity disorder (ADHD) should be recognized as a chronic condition. A long-term treatment plan for children and adolescents with ADHD should be developed as for other children and youth with special health care needs. Management of children and youth with special health care needs should follow the principles of the chronic care model and the medical home, which will be discussed later in this chapter.

- Attention-deficit/hyperactivity disorder treatments can be effective for preschoolers through adolescents, but different considerations should be applied to children of different ages.

- Clinicians should prescribe medications for ADHD approved by the US Food and Drug Administration (FDA) and/or scientifically proven parent- and/or teacher-administered behavior management therapy as part of the treatment for ADHD. Recommendations regarding the school environment, program, or placement may also be part of the treatment plan.

- When medications are part of a treatment plan, clinicians should adjust doses of an FDA-approved medication for ADHD to achieve maximum benefit with minimum side-effects.

Adapted from American Academy of Pediatrics. Clinical practice guidelines: diagnostic, evaluation, and treatment of the child and adolescent with attention-deficit/hyperactivity disorder. *Pediatrics.* In press.

ADHD as a Chronic Condition

Untreated ADHD can continue to cause symptoms and problems in managing day-to-day functioning in many individuals over long periods—even when they are adults. It affects many areas of a child's life, and managing these areas needs to be coordinated. The model for treating chronic conditions has been effective for other long-term conditions, such as asthma and cystic fibrosis. Parents, children, and adolescents need a program for ongoing education about ADHD and related issues and for adapting treatments to their needs over time. The treatments presently available address symptoms and functioning but are not curative.

The Medical Home Model

The pediatric family-centered medical home model has been accepted as the preferred standard of care for chronic conditions like ADHD. The medical home model recognizes that appropriate care for ADHD requires attention to multiple areas of a child's and family's life, including home, school, friendships, health care, emotional care, and self-esteem. This kind of care needs to be coordinated to be the most effective. Parents and children are partners in an overall treatment plan with physicians, teachers, therapists, and other key individuals. In this model, all parties work together to identify specific goals or target outcomes, and then they work together to make decisions about treatment. In the pediatric family-centered medical home model, care is provided to children and families that is accessible, continuous, comprehensive, family centered, coordinated, compassionate, and culturally effective. It addresses care needs at all levels.

Family-centered care includes partnering between parents and health care professionals in

- Providing information about the child's condition to parents and children.
- Updating and monitoring family knowledge and understanding on a periodic basis.
- Counseling families about how they respond to ADHD.
- Providing appropriate education to the child about the condition that is appropriate to the child's level of understanding. Patient education is updated as the child grows older and treatment soon includes the child in decisions about her treatment.
- Having the pediatric clinician available to answer family questions.
- Ensuring coordination of health and other services like education and behavioral treatments.
- Helping families set specific goals in areas related to the child's condition and its effect on daily activities.
- Linking families with other families with children who have similar chronic conditions as needed and available.

- Working in collaboration with mental health clinicians if the child requires a consultation.

- Addressing transition periods in the child's life and developing a transition plan as primary grade students transition to middle school, middle school early adolescents transition to high school, and adolescents approach adulthood.

Identifying the Treatment Team

To successfully develop a treatment plan and put it into action, you will need to create a treatment team. This entails identifying the people most directly involved in your child's care and education. Their combined efforts will lead you to develop and carry out the most thoughtful, informed, and effective treatment plan. The team will optimally include you (the parent[s]), your child, your child's pediatric clinician, and your child's teacher. It may also include other adults at school and any involved mental health professionals. Why a team? It will promote communication and the development of an agreed-on unified approach. Like all good teams, the treatment team should be more valuable than the sum of each member's individual contribution to your child's success. You are an essential facilitator of communication among team members.

Creating a List: Defining Target Outcomes

Before you, your child, her pediatric clinician, and other members of her treatment team can create an appropriate treatment plan, you will want to carefully consider which behaviors are most problematic for your child and most in need of attention, and which can be addressed later. A good way to begin this process is to identify your child's day-to-day problems with functioning at school, at home, and elsewhere. Think in terms of *addressing your child's problems* in the context of your family and available community resources, rather than "treating her ADHD." Consider a full picture of your child. Start with her strengths and identify preferences, dislikes, and problems. Are there accompanying diagnoses that were identified during her evaluation? How does your family function? Are there other major demands on family members that may affect your child's situation? What helpful resources are available in your community?

In this broad context, you and your child's pediatric clinician can together decide the best treatment plan that will work for your child's unique circumstances. Your next step in creating a treatment plan is to initially identify a few areas, goals, or targets that would most improve your child's functioning and self-esteem. Such targets may include

- Improved relationships with parents, siblings, teachers, and friends
- Fewer disruptive behaviors
- Better academic performance through improving organizational skills and managing the volume, efficiency, completion, and accuracy of her work
- Greater independence in self-care or homework
- Improved self-esteem and self-perception
- Safer behavior in the community, like when crossing streets, riding bicycles, and driving
- Making better behavioral choices—more thinking before doing

Once you, your child, and the other members of her treatment team have agreed on this list, you can turn these types of broad targets into specific behaviors and criteria that will help you know if your child is meeting the goals that you set. For example, if the broader area is "improved teacher relationships," your target outcomes might be

- Appropriately accepts feedback (eg, no more than 2 arguments per day following feedback)
- Appropriately asks for adult help when needed (eg, knows how to do the homework assignment before leaving class)
- Maintains appropriate eye contact when talking to an adult, with fewer than 2 prompts to maintain eye contact
- Respects adults (eg, talks back fewer than 2 times per class period)
- Complies with at least 80% of teachers' requests with fewer than 2 noncompliances per class period

Courtesy of William E. Pelham Jr, PhD

Try to make each behavioral goal specific and countable. Also, be aware that if you use words like "appropriately," you will need to define what it means for you, your child, your child's teacher, and any other adults who will be involved with the treatment plan. After you have defined these targets, you can arrange them in order of priority. Make sure that you are not taking on too much at once. Highest priority issues will be those that most interfere with your child's functioning to the greatest degree at school, at home, or with her peers; those that impede her development; or those that have proved largely unmanageable so far. A problem that creates much stress for your family may also affect the level of priority you give it. Your child's teacher can be an especially valuable contributor to this discussion because the teacher observes your child daily within the context of a typical range of same-aged children and, thus, may have a good idea of how much a particular behavior interferes with your child's classroom learning.

Try to be certain that your target goals are realistically within your child's and family's abilities to achieve. Your child's pediatric clinician or other medical or mental health professional will be able to advise you on which goals are realistic and what types of results you can reasonably expect from which types of treatments. Expecting all As on your child's next report card may not be a realistic expectation no matter what treatment is chosen, but changes from Ds to Bs in certain academic subjects may be realistic, possible, and rewarding.

One of the major effects children with ADHD face is the loss of self-esteem as they experience academic failure, teasing from peers, and other upsetting effects of their inability to manage their behavior. Setting the bar a bit lower than ideal as you create a first set of goals will make it easier for your child to succeed, which may give her a boost in confidence at a critical moment and could ensure greater success down the road.

Involving Your Child and Getting Her Buy-In

Once your child's target outcomes have been identified, placed in order of priority, and screened for feasibility, take a moment to make sure that she understands them as fully as possible given her level of understanding. *Treatment for ADHD should never be a process that is done to your child but one that is, as much as possible, implemented by your child with your support, guidance, and educated assistance, as well as support from the rest of the treatment team.*

For any treatment plan to succeed, your school-aged child or adolescent needs to understand the nature of ADHD, think and talk about ways in which she would like to improve her functioning, and feel comfortable participating in the treatment process to the extent that she is able. Your child should be present whenever possible for at least part of meetings that concern her, and parts of the discussion should be addressed directly to her at her level of understanding. Adolescents also benefit from time alone with the doctor without parents present. Your child's reports on her day-to-day experiences with issues related to ADHD should be listened to and carefully considered. Her prioritizing of ADHD-related problems should be taken seriously and addressed. By teaching your child to consider her strengths, obstacles, and abilities to function in different situations and to monitor any changes, you are helping her prepare for the day when she will be in charge of her own care.

Becoming the Care Manager

Identifying target outcomes is only the first step, but it is an important one. Even though your child's pediatric clinician, teacher, and psychologist will take the primary responsibility for coordinating aspects of your child's care from time to time, as your

Your child should be present whenever possible for at least parts of meetings that concern him, and the discussion should be addressed to his level of understanding.

child's parent you should still expect and need to serve as the primary overall coordinator. In a family-centered medical home model, you would ideally partner with a care manager and all those who are caring for your child to successfully coordinate the treatment plan. As time goes on you will need to take on many functions of care management, such as soliciting teachers' comments, providing your own observations and feedback, reviewing new evaluation results with medical personnel, and seeking out the emotional and behavioral support that you, your child, and other family members need. The more active you are in coordinating this care among team members, the more organized your child's treatment is likely to be. Many of the details of this role are discussed in Chapter 5.

What Works and What Does Not— What We Know About Treatment

Once you, your child, and the treatment team have identified the target outcomes you hope to achieve, you will create a treatment plan to address those goals. With the help of the professionals on your treatment team, you will need to educate yourself on the various treatments that are available and what effects and limitations each is likely to have.

As you begin to make decisions about treatment, keep in mind this fact about treatment for ADHD: Nothing is written in stone. Because ADHD symptoms tend to change over time, your child may have different target outcomes at different stages of life and require different types of treatment. What worked well during third grade may not work well or be appropriate for fourth grade. Because individual children respond to different therapies in a variety of ways, it may take several tries before you find a treatment program that works well. For all these reasons, your child's treatment plan will consist of an ongoing process of treatment decisions, observation, review, and treatment revision.

Choosing One or More Types of Treatment

In the years since ADHD symptoms were first described, a variety of treatment approaches have been tried and tested for their effectiveness. *Only 2 of these approaches—use of medication and behavior therapies (a set of systematic, consistent techniques that parents and teachers can use to help a child better manage her behavior)—have been shown in well-done studies to have consistently positive effects.* The key is to find a balance between medication and behavior therapies—using the medication recommended by your pediatric clinician, as well as relying on behavioral management techniques that will help address behaviors such as not paying attention, hyperactivity, tantrums, and oppositional behavior (also see Chapter 6). These approaches are often most effective when used in combination (see An Overview of Medication and Behavior Therapy for ADHD: The Mainstays of a Treatment Plan section later in this chapter).

Medical professionals and other experts have studied traditional psychotherapy, special diets, nutritional supplements, biofeedback, allergy treatments, vision training, sensory integration therapy, chiropractic, and many other methods. These approaches cannot be recommended. They have either not been studied adequately enough to be recommended or have been shown to have minimal or no long-term effect. Some will be discussed in more detail in Chapter 10. Table 3.1 summarizes the most proven treatments for ADHD and accompanying problems.

An Overview of Medication and Behavior Therapy for ADHD: The Mainstays of a Treatment Plan

Stimulants such as methylphenidate and amphetamine have been the widest and best studied of any group of medications for the behavioral and emotional problems faced by children. Taken as recommended, they are effective and safe for most children with ADHD. Side effects mostly occur early in treatment, tend to be mild and short-lived, and, in most situations, can be successfully managed through adjustments in the dose or schedule of medication.

Parents are often confused by the fact that *stimulants* are the most frequently prescribed medications for ADHD. Why use stimulants, they wonder, when their child seems already overactive and overstimulated? *Stimulant* is an old name for these medications and does not describe accurately how they work in ADHD.

These medications work by helping the brain to provide more of the neurotransmitters, or brain chemicals, that are necessary to help all of us focus our attention, control our impulses, organize and plan, and stick to routines. With effective stimulant medication treatment, children with ADHD are better able to manage academic work and social interaction, attend to behavior modification techniques, and follow rules.

Table 3.1. ADHD Treatments: What the Evidence Shows	
Treatment For	**Possible Treatments[a]**
ADHD as a chronic condition	■ Education for parents and treatment ■ A team approach among all the child's caregivers, including parents and pediatricians (the kind provided in a family-centered medical home) ■ Empowerment of children and adolescents to "own" and help carry out their own treatment plan ■ Careful setting, monitoring, and reassessment of treatment targets, goals, and plans
Core symptoms of ADHD (inattention, impulsivity, hyperactivity)	■ Stimulant medications (methylphenidate or amphetamine) (first-line treatment) ■ Proven behavior therapies ■ Atomoxetine, or α2 agonists (extended-release guanfacine or clonidine) (second-line treatment) ■ IEP based on IDEA legislation or a plan based on Section 504 of the Rehabilitation Act

Oppositional and defiant behavior and serious conduct problems	■ Behavior modification and management techniques
	  ■ Parent training in behavior management
	  ■ School behavioral programs
	■ Medication management, if appropriate

Depression, anxiety, posttraumatic stress disorder, and problems with self-control and anger management	■ Cognitive behavior therapy ■ Selective serotonin reuptake inhibitor or other antidepressant medication management, if appropriate
Significant difficulties in family functioning	■ Family therapy

Underachievement and learning and language disorders	■ School IEPs that include
	  ■ Educational management
	  ■ Optimizing the classroom environment
	  ■ Addressing individual learning and language abilities and learning style

Abbreviations: ADHD, attention-deficit/hyperactivity disorder; IDEA, Individuals With Disabilities Education Act; IEP, Individualized Education Program.

[a] These treatment options will be described in detail in chapters 4 through 7 and 9.

Often parents view placing their children on stimulant medication as a last resort, after all other measures have been tried. Many years of research has consistently shown that other treatments are more likely to work if the child is also taking stimulants. By helping your child focus, stimulants *lay the groundwork* for her to be able to respond better to behavior management techniques, academic instruction, and other demands on her attention.

Stimulant medication can be prescribed in a variety of doses and schedules. A child's response to the 2 types of stimulants (methylphenidate and amphetamine) and the most effective dose for each child varies greatly; some children only respond to one type of medication, and some smaller children may require a higher dose than some bigger children. This is why determining the best dose may take a while. Studies show that the best results from medication treatment are achieved by the dose that shows the *most* improvement with the *fewest* side effects. It is a common error to use only the lowest dose of stimulant medication that leads to any improvement.

Children for whom neither type of stimulant (methylphenidate or amphetamine) has worked may need to be prescribed 1 of the 2 non-stimulant medication types (atomoxetine) or 1 of the 2 α2 agonists (extended-release guanfacine and clonidinde) instead. These drugs are also used for the rare child with ADHD who has another medical condition and cannot use stimulants. Children who were originally prescribed stimulants who show some but not adequate improvement may add extended-release guanfacine or clonidine. Those who do not respond or have serious or pretty bothersome side effects can be treated with atomoxetine or α2 agonists (extended-release guanfacine or clonidine) as a second-line treatment. These non-stimulant medications have been shown to have work adequately on the core symptoms of ADHD but not as consistently as stimulants. The advantages and disadvantages of stimulant and non-stimulant medications will be discussed in greater detail in Chapter 4.

Behavior therapy is another proven first-line treatment for ADHD. Behavior therapy emphasizes ways in which adults can better manage and shape their child's behavior by using tested and effective behavior management principles. These treatments teach techniques for giving instructions and commands in a way that builds children's self-control and self-esteem.

Programs that teach behavior therapy focus on how to give clear commands, use time-outs effectively, create effective rewards systems, and otherwise structure a child's environment in ways that work. This approach focuses on how adults can help children develop more appropriate and positive behaviors. Both parents and teachers can learn to use these techniques effectively. Traditional child-focused counseling approaches have not been shown to be effective for ADHD, but parent and teacher behavior therapy is proven to work. You will learn more about the specifics of behavior therapy in chapters 6 and 7.

Evidence for the effectiveness of behavior treatments in children with ADHD comes from a variety of studies. The long-term positive effects of these treatments may be boosted when a chronic care model for child health has been implemented. Some of the proven effective, evidence-based behavioral treatments for children with ADHD are listed in Table 3.2.

Table 3.2. Evidence-Based Psychosocial Treatments for ADHD		
Treatment Type	**Description**	**Treatment Can Result In**
Parent training in behavior management	Behavior modification principles provided to parents for implementation in home settings	■ Improved compliance with parental commands ■ Improved parental understanding of behavioral principles ■ High levels of parental satisfaction with treatment
Behavioral classroom management	Behavior modification principles provided to teachers for implementation in classroom settings	■ Improved attention to instruction ■ Improved compliance with classroom rules ■ Decreased disruptive behavior ■ Improved work productivity

(continued)

Table 3.2 (*continued*)		
Treatment Type	**Description**	**Treatment Can Result In**
Behavioral peer interventions	Interventions focused on peer interactions/relationships. These are often group-based interventions provided weekly. They include clinic-based social skills training employed either alone or concurrently with parent training in behavior management and/or medication.	When these treatments are provided in offices instead of schools, they have produced minimal effects. Interventions have been of questionable help in everyday life, even though they may be helpful in the groups themselves. Some studies of behavioral peer interventions combined with clinic-based parent training in behavior management report positive effects on parent ratings of ADHD symptoms.

Abbreviation: ADHD, attention-deficit/hyperactivity disorder.

Adapted from Pelham WE Jr, Fabiano GA. Evidence-based psychosocial treatments for attention-deficit/hyperactivity disorder. *J Clin Child Adolesc Psychol.* 2008;37(1):184–214. Reprinted by permission of Taylor & Francis Group, https://www.tandfonline.com.

Behavior therapy programs coordinating efforts at school as well as home may enhance the effects. School programs may be able to provide enhanced training to help your child master skills or at least provide classroom adaptations, such as preferred seating, reduced work assignments, and test modifications including the location where tests are administered and the time allotted for taking the test. Adolescents documented to have ADHD can also get permission to take college boards in an untimed manner by following appropriate documentation guidelines. These recommendations will be discussed further in Chapter 11.

The largest study of combined medication and behavioral long-term treatment for ADHD to date is the Multimodal Treatment Study of Children with Attention Deficit Hyperactivity Disorder (MTA), whose primary results were published in 1999. The MTA researchers found that stimulants used as the sole form of treatment lead to significantly better results for the core symptoms of ADHD than behavior therapy used alone. A *combination* of the 2 approaches, however, has been shown to lead to the best overall improvement in several aspects of ADHD. Improvements were found in reduction of oppositional and aggressive behavior and in improved social skills, parent-child relationships, and some areas of academic achievement. The use of behavior therapy can also lower the rate of medication required in some cases. Parents in the MTA whose children used this combined approach were often significantly more satisfied with the treatment plan than those whose children received medication alone.

In this study, medication management and behavior treatment guidelines were carefully developed and followed. When the study guidelines were followed in this way, about 60% of children treated with medication alone could not be distinguished from their peers who did not have ADHD at the end of this 14-month study, longer than any prior study. When children were treated with medication and the highly specific behavior treatments, this number increased to 70%. With this combination treatment, children with ADHD had fewer anxiety symptoms and fewer problems with academic performance and social skills.

After the initial 14-month study, the children returned to their own care from community providers but continued to be followed for 8 more years to track their progress. The following additional observations have been published:

- Changes in starting or stopping medication did not seem to be affected by whether the children had been in the medication only, behavioral treatment only, or combined medication and behavioral treatment groups in the original study.

- Three patterns of outcomes were identified and remained consistent during follow-up care.

  - About one-third of children showed gradual improvement throughout the first 3 years and had more consistent use of medication at 3 years.

  - About half of the children showed a large improvement at 14 months, which could still be seen at the 3-year follow-up. This group also had the best outcomes at 6 and 8 years, and this did not seem to be due to the extent of their medication use.

  - The third group, of about 15% of children, showed a large initial improvement followed by a trend of deterioration over time regardless of medication use.

- Children who continued to use medication over the 8 years of follow-up tended to have a minor decrease in their rate of growth for 2 years of medication treatment but then stabilized. However, no catch-up growth was found, although the follow-up reported to date did not take the children through their full growth period.

It is not known what the outcomes would be if a group of children received the same careful treatment and medication adjustment that they had received in the 14-month initial study period. It is also unclear what the outcome would have been if these children had also received care according to the sound family-centered medical home principles discussed previously.

All medication and behavior approaches are not the same—one size does not fit all. The most successful approaches, like those in the MTA, are evidence based. This means they have been carefully researched and found to work. More evidence-based approaches for the treatment of ADHD will be reviewed in the chapters that follow. Untested treatment approaches are not as reliable.

Other Components of the Treatment Plan

Other treatments, including psychotherapy and family or marital therapy, may provide valuable assistance to families who have problems that are not directly caused by their child's ADHD. Such problems are often related to ADHD and can worsen ADHD symptoms. The stress that a child's behavior may place on the family may prevent them from carrying out a treatment plan unless such issues are addressed. Because ADHD runs in families, one or both parents or a partner may also have ADHD. If a parent's ADHD has not been recognized, diagnosed, or effectively managed, even more stress is placed on family functioning.

Children with ADHD may also have learning disabilities and other learning-related conditions. Important and necessary academic interventions can make a difference for your child, even if it does not directly affect her ADHD symptoms. Children with clearly diagnosed learning disabilities qualify for special education services in school. In this situation, schools are federally mandated to develop Individualized Education

Programs, or IEPs, that detail exactly what services will be offered and how they will be delivered. The same is true for children who have behavioral needs too severe to be handled in a regular classroom with a Section 504 plan.

Students who have learning or behavioral needs related to their ADHD symptoms but do not have diagnosed learning disabilities or such severe behavioral needs can also receive services (see Chapter 7). While such programs, strategies, and considerations do not directly address the core symptoms of ADHD, they support the child with ADHD academically and behaviorally and, thus, help maintain their success and self-esteem.

Because each of the treatments discussed targets different results, it is most common to use several types of treatment together. While most children's treatment plans may begin with medication and behavior therapy, additional approaches, such as academic intervention and family therapy, may provide added support when they are indicated. When choosing from the menu of treatment options, you will need to consider whether

- You have the work schedule, time, confidence in the treatments, and energy necessary to adhere to them.
- They address one of your child's most important target outcomes.
- The therapies are available in your community, which isn't always the case.
- Your family can realistically afford them, particularly since behavior therapy often isn't adequately covered by health insurance.

Consider how good a match each of these approaches is for your child and whether the results can be satisfactorily monitored. How smoothly can each treatment be combined with the others that you plan to implement? How available are these techniques or programs in your community? How long are the benefits likely to last after the treatment has ended? Are there any possible negatives or side effects? How well do the positive effects translate to your child's everyday life? Are you still using the parenting techniques 3 days after the training session and are they helping with your child's behavior? How well does the treatment method coincide with the values and goals of your family as a whole? Most importantly, how does your child feel about this type of treatment? Will she feel stigmatized by her friends or family because of it?

In the end, no matter how effective the other members of a treatment team believe a certain approach to be, it will most likely break down unless the child herself understands its purpose and is committed to making it work. For this reason, unless a mode of treatment promotes your child's self-confidence, improved self-management, and higher self-esteem, it is not likely to work and probably should not be considered. It may take more than one try to create this type of treatment plan, and you should expect to be constantly reshaping it, but the potential benefits are worth the effort.

Follow-up Plan

Your pediatrician or other pediatric clinician will want to periodically provide a systematic follow-up for children and adolescents with ADHD. One good model could be for a child to be initially seen by the clinician prescribing medications each month after treatment is prescribed until the desired effects are seen. Follow-up may then be every 3 to 4 months in the first year of treatment. Many pediatricians continue to see children with ADHD twice annually, once for their health supervision (well-child) visit and 6 months later for an additional ADHD check.

The prescribing pediatrician will generally consult with parents, teachers, and the child about how well target outcomes are being met and what, if any, unexpected or negative effects have been experienced. Family input will allow the treatment team to further tailor your child's treatment plan in ways that can make it more effective. If the target outcomes are not met, the treatment team will reevaluate the original diagnosis, treatments used, whether the treatment plan is being carefully followed, and presence of any coexisting conditions (see Chapter 9).

Setting a Plan for Your Child's Follow-up Visits

The American Academy of Pediatrics recommends that pediatricians periodically provide systematic follow-up for your child. You can help structure each visit so that you and your pediatrician can include as many of the following steps as possible:

1. Discuss and review your own observations of your child, his most recent teachers' reports, and the results of any rating scales completed since the last visit.
2. Share information about the target behaviors and how they might have changed since the last visit.
3. Review the plan agenda, the target behaviors, and the current methods of treatment.
4. Screen for new coexisting conditions.
5. If your child is taking medication, review any possible side effects.
6. Review your child's functioning at home, including his behavior and family relationships.
7. Review your child's functioning at school, especially relating to academics, behavior, and social interaction. Make sure that some information is obtained directly from your child's teacher. This is particularly important before changing any medication dose.
8. Discuss your child's self-esteem and review his behavioral, social, and academic self-management issues.
9. Assess and supplement your child's understanding of attention-deficit/hyperactivity disorder, coexisting conditions, and treatment as appropriate for his age.
10. Discuss any current problems relating to organizational skills, study skills, homework management, self-management skills, anger management, etc.
11. Make sure that you get all the information you need to enable you and your child to make informed decisions that promote his long-term health and well-being.
12. Review and revise your child's treatment plan.
13. Make sure that there is a system in place for communication among you, your child, his teachers, and the pediatrician between visits.

A Parent's Story

A Team Effort

"At first I was surprised to hear from other families how often kids switched their medication or tried new doses or schedules," writes the father of a 9-year-old. "I guess my first reaction was, 'Don't the doctors know what they're doing? Why can't they get it right the first time?'

"After we started the treatment process, though, I found it very reassuring that Tina's pediatrician wanted our feedback on how the medication was working and how we were doing with the behavior therapy. Tina experienced some irritability in-between doses with her first prescription, so we switched to a long-acting medication where she only had to take one dose per day. That worked a lot better, and then we figured out that working more in concert with her teacher on the behavior techniques improved the situation even more. As Tina started doing much better, she became more eager to participate in the plan. By the end of the first year I felt like we'd all worked as a team to put together the best program we could for her. It was great knowing we had all these people's support and that as Tina's life changed her treatment could change along with her."

John, Tampa, FL

Follow-up visits cover all the ground since your last visit. This includes sharing your own observations of your child's recent behaviors, ongoing problems, and any new concerns. Screening may be necessary for any new coexisting conditions. You and your child now have the opportunity to ask questions and may be informed about any major new research or other information pertaining to her condition or treatment.

The most recent rating scales, teachers' observations, and other progress reports are reviewed. Finally, your child's target outcomes can be reviewed and, if your child is clearly not meeting the current goal for each one, her treatment can be reassessed.

If your child is not meeting her specific target outcomes, you, your child's pediatrician, and your child should consider the following issues:

- Were the target outcomes realistic?
- Is more information needed about your child's behavior?
- Is the diagnosis correct?
- Is another condition hindering treatment?
- Is the treatment plan being followed?
- Has the treatment failed?
- What coping strategies can you learn to deal with target behaviors that cannot be fully resolved through appropriate treatment?
- Are there changes for your child at school or with her friends? Is she being bullied?

No treatment for ADHD is likely to completely eliminate all the symptoms of inattention, hyperactivity, and impulsivity and associated problems and conditions. Children who are being treated successfully may still have trouble with their friends or schoolwork. But you should see signs of progress relating to your child's specific target outcomes or general behavior. If not, your child's diagnosis and treatment should be reviewed. The diagnosis of ADHD and possible co-occurring conditions need to reconsidered. A revised diagnosis is not a sign of failure in you, your child, or your child's pediatrician. It is merely a signal that your child's treatment team has yet to create the optimal response to her symptoms.

Treatment of ADHD is, in many cases, largely a matter of continually monitoring and reshaping the plan, and you can expect treatment to change as your child adjusts to treatment, grows, and develops over time. As these changes are made, continue to make sure that any and all treatments are aimed at fostering good self-esteem and that your child understands them to the extent possible given her developmental level. Follow-up visits should be geared in large part toward educating your child and empowering her to participate more and more in decision-making as she approaches adolescence.

Adolescents who "own" their problems and treatment plans are much more likely to make progress. Those who feel that treatment changes are being "shoved down their throats" will naturally resist or abandon treatment and are at higher risk for school failure, poor peer relationships, low self-esteem, substance use, and conduct problems.

Treatment for ADHD is generally considered to have failed only in cases when a child shows no response to appropriate trials and alterations in medication at maximum doses without side effects, when she cannot learn to control her behavior in spite of appropriate behavior therapy, or when a coexisting condition persistently interferes with the meeting of target outcomes. In each of these cases, the diagnosis would need to be carefully reconsidered and additional consultations might be called for. In treating, monitoring, and following up on treatment for your child with ADHD, communication is key. As treatment continues in one form or another throughout your child's early years, you will need to make sure that

- She understands and supports the goals and methods of her treatment.
- Other family members are equally informed and supportive.
- Each new school year teachers continue to work with her in effective ways and pass their observations on to her and you.
- Pediatricians and other medical personnel receive this feedback from you, your child's teachers, and others who spend time with your child.
- You and other members of the treatment team remain up-to-date on the legislation and medical, educational, and psychological issues that affect your child.

A child who knows as much as possible about ADHD will be better prepared as she faces challenges at home and school. A sibling who understands the steps involved in the treatment process may be more patient when you need to take time out for parent behavior management training. Pediatric clinicians who are informed of any new family problems or stressors can make better decisions about your child's treatment. Finally, educators who know that you and your child understand the nature of ADHD are often more eager to work together to manage it.

Attention-deficit/hyperactivity disorder is not curable, but it is certainly treatable. With attention, dedication, and a long-term outlook, you and your family may be able to look forward to continuing progress in the target areas you have defined.

Q & A

Q: *My son was recently diagnosed with ADHD, and we have worked out a treatment plan with his pediatrician. The problem is, the plan involves having my son take medication twice each day, implementing a number of new parenting practices, changing his homework habits, and dealing with the fallout with my other children and my wife. Frankly, since the diagnosis I feel like my entire family is falling apart. We can't seem to handle this responsibility on top of all the pressures of daily life. Is there anything we can do to get better organized?*

A: The initial steps in starting and carrying out a treatment plan for ADHD can be stressful for all families. It is not at all unusual for a family undertaking a complex treatment program—learning to administer medication on time, consistently applying new behavior-modification techniques, and making and keeping appointments with various specialists—to feel at first that it is almost impossible to get through a single day. That is why it is so important to define a limited number of target goals and treatments that are achievable and can fit into your family's daily life. If the treatment plan overwhelms you and your child, the chances of it succeeding will significantly decrease. If the plans you make around these goals are successful, it will give you more energy to take on the next steps. Through all this, make sure that you keep your support systems in place—other family members, members of the treatment team, and community support groups. Also make sure that you emphasize more than ever the things that you and your family value and enjoy.

Q: *My 14-year-old daughter has recently begun treatment for inattentive-type ADHD. From the beginning, we have involved her in her own diagnosis and treatment and have asked for her input as we created a list of behavioral goals and put together a treatment plan. She is now responding well to treatment, but I'm not sure that she really comprehends the nature of her condition. She keeps asking us, "When can I stop my medication?" and "Why does everyone say there's something wrong with me?" We know how important it is for her to understand and participate in her own care. What can we do to make this happen?*

A: Receiving a diagnosis of ADHD can be a blow for most children and adolescents, and some take longer than others to adjust in a positive way. That is why it is so important to involve children and adolescents in as many of the steps in evaluation and treatment as possible. Adolescents, particularly, do not want to stand out from their peers in any way, so obtaining buy-in to the target goals and treatment plan is especially important at this age. Part of the treatment for your daughter should include ways of keeping the diagnosis and treatment plan as private as she wants. This might include decisions—that she is part of— to figure out a medication schedule that does not involve taking medication at school, or arranging for tutoring outside of school hours. And, of course, the more good information she has about ADHD and its treatment at every stage, the better.

CHAPTER 4

The Role of Medications

If your child has been diagnosed with attention-deficit/hyperactivity disorder (ADHD), you may be considering using medication as part of his treatment plan. As discussed in Chapter 3, stimulant medications have been shown to provide a proven safe and effective way to manage the hyperactivity, inattention, and impulsivity symptoms of ADHD. Stimulant medications are a first-line treatment recommendation for most children with ADHD who are 6 years and older. Medications are often used in combination with parent behavior management training.

The use of stimulants has been compared to wearing glasses for a person with poor vision. Stimulants help "put things into focus" for a child when they are active in his system. But just like when glasses are taken off, when stimulant medications wear off things "go out of focus again." Stimulants can help children improve their functioning in measurable ways, but stimulants do not make a child perform better. They help him focus so he can do his work—with your help and his teacher's help.

Choosing to use medications for your child's ADHD is an important decision, and it probably feels like a big decision. It is likely that family and friends will offer their opinions on how you could decide, even if you don't ask for their input.

You learned in Chapter 3 that stimulants are safe and effective. There are very few situations in which ADHD medications should not be used. Only a small number of children experience serious side effects when stimulants are used at appropriate doses.

It is important to have factual information so that you might be well educated about ADHD medications. You and your family will weigh the pros and cons of choosing medication as part of the treatment plan for ADHD. To assist you in this important decision, in this chapter you will learn

- What types of medication are approved by the US Food and Drug Administration (FDA) to treat ADHD
- How your child's medication dose and schedule will be determined, monitored, and adjusted
- What types of medication are available for children and adolescents with ADHD
- How to talk with your child about the use of medications to help with his ADHD
- How to make the most of the benefits that medications provide

A Parent's Story

Missed Clues and Lost Opportunities

"Like most parents, I didn't like the idea of my 10-year-old using stimulant medication to manage his ADHD. But I was very concerned about his behavior and ability to learn, and I felt we needed to do whatever was necessary to help him in those areas. We tried stimulant medication, and within the first few days we began to see an amazing difference. His concentration improved. He stayed focused on his tasks. We still had to try several different types of stimulant medication during that early period and adjust the dose a few times, but eventually he was able to learn better than before and complete his assignments. Where there was once frustration, I began instead to see a happier, more successful, and more confident child.

"Once I saw that medications could help him succeed, I felt we had made the right decision. When people ask me about medication now, I tell them they're a helpful treatment that gets a bad rap for reasons that now I don't entirely understand.

Still, I think families rely too much on them sometimes. Parents still need to learn how to help their child improve his behavior, learn organizational skills, and take advantage of school support to figure out the best approaches to learning. Medication can help, but as I see now, that's mostly because the child and his family have also put in a lot of hard work."

Margaret, Sacramento, CA

What You Need to Know About Stimulant Medications

Stimulant medications are thought to work by stimulating the brain to make available slightly more of the brain chemical *dopamine*, a neurotransmitter that helps our brain cells communicate more efficiently. This increased efficiency allows us to better focus our attention, control impulses, organize, plan, and stick to routines. As a result, stimulants generally reduce the core ADHD symptoms of hyperactivity, inattention, and impulsivity.

Parents of a child with ADHD who is taking stimulant medication may notice a decrease in the number of accidental injuries their child experiences as his impulsivity declines. They may also observe that his social relationships may improve as his intensity decreases and his social judgment improves. He may respond more positively to others, and he may be able to communicate more effectively. School behavior can improve significantly, even to the point that it is not different from that of his classmates. This is particularly satisfying to most children and their families. Children treated with stimulant medication for ADHD can also enjoy a longer attention span and an increased ability to stay focused on a task, as well as more productivity and accuracy in schoolwork.

Stimulant medications are almost always highly effective and safe. However, the US Drug Enforcement Administration considers them Schedule II drugs, meaning medications that have been approved for medical use but have a significant potential for abuse in adults if they are not used properly. Because of this, the rules for prescribing stimulant medications differ from those for other medications, such as antibiotics, and vary from state to state. In spite of the potential for the abuse of stimulant medications, they *do not* produce stimulation or euphoric effects in children or adolescents when used properly and restricted to FDA-recommended treatment doses. Importantly, the use of stimulant medications by children with ADHD has not been found to put adolescents at an increased risk for street drug use or abuse. Some studies indicate that proper treatment of ADHD reduces later risk of drug misuse.

Responses of individuals to stimulant medications vary greatly regardless of the severity of symptoms. Some children with mild symptoms may need higher doses of medication, while others with more severe symptoms require lower doses. Needing a higher dose than another child means that your child's ADHD is more severe. Responses to stimulants are also not dependent on the size or weight of the child.

Stimulant medications can be described by their generic (chemical) names but are most often known to parents by their brand names. The 2 generic classes of stimulant medications proven to be effective for the treatment of ADHD are *methylphenidate* and *amphetamines*. Both classes of stimulant medications have similar effects and side effects. Different preparations have varying lengths of time that they work effectively, termed *duration of action*. Comparing doses of different medications can be confusing to parents. The amount or number of milligrams for each medication prescribed *is unique to that particular medication*. For example, 5 mg of methylphenidate (eg, Ritalin) is only about half as strong as a dose of 5 mg of dextroamphetamine (eg, Dexedrine). Stimulant medications come in a variety of formulations—pills, chewable pills, liquid, dissolvable tablets, and capsules—and can last from 3 to 12 hours.

Durations of action can be short acting, lasting around 4 hours; intermediate acting, effective for 6 to 8 hours; and long acting, which may work for up to 10 or 12 hours. Short-acting preparations are very well studied, begin acting rapidly, and are the least expensive. Their limitation is that they have to be taken 2 to 3 times each day to cover a 12-hour period. This means they will need to be given while in school. This can lead to forgetting doses, and many children do not like to be seen taking medication in school. Intermediate-acting preparations usually can span a school day but won't be active for after-school homework.

Stimulant medications begin to work rapidly. Once your child's appropriate dose has been determined, you will usually see the effects of the stimulant in less than an hour; the medication is essentially out of your child's system by the next morning. These medications do not build up in your child's system; their effects and possible side effects stop when the medications wear off at the end of the day. Stimulant medications can be stopped abruptly, and some families and patients choose to not give their child the medication on weekends or during vacations. Families are encouraged to discuss this with their child's pediatric clinician. This decision should consider your child's behavior on and off medication, his need for performing in different settings, and the extent of any side effects.

Costs of stimulant medication can vary widely, and even if your family has health insurance, paying for prescriptions can be a challenge. Wholesale prices of different preparations of the same FDA-approved medication for ADHD can also differ significantly. If you find yourself unable to afford the cost of medications, contact your state's pharmacy assistance program to see if you are eligible for assistance.

Short-Acting Stimulants

Different preparations of stimulant medication will have different advantages. There are short-acting medications available as chewable tablets and oral solutions for children who have difficulty swallowing pills and capsules. However, pills and capsules are the least expensive.

Young children between 4 and 6 years of age are usually prescribed short-acting preparations because they often work longer in younger patients. Because young bodies break down and remove the drug from the body more slowly—described as a *slower rate of drug metabolism*—a short-acting form often stays in effect for the time it is needed.

In older patients, short-acting doses may also be used to extend the hours of medication effect. For example, if an intermediate-acting medication is given that lasts for 8 hours, a short-acting medication can be used when homework needs to be done in the evening.

Longer-Acting Stimulants

Longer-acting stimulants are just as effective as the short-acting preparations but limit the need for multiple doses during the day. For many children, this prevents the possible embarrassment of having to take medication doses in school. These medications are often more expensive than the short-acting forms and may be regulated by health insurance company prescription policies.

Not all longer-acting stimulants are alike. Sustained-release preparations with the stimulant suspended in wax vary in how well they work, so their use is *not* encouraged. Examples are brand names Ritalin SR, Metadate ER, and Methylin ER. All need to be swallowed whole to remain long acting, and they are slower in how quickly they start to work.

Preparations using beads or tiny pearls of medicine generally contain half of the microbeads to be released immediately and the other half as coated delayed-release bead medication. The products using this technology include, but are not limited to, Dexedrine Spansule, Focalin XR, Adderall XR, Ritalin LA, Aptensio XR, and Metadate CD. Beaded preparations are helpful for children who have trouble swallowing pills because the capsules can be opened and sprinkled into teaspoons of applesauce, yogurt, or other foods. *Beads should not be chewed.*

Lisdexamfetamine (eg, Vyvanse) is a *prodrug*. A prodrug requires ingestion by mouth for it to be converted to the active drug. It is a liquid within a capsule that, like the microbeads, can be opened and sprinkled on food.

The long-acting methylphenidate Concerta is in a capsule with a pump technology that delivers 1 dose immediately and also has long duration components. It acts as the equivalent of 3-times-daily dosing of shorter-acting preparations. These capsules cannot be chewed. They do not dissolve, so empty capsules can be found in children's stools. They should not be used in children who have had abdominal surgery where there is the risk of causing blockage related to the previous surgery.

Dyanavel XR (amphetamine) and Quillivant XR (methylphenidate) are in liquid form.

QuilliChew ER (methylphenidate) is a chewable form and Adzenys XR-ODT (amphetamine) is a tablet designed to melt in a person's mouth.

Methylphenidate can also be absorbed through the skin. Patches are helpful for children who can't tolerate any of the oral forms of stimulants. The brand Daytrana is currently the only methylphenidate that comes as a patch. Absorption from a methylphenidate patch may not reach a peak until 7 to 9 hours, and symptoms of ADHD may not be noticeably helped until 2 hours after the patch is applied. In addition, the medication action continues for about 2 to 3 hours after the patch is removed. Effective timing for use of the methylphenidate patch, then, is to *apply it at least 2 hours before the start of school* and to *remove it at least 3 hours before bedtime* or the desired time that the family and patient wish the methylphenidate to stop working. Insurance coverage for Daytrana is often not predictable. Some children develop skin rashes from the patches, but this can be avoided by placing patches on different parts of the body.

Studies have shown that the stimulant medications methylphenidate and amphetamine are equally effective in treating the symptoms of ADHD. However, individual children may respond better to one particular stimulant or be limited by side effects from taking another. This is why it is necessary to begin with one stimulant and monitor the dosing and results. With your pediatric clinician's guidance, you might be asked to slowly increase or titrate the dose until optimal results are achieved. If good results are not found, a switch of stimulant medications may be suggested.

No laboratory tests, electrocardiogram monitoring, or psychological tests are routinely necessary for monitoring the use of these medications. It is recommended that you tell your pediatric clinician if your child has any history of heart disease. There is special concern if there is a family history of heart disease or conditions that cause the heart to have irregular heartbeats, especially long QT syndrome or Wolff-Parkinson-White syndrome. These genetically important illnesses will almost certainly be known to your family if anyone has them. In these situations, it is helpful to consult with a pediatric cardiologist before starting the medication.

Non-stimulant Medicines for ADHD

Atomoxetine (Strattera) is not a stimulant. It is a different type of medication for ADHD that is approved by the FDA for the treatment of ADHD. It is discussed in the What Other Types of Medications Are Available? section later in this chapter.

Other medications approved for ADHD are extended-release guanfacine XR (Intuniv) and extended-release clonidine XR (Kapvay). These α-agonist drugs are FDA approved as non-stimulant medications for treating ADHD. They can also be used in combination with a stimulant medication when the stimulant medication has provided some but not enough benefit.

How Will My Child's Medication Treatment Be Determined?

You and your child's pediatric clinician will usually wish to consider 4 elements when arriving at the best stimulant medication choice for your child: the type of stimulant medication, the dose, the medication schedule, and the cost. Other issues that may be considered include the time of day when the targeted symptoms occur, when homework is usually done, whether medication remains active when teenagers are driving, and whether medication makes it hard for your child to fall asleep.

The short-acting forms of methylphenidate and amphetamine come in generic forms and are the least expensive. Some of the extended-release forms are also generic, but some are still name brand only and more expensive. It is important to ask how much the medication will cost, if your insurance will pay (if you have insurance), what insurance will pay, and what amount you will need to pay (ie, co-pay) even if you have insurance. You may need to discuss this with your pharmacist. In addition, it can be helpful to let your pediatric clinician know if you or other family members have taken stimulant medications and how they worked. This information might be considered to help you and your pediatric clinician to determine which medication to try first.

Dosage

You may already be aware that the dosage of many medications, including antibiotics, cold medications, and other over-the-counter drugs, is determined by a child's weight. This is *not* the case with stimulant medications. Individual children respond differently to different stimulant medications; each child requires a specific dosage that cannot be predicted in advance.

The best dosage for a child with ADHD is the one that achieves the *best possible* results without troublesome side effects—*not the minimum dose that leads to any level of positive response.* Because the dosage is determined by how well it works, and because it varies so widely among children, your child's pediatric clinician may need to adjust the dosage a number of times, or *titrate* the dosage, to find the best level for your child.

Your child's pediatric clinician may choose to start with a low dose and progress through a series of dose increases, monitoring the results by feedback from you, your

You can expect medication changes until you and your child's pediatric clinician arrive at the most effective medication and dosage for your child.

child, and your child's teacher. Often, rating scales are given to parents and teachers to organize their observations concerning each dose. The effects occur quickly so that you can often know about the effects within a week. Dosage adjustments can be made through weekly phone calls or secure email portal contact. Many physicians use rating scales like the Vanderbilt scales to organize parents' and teachers' observations. Behavior rating scales may be completed by you and your child's teacher and reported back by phone, fax, or electronically with secure email.

In general, you and your child should see your pediatric clinician for a follow-up visit by the fourth week of medication use to review your child's response to the medication. Together you will assess its effects on core symptoms, monitor any side effects, and check your child's blood pressure, pulse, and weight. Remember that you have already targeted specific behaviors that you hope to see improve with medication management, so you will review these together. At times it will be of value to ask for teacher input on these targets in the form of a rating scale, phone call, or written report. Some teachers choose to create a daily report card that can track their observations about each target. Online programs have been developed to help make this type of communication easier. The more objective these reports can be, the better;

for example, how many times in a half-hour period a child blurts out answers without raising his hand, or how many math problems were completed correctly in a 15-minute period. These reports can then be brought to the follow-up visit for review.

As you review together any changes in your child's core symptoms and target behaviors, the medication dose might be gradually adjusted upward until the best results are achieved. As previously discussed, it is not recommended to stop increasing the dose when you first notice a positive result. Increases continue until the best results are found. If a higher dose produces side effects or no further improvement, the dosage might be reduced. This gradual titration method of arriving at the proper dose will generally minimize initial side effects that might have occurred if your child had started with too high a dose in the beginning.

In some cases either methylphenidate or amphetamine will not have sufficient effect. If this is the case with your child, the other stimulant medication will usually be tried. If you start with a methylphenidate medication, you would switch to an amphetamine medication, or vice versa. It is uncommon for both medications to fail to be effective. If this is the case, a review of your child's diagnosis may be in order. Switching to or adding a non-stimulant medication may also be considered.

Medication Schedules

As listed in Table 4.1, stimulant medications are available in short-acting (about 4 hours), intermediate-acting (6–8 hours), or extended-release (10–12 hours) forms. This allows the dosing schedule of your child's medication to be adjusted to his day and routine. You and your child might choose to combine short-acting simulants with intermediate-acting or extended-release stimulants to create a schedule that works best for him.

Many children prefer to take a longer-acting preparation (8–12 hours) before leaving for school in the morning because this makes it unnecessary to take any medication at school. With this approach their classmates will not know they are taking medicines. If your child has after-school activities that cause him to put off doing homework until after the longer-acting medication has worn off, an additional short-acting dose might be added later for study time. For example, your child could take an 8-hour dose in the morning before school and another 4-hour dose half an hour before beginning his homework in the early evening.

Some college students prefer 4-hour medications because they can schedule these doses for the times during the day when they most need the medication. Especially for older students with ADHD, it helps to think of stimulant medications as helpful tools: use them at the times of day when needed to improve focus or achieve other target outcomes, and perhaps not use them at other times. While continuous coverage throughout the entire day with minimal side effects might be ideal, there is no stimulant at this time that provides this.

Table 4.1. Stimulant Medications			
Medication Brand Name	**Medication**	**Type of Medication**	**Medication Length**
Metadate CD, Focalin XR, Ritalin LA, Aptensio XR	Methylphenidate	Beaded preparation. The pill can be opened and spread with applesauce or yogurt. Beads should not be chewed.	About 8 hours
Concerta	Amphetamine	Capsule with pump delivery that delivers 1 dose immediately. You cannot chew this pill.	About 12 hours
Daytrana	Methylphenidate	Transdermal patch. Needs to adhere to the skin.	About 12 hours
Quillivant XR/ QuilliChew ER	Methylphenidate	Long-acting liquid and chewable	About 10–12 hours
Cotempla XR-ODT	Methylphenidate	Disintegrating tablet	About 8 hours
Dexedrine Spansule, Adderall XR, Mydayis	Amphetamine	Beaded preparation. The pill can be opened and spread with applesauce or yogurt. Beads should not be chewed.	About 12 hours
Vyvanse	Amphetamine	Concentrated liquid that can be opened and spread on food	About 12 hours
Adzenys XR-ODT	Amphetamine	Disintegrating tablet	About 12 hours
Adzenys ER	Amphetamine	Liquid	About 12 hours
Dyanavel XR	Amphetamine	Liquid	About 12 hours

General Considerations When Beginning to Take Stimulant Medications

- Stimulants are considered quite safe and effective for the treatment of attention-deficit/hyperactivity disorder.
- Your child's growth in height should be monitored regularly. Children taking stimulants may have modest slowing of their rate of growth for the first 2 years, especially if they are using high doses of stimulants and taking them over long periods.
- Your child's blood pressure and heart rate should be checked before and during treatment with stimulant medications.
- If your family history includes sudden unexplained death, especially in younger adults, let your pediatric clinician know. In that case, or if your child has a history of severe heart palpitations, exercise intolerance, fainting spells, or chest pain, your pediatric clinician will do a careful physical examination, may obtain an electrocardiogram, and may check with a cardiologist before starting stimulant medication.
- Your pediatric clinician will also likely consult with a cardiologist prior to starting medication if your child has a serious heart problem.

Many families find that continuing the medication schedule outside of school hours and school days helps family relationships by supporting better listening skills. This approach can help a more hyperactive and impulsive child better enjoy social experiences such as scout meetings, church activities, and sports. "Medication holidays" were popular in the past but have been found to offer little advantage and often bring problems. In adolescents, it is also important to remember that there is clear evidence that adolescents and adults with ADHD drive more safely if they are on medication when they drive.

Side Effects

The dose of your child's medication will be increased until optimal results are achieved without significant side effects. Only a small number of children who are introduced to stimulant medication in this careful way experience unwanted side effects. Taking medication only as prescribed by your pediatric clinician is also important to prevent side effects. Any side effects that do occur are likely to be mild, and most can be relieved by adjusting the dose or schedule of medication or by switching to another stimulant.

While any medication can potentially create side effects in some children, there is no way to predict which child will experience side effects with any one medication. One child may experience side effects while taking dextroamphetamine but not methylphenidate, for example, while another may report opposite results. Careful introduction of stimulant medications and monitoring the results of any dosage change is the best and safest way to deal with possible side effects.

Side effects caused by stimulant medications tend to occur early in treatment and are generally mild. The most common side effects include a decreased appetite, stomachaches, headaches, difficulty falling asleep, and jitteriness. These symptoms often resolve in a few weeks as your child's body adjusts to the medication. Social withdrawal is a rare and concerning negative effect that is immediately reversed with dose adjustment. In this situation children are overly sensitive to stimulant medications or on too high a dose. They can become overly focused and seem dull. Should this occur, notify your pediatric clinician so that you can discuss a quick remedy for this unpleasant side effect.

Other less common side effects include dizziness and rebound effects as the medication wears off. Increased activity, irritability, or sadness is sometimes seen for a short time at the end of the medication's effective period. Some children experience what many families have termed "the hangries": the stimulant is wearing off and the medication's appetite suppression is weakening, and the children are hungry—really hungry. Remember, this is not harmful and will be brief, but it can be unpleasant for your child and those around him. The hangries tend to be predictable, at about the same time every day. Often they can be fixed by offering a healthy snack 15 minutes before the irritability is anticipated. Finally, there might be truth that "an apple a day" really works!

Another less common side effect is transient tics, such as repetitive eye blinking or shoulder shrugging. These usually occur when a new stimulant is first taken and almost always resolve quickly. In some children with Tourette syndrome (see Chapter 9) stimulants may make their tics worse.

Your child's pediatric clinician can help you manage most of these side effects through adjustments in dose amount or schedule, the use of alternative medication preparations, or, occasionally, by adding other medications. It is important to pay attention to the timing of side effects. For example, if the irritability occurs 8 hours after an intermediate-acting medication, it may indicate a withdrawal or rebound effect. This way families will know the time to give the "apple a day"!

Eating Challenges

Decreased appetite and weight loss are common side effects of stimulant medication use early in treatment. *This does occur commonly, is not a cause for concern, and is usually short-lived.* If you are concerned that your child is losing weight or not eating enough, consider the following tips. Remember, your child's pediatric clinician will want to help you manage eating challenges, so be sure to share any concerns.

- Encourage breakfast with calorie-dense foods. Examples include yogurt, eggs, fiber cereals, and oatmeal. If possible, give the morning dose of medication with or after breakfast.
- Provide nutritious after-school and bedtime snacks that are high in protein and complex carbohydrates. Examples include apples or other fruit, whole-grain crackers and cheese, whole-grain pitas with hummus, and nutrition bars.
- Shift dinner to later in the evening when your child's medication has worn off. Or allow "grazing" in the evening on healthy snacks, as your child may be hungriest right before bed.

Derived from American Academy of Pediatrics. *ADHD: Caring for Children With ADHD: A Resource Toolkit for Clinicians.* Elk Grove Village, IL: American Academy of Pediatrics; 2005.

Special Circumstances: Preschool Children

In preschool-aged children, parent behavior management training approaches should be tried before considering the use of stimulant mediations. Up to one-third of young children (aged 4–5 years) experience improvements in symptoms with parent behavior management training alone. Although stimulant medications appear to be safe in preschool children, there has been little study in this specific age group. They have been widely used in this age group for some time, leading to their acceptance. However, information available about the effects of stimulant medications on growth and brain development in preschool children from research studies is limited.

Many 4- and 5-year-olds with ADHD *will* require medication to achieve maximum improvement. The decision to consider using stimulant medication at this age depends in part on how severely a child's symptoms of ADHD are interfering with his development and other aspects of his life, such as safety risks, consequences for school, and limitations on social participation.

A Parent's Story

An Early Start to Treatment

"I began seeing plausible signs of ADHD in my son when he was only 4 years old. He was very active and overreacted to any bit of frustration in his life. When we tried to talk to him, he didn't seem interested in listening and had trouble paying attention. He went to preschool but was actually thrown out because he was so out of control.

"His pediatrician diagnosed him as having ADHD, and although she told me and my husband that medication was an option that we could consider, I was very hesitant. I was nervous about side effects of medicines and initially didn't want to go there. So with my doctor's guidance, we tried behavioral approaches like setting up reward systems. But none of them made much of a difference. We became more concerned that he was not able to follow directions at home, had great difficulty playing with friends, and didn't seem to be learning what other preschoolers usually know, even though we've always considered him really bright. We were also worried that he might not be able to handle a kindergarten classroom.

"That's when we agreed to try medication. We tried low doses of methylphenidate. My son has been taking it for more than 4 months now, and we've seen a dramatic improvement in his behavior. He's back in preschool and, after a lot of struggling with this, we feel like we made the right decision."

Diane, Los Angeles, CA

Monitoring the Treatment Results

When stimulants are introduced with careful titration at least 80% of children will respond well. The medication must be initially prescribed according to a reliable plan. After the initial dose has been established, titration involves adjustments in response to frequent, regular feedback provided by parents and your child's teacher. To avoid the natural tendency to believe a method is working just because it is being used, your child's pediatric clinician will

- Ask your child if he feels the medication he is taking is working. The pediatric clinician will also ask parents for their observations and feedback.
- Regularly ask specific questions about behavior and academic performance.
- Help you develop processes to measure progress at home and school with the target outcomes you have selected.
- Ask your child's teacher to complete structured behavioral and performance rating scales, rather than simply asking you if your child is doing better. This careful teacher input is especially important when starting medication or changing the dose.

Structured rating scales from teachers are useful to assess improvement in your child's treatment targets, such as classroom productivity, on-task behavior, and other function-related goals. Many of the better rating scales your child's pediatric clinician will recommend have been used with hundreds of children with ADHD the same age as your child. This allows comparison of your child's performance with peers and classmates.

Keep in mind that children respond at different rates in different target areas. Remember that not all goals that you set for your child can be helped by medication. Almost everyone who is hyperactive improves rapidly with a proper dose of stimulant medication. But, for example, if inattention has led to falling behind in reading, it may take several weeks or months to see reading skills improve. On the other hand, if the reading lag is due to a learning disability (see Chapter 9), it will not be expected to respond to medication. In this situation, the reading troubles are not caused by inattention. Special educational interventions are likely to be needed.

Pay attention to the improvements in your child's ability to function in the target areas you have identified. Assess behaviors that can be counted and measured, rather than relying on more vague impressions about improvement in "his ADHD." When attending follow-up visits with your child's pediatric clinician, come prepared to discuss specific and, if possible, countable examples of changes in his target areas that you are measuring. You might also ask your child's teachers to prepare a brief note reporting on your child's progress since your last visit, or fill out the rating scales your child's pediatric clinician may ask you to use to help make decisions about medication management. The more frequently good feedback from home and school is obtained at follow-up visits, th e greater improvement your child is likely to experience.

Your Child's Treatment: What We Can Learn From the Multimodal Treatment Study of Children With Attention Deficit Hyperactivity Disorder

In the Multimodal Treatment Study of Children with Attention Deficit Hyperactivity Disorder (MTA; described in Chapter 3), special care was taken to find a best dose of medication according to specific study guidelines during the first few weeks of treatment. These best or optimal doses for the children in the study were usually higher than doses given to children who were being treated by the individual plans of their own physicians. In addition, the dosage in the study guidelines spanned the school day as well as the early evening, unlike the common practice of prescribing just enough medication to cover the school day.

Once treatment began, children and families in the study met with their physician for half an hour each month to discuss concerns and review the teacher's monthly report. During these sessions a great deal of parent and child education was carried out. Changes in the child's treatment were then made, if necessary, in response to feedback from parents and schoolteachers. If the child was not responding, the physician adjusted the medication, and these adjustments occurred frequently.

In contrast, the MTA children with ADHD who were not part of the study group but were being treated by their own physicians in the community generally met with their own physicians only once or twice a year. The study found that they also had shorter and less comprehensive visits, their teachers were not as consistently involved in the treatment process, and they were on lower doses of stimulant medication.

The MTA teaches us that a major reason for frequent follow-up visits with your child's pediatric clinician is to make certain that your child's medication dose is optimal. As was pointed out in the MTA discussion in Chapter 3, about 60% of children with ADHD who received the optimal dose of medication and who had frequent and regular doctor visits and careful monitoring by parents and teachers were rated by teachers as indistinguishable in many areas from their peers without ADHD. This means that in many, if not all, aspects of their school experience their ADHD was controlled; their function was near normal or typical. This was even more true if they received a combined medication and an in-depth behavioral approach. However, only about 25% of children being treated for ADHD by their own, non-MTA physicians were so rated. This was the case even though most of the treatments included medication. Experts feel that this may be due, to a large extent, to not following the kind of careful and organized approaches discussed previously.

Of course, we live in the real world, not under the ideal conditions of a study. Monthly visits are often not practical. But, by using the principles used in the MTA, you can achieve the best evidence-based medication regulation possible for your child. That means choosing a medication dose that causes the most improvement rather than the lowest possible dose, making sure that homework time is also covered by medication, and setting up reasonably frequent and highly structured follow-up visits.

What Other Types of Medications Are Available?

If your child has tried both stimulant medications and neither has helped, if your child had side effects that could not be controlled, or if you have a strong reason why you don't want to try a stimulant medication, other types of medication are available for consideration with your child's pediatric clinician. Stimulants may not be an option for children who are taking certain other medications or who have certain medical conditions.

Proven alternate choices to stimulant medications include atomoxetine (Strattera), guanfacine XR (Intuniv), and clonidine XR (Kapvay). They have not been studied as well or used as much as stimulant medication, so these medications are considered second-line or second-choice treatments. Occasionally, non-stimulants may be appropriate for children who have been diagnosed with ADHD and certain coexisting conditions.

Atomoxetine

Atomoxetine (Strattera) is a non-stimulant medication approved by the FDA for the treatment of ADHD (Table 4.2). It is in the class of medications known as *selective norepinephrine reuptake inhibitors.* Because atomoxetine does not seem to have a potential for abuse, it is not classified as a controlled substance. Because atomoxetine is a newer medication, the evidence supporting its use is adequate to meet FDA requirements for approval, but studies and evidence are more limited for atomoxetine than for stimulant medications. Atomoxetine may be helpful in the treatment of some children who have both ADHD and anxiety.

Table 4.2. Non-stimulant Medications Used for ADHD

Generic Class (Brand Name)	Daily Dosage	Prescribing Schedule
Atomoxetine (Strattera)	Once a day to twice a day	0.5 mg/kg per day increasing to 1.4 mg/kg per day
Guanfacine Long acting (Intuniv) Short acting (Tenex)	1–4 mg daily 1–2 mg 2–3 times daily	Start at the lowest doses.
Clonidine Long acting (Kapvay) Oral tablets Film patches	0.1–0.2 mg 2 times daily 0.1–0.3 mg 2–3 times daily 0.1–0.3 mg patch daily	Start at lowest doses.

Abbreviation: ADHD, attention-deficit/hyperactivity disorder.

Unlike stimulants, atomoxetine is active around the clock. However, atomoxetine has been found to be only about two-thirds as effective as stimulant medications. It works well for some patients but does not work as well for as many patients as the stimulant medications. After starting atomoxetine, it may take up to 6 weeks before it reaches its maximum effectiveness.

Atomoxetine carries a treatment warning on it that it may, in a very small number of cases, have some potential for causing suicidal thoughts in the first few weeks of treatment, although no suicide attempts were reported. Side effects are generally mild. They can include decreased appetite, upset stomach, nausea or vomiting, tiredness, problems sleeping, and dizziness. Because the side effects are more common and troublesome in the first week of treatment, your child will start at half of the expected dose for that week. Jaundice is also mentioned as a treatment warning on the medication but is extremely rare. Taking atomoxetine with food can help avoid nausea and stomachaches. Atomoxetine should be used in lower doses in children also taking certain antidepressants like fluoxetine or other selective serotonin reuptake inhibitors, which can raise the atomoxetine levels in the bloodstream.

Parents concerned about the possibility that stimulant medications may be misused by their child or his peers as a substance for abuse may choose atomoxetine for their child. It is also a medication to consider in children who are going off to college, where concerns about misuse or abuse are greater.

To be effective, atomoxetine needs to be taken daily, on a consistent basis. Like stimulant medications it can be stopped abruptly, without having to be tapered.

Long-Acting Guanfacine and Long-Acting Clonidine: The Other α-Agonists

Long-acting guanfacine XR (Intuniv) and long-acting clonidine XR (Kapvay) are in the group of medications known as α-agonists. α-Agonists were developed for the treatment of high blood pressure but have also been used to treat children with ADHD, and especially those who have tics, sleep problems, and/or aggression. The FDA has not granted approval for the use of α-agonists in these situations.

More recently, the long-acting forms of guanfacine and clonidine have been approved by the FDA for the treatment of children with ADHD. Long-acting guanfacine and clonidine are pills, but they cannot be crushed, chewed, or broken. They must be swallowed whole. Like atomoxetine, they are not controlled substances.

α-Agonists cause little, if any, appetite suppression; they may be a good choice for the rare children who have lost a significant amount of weight while taking a stimulant. Side effects can include sleepiness, clonidine especially. Headaches, fatigue, stomachaches, nausea, lethargy, dizziness, irritability, decreased blood pressure, and decreased appetite are reported very rarely. Although sleepiness occurs in a large number of children when they start taking long-acting guanfacine or, more likely, clonidine, it usually gets better after the first week of continued use. It may take 3 to 4 weeks to see medication benefit. Families are cautioned that a 1-month prescription bottle of either of these medications contains a lethal dose. However, to put this in family context, so does a large bottle of acetaminophen (Tylenol).

The long-acting α-agonists can be used in addition to stimulant medications when the stimulant medication provides some but not optimal improvement. Shorter-acting guanfacine and clonidine are available for use along with stimulants but are not approved by the FDA for this use. Short-acting clonidine has been used by a number of clinicians to address sleep problems, but it is not FDA approved for this use.

If no FDA-approved medication has been found helpful for your child, it is essential to consider whether ADHD is the correct diagnosis, or if additional coexisting conditions (see Chapter 9) are complicating your child's ADHD management.

How Can I Talk to My Child About Medication?

Your child's pediatrician will almost always explain ADHD to your child when the diagnosis is confirmed. This conversation will include what ADHD is and what it is not. And more importantly, your child, you, and your pediatrician are now a *team* to address this problem together. Almost all children with ADHD are fully aware that they are having difficulties, and they would like some help with any behavior or school problems.

As part of this diagnosis discussion, your child's pediatrician might describe how his hyperactivity, impulsiveness, and inattention are just how his brain works. The behavioral strategies and medications that are recommended will give him a chance to be a bit calmer, think before he acts, and pay better attention. Pediatricians often will tell younger children that their stimulant is *not* a "smart pill"—rather, "It's a pill that helps you pay attention, so that now you can show us how smart we know you really are!" And it's *not* a "good behavior pill," but "it gives you a moment to stop, think, and make better choices."

So, it is a good idea to let your pediatric clinician lead this first conversation. He or she has done it before and can help you with how you further discuss this with your child.

The more information you can give your child about medications, the more actively and productively he can participate in his own treatment decisions. And while on medication he will likely have better insight about his own behavior and performance. His increasing understanding will help him become an active member of his treatment team.

Parents sometimes worry that their child will begin to attribute successes only to the medication. Not infrequently, children with ADHD do not notice any changes in themselves but will notice that they get into less trouble or complete more of their work. In fact, children on medication most often cite their own efforts or abilities as the explanation for their success, and not the medication! This is important because children's active participation in their own treatment plans leads to better treatment results.

Even younger children will need to know something about what stimulant medications are, what effects they are likely to have, how long most children continue to take them, how doses and schedules can vary, and how their treatment team will be working together. Medications may be discussed as tools to achieve behavior or learning goals. As you and your child's pediatric clinicians explain these issues, encourage your child to ask questions, voice any fears or concerns, and incorporate his ideas into the medication treatment plan.

Your child's pediatric clinician can help your child to adjust to his medication and overcome many or most ADHD problems. Be sure to ask for the pediatric clinician's help with your child's concerns. Common complaints from children at the start of ADHD treatment include

- Worries that other children will make fun of him for taking medications.
  - Remind your child that he does not need to tell any of his friends about his ADHD medication. Explain to him that that long-lasting stimulant medication he takes means he wouldn't have to take it during school hours.
  - When you help to educate your child about his medication it helps him understand and will help bolster his confidence, making him less vulnerable to this type of teasing.
- Complaints about having to take pills every day. You can ask him if he has ideas about his dosage regimen.
- Complaints that he "feels different" when he takes his medication.
  - Consider whether he is reporting side effects or just describing the hoped-for positive effects of the medication.
  - As your child begins the process of taking medication, listen carefully to how he feels.
  - Remind him that you don't want to change any of his positive personality traits, but you do want to help him focus and think about his choices and together pick the best one.

Helping your child become knowledgeable about the desired effects and side effects of medications will almost always lead him to greater involvement in his own treatment. One of the ways in which he can maximize the potential of his prescribed medication is to monitor his own responses to it and report them to the other members of his treatment team. Your child is probably aware of any side effects that he experiences. Help him learn that he can and should report them to the treatment team if and when they occur.

Eventually your child will come to understand that medication is only part of his treatment. Medication certainly helps with the core symptoms of ADHD. He can use this help to improve his function and to overcome social, academic, and behavioral challenges.

As your child approaches adolescence, it will be appropriate to gradually transfer much of the responsibility for his medication regimen. The more empowered he feels in his own treatment, the more likely he is to be an active participant. Some adolescents may begin to have a hard time accepting the idea of taking medications. In their age-appropriate desire for independence, they become resistant to adult direction and wish to conform to their peers.

Listen even more openly to your child's opinions and feelings about his ADHD to allow him as much control of his treatment as possible. Teenagers who "own" their own problems, successes, and treatment plan do much better with treatment decisions. By high school, depending on study habits and extracurricular activities, your child may ask that his medication plan be changed. For example, the 12-hour dose from 7:00 am to 7:00 pm that worked well in junior high school may need to be reconsidered if his homework now usually gets done between 7:00 and 11:00 pm.

As your adolescent plans his future as an adult, he will be considering his long-term use of medication. If he is going off to college or working in a different state and he is taking a stimulant medication, he is likely to need to identify a new clinician to work with him in his new home. As an alternative for college, it may be worthwhile for your child to try a non-stimulant medication that could still be prescribed by his current pediatric clinician. If he continues to take a stimulant medication, he needs to be aware of the importance of not sharing any prescription medicines with friends.

Beginning to practice self-management is a healthy sign of growth that is to be encouraged with your careful attention and guidance. As an adult, your child will need to be able to routinely manage his own medication and other issues related to his ADHD. Prepare him for this by involving him in all areas of decision-making related to his medication management.

Making the Most of Medication

It is important to remember that medication is only one component of your child's treatment. Attention-deficit/hyperactivity disorder medications can provide a powerful springboard from which your child can begin to master the challenges of ADHD. While it can be difficult at first to understand and properly use any type of medication, you and your child will soon grow comfortable with the routines that can make his treatment most effective.

You, your child, and your child's teachers must actively monitor its effects and discuss them with your child's pediatrician. To get the best results, effective parenting techniques and teaching and self-management tools (see chapters 5 and 6) may also need to be used.

You will find that participating in and actively monitoring your child's treatment can be extremely rewarding for both of you. You can expect to watch his day-to-day functioning, performance, and self-esteem improve. In the meantime, as you become acquainted with the process of using medications, consider sharing your new experiences with other families in your situation. Your local support group for children with ADHD and their parents can provide you with validation and practical advice during this challenging time. As you will discover, many families have been where you find yourselves today. Most will tell you how glad they are that they informed themselves about their child's treatment as they took important steps for their child's future.

Q & A

Q: *I've noticed that, especially on days when my son hasn't had a lot of sleep or he's under some kind of stress, he tends to lose control of his behavior in extreme ways toward the end of his dosage. Any disruption in his life—a change of plans or a time-out—will cause him to go into a tantrum or lash out against family members. Is this a side effect of the medication, and is there any way to avoid it?*

A: Some children do experience the kind of "behavioral rebound" effect you describe— most often in the early days of medication use as they are adjusting to the medication. It is important to report these symptoms to your child's physician who prescribed the medication and to monitor the effects from day to day and over time. In most cases, this rebound effect lasts for only a short period right around the time that the medication is wearing off. If you schedule your child's day to have a less demanding time for that 30 to 60 minutes, it can be helpful. Try a healthy snack about 15 minutes before this predictable time.

This usually becomes much less of a problem within a period of several days after starting a particular medication or changing a dose. If rebound remains a problem, it can usually be helped by changing the time of medication administration, changing the medication preparation to a longer-acting form, or adding a small dosing about 30 minutes prior to the onset of rebound symptoms. Discuss this with your child's pediatric clinician. If these measures do not help, an alternative medication might be considered. Remember that sleep deprivation can add to difficulties. What is bedtime? And how effective is his bedtime routine? Be sure to limit screen and media time at least an hour before bedtime.

Q: *My 14-year-old daughter began taking stimulants for her ADHD 6 months ago. Although we were all hesitant at first to try medication, the results were so clearly positive when she did try it that we had no problem continuing. Lately, though, my daughter has begun "forgetting" to take her pill in the morning. The more we remind her, the more resistant she gets. Her typical response is, "OK, Mom, I'll take it! Do you think I forgot for a minute that I have ADHD?" So far, she hasn't missed her medication more than 1 or 2 days in a row, but we fear these lapses may grow more frequent if we don't figure out why they're happening. Is this kind of resistance common with most kids with ADHD?*

A: Medication continues to carry with it a stigma that many children with ADHD—particularly early adolescents—feel acutely as they try to fit in with their peer group in the neighborhood and at school. In addition, adolescents with ADHD must negotiate the same process of seeking independence from parents that all teenagers do.

Your daughter's resistance to taking medication—despite its obvious benefit—is not unusual, though it is an issue that needs to be addressed. While there is no one-size-fits-all solution to your situation, you should work with your daughter and the rest of your treatment team toward a positive approach. This may involve allowing her more control of the medication process. Your pediatric clinician can engage her to help make decisions about the dosage schedule as well as when and where she takes the medication. It is important to be sure she understands that she *cannot* carry the medicine to school to take later in the day. Most states have strict regulations requiring that school nurses *must* administer all medications at school.

Because your child is first starting medication in her teenage years, it is important that she has buy-in to the initial trial of medication and that it is carried out in a manner that clearly demonstrates to her that the medication has a clear, positive effect. It is also important that she remain as informed as possible about the medication and all aspects of her medication management.

CHAPTER 5

Managing ADHD at Home

Specific home measures and parenting techniques have been shown to significantly improve the functioning of many children with attention-deficit/hyperactivity disorder (ADHD). When consistently and properly applied, these approaches may not only help reshape your child's behavior at home and in public but also decrease tension, strengthen family relationships, improve school performance, and lead to an increase in your child's self-esteem. Introducing and maintaining new routines and styles of interaction may not always be easy, but it is worth the effort. Children with ADHD can and do learn, adapt, and succeed!

Medication management and parent training in behavior management are the most proven, evidence-based mainstays of treatments for ADHD. They can measurably improve the lives of many children with ADHD and their families. There are also many other helpful approaches to parenting and to your child's everyday life at home that can increase positive behaviors, create a supportive and structured home environment, foster positive family relationships, and bolster your child's self-esteem. This chapter will review these measures.

In this chapter, you will learn how to

- Help your child focus on his strengths rather than directing attention to his disabilities.
- Simplify, organize, and structure his home environment to help him succeed.
- Monitor your child's daily routines and rhythms and use this knowledge to help him become better regulated.
- Avoid triggers that lead to problem behavior.
- Facilitate better communication with your child and within the family.

- Organize your own life in ways that will allow you to manage your family's challenges and have time for yourself.

- Help your child establish and maintain new, rewarding relationships.

Focusing on Strengths

All children, with or without ADHD, do best when their parents recognize and build on their strengths. By identifying and nurturing your own child's special abilities and talents, you can encourage the self-esteem, confidence, and the competence necessary for him to succeed in life despite the obstacles that stand in his way. In a child with ADHD these strengths might include being fast on his feet, seeing things that others do not, using creative thinking, and being family oriented. And he may have many other talents that will serve him well throughout childhood, adolescence, and his adult life.

One of the best ways to help your child celebrate what he can do, rather than feel shame about what he cannot, is to help him experience as many concrete successes as possible. The more he sees what he can accomplish in his world, the more optimistic and confident he is likely to feel. Instruction in any of your child's evolving interests—sports, art, computers, woodworking, music, martial arts, or any other area—can lay the groundwork for such achievement, especially when combined with your praise for his efforts as well as his successes. If your child's interests are not clear, help him discover and define some by actively finding areas where he can succeed. Talking with your child and supporting what he most enjoys and is best at may help him start to think about who he is and what he can do instead of who or what he is not. "Catch him being good," and tell him you are proud.

The Primary Need for Your Child to Be a Child

The richness of childhood includes being allowed to play, explore, and test; to make mistakes as well as good choices; to be oppositional as well as well-behaved; etc. Part of allowing developmentally appropriate growth in children is to engage in daily activities without being constantly corrected.

For example, appropriate television shows and video games might be an important aspect of many children's social life, ability to make friends, and share interests. On the other hand, few experts or parents would disagree with limiting television, video games, and media time. There is evidence that children with ADHD clock more hours of video watching and video games than other children. Excessive video viewing in early childhood may be associated with a higher risk for developing ADHD or worsen its symptoms. There is also evidence that excessive media consumption, especially video game playing, can impair sleep patterns and verbal cognitive performance in children.

A reasonable approach to these issues might be to limit screen time and to let this time be dependent on completing household tasks and homework. All parents need to constantly walk this fine line.

It may be tempting for parents with children with ADHD to become overly cautions or restrictive, or rule-bound. But will that always be best? Probably not. A good question to ask for any plan that you consider adopting is, "How does it encourage and foster healthy development and also relationships with family members?"

Simplifying, Organizing, and Structuring the Home Environment

You will find that your child's ability to progress in nearly all areas of self-management and social interaction increases when his environment is organized and structured to meet his unique needs. If your child is physically impulsive or accident-prone, uncluttering and safety-proofing your home may keep him safer and at the same time be easier for you. Some children with ADHD may benefit from an orderly physical environment with a place for each object, while keeping your child's room organized may be a hopeless task for others. Try helping your child organize his room at a level he can manage, but don't forget the proverb that "perfect is the enemy of good."

Daily routines are a necessity for many children with ADHD. It is also useful to offer choices. For example, rather than asking, "What do you want to eat?" and risking that he will request something unhealthy, consider asking, "Do you want an apple or a boiled egg?" Now the snack is healthy and an argument over unhealthy choices might have been avoided. Written lists of chores or other daily tasks can be especially useful in helping your child keep track of what he needs to do and is an excellent habit for him to carry into adolescence and adulthood. Consistent limit-setting with predictable consequences also makes your child's world more manageable and helps him meet his goals.

Tips for Structuring Your Child's Home Environment

Remember that the success of rules and strategies within your home is influenced by the quality of the relationship that you have with your child or adolescent.

- **Keep your child on a daily schedule.** Try to keep the time that your child wakes up, eats, bathes, leaves for school, and goes to sleep about the same each day.
  - Be prepared for transitions and shifts in routines or projects.
  - Try to give time warnings when an activity or event is going to be taking place. Give 15-, 10-, and 5-minute warnings for changes in activity. Examples are coming to dinner, doing homework, turning off the television set, and bedtime.
  - Schedule unconditional "fun time" regularly. And enjoy spontaneous "fun time" whenever you can.
- **Cut down on distractions.** Identify the things that distract you and your child the most at important times, like during homework. Be careful to not jump to conclusions; the distractions for each child are different. As you identify them, remember that some are under your control and you can fix right away, while with other distractions, you and your child need to negotiate together how to remove them. Gradually eliminate them one by one.
- **Develop a homework plan with your child.**
  - Create a special homework space with your child and stock it with supplies for projects and homework.
  - Keep in mind, some children like having a mini office set up. Others need to be close to mom or dad.
  - Use a homework incentive chart with rewards.
  - Divide homework into small working parts with short breaks to reward effort.
  - Consider using special timers to keep your child on track.
  - Share the task of managing the homework routine with other family members. Praise your child in front of other family members for her efforts and successes.

- Save a spot near the door for your child's school backpack so she can grab it on the way out the door. You may want to place a hook on the wall near the door to hang the backpack up after homework is done and in the backpack.
- **Organize your house.** If your child has specific and logical places to keep his schoolwork, toys, and clothes, he is less likely to lose them.
  - Develop "house rules," monitor daily, and reward for compliance with rules. Pick one new house rule weekly to review and discuss as a family.
  - Provide a safe space in the home for active play.
- **Use charts and checklists.** These written reminders can help your child track his progress with chores or homework. Keep instructions brief. Offer frequent, friendly reminders to check his list and make sure each task has been completed.
  - Implement the use of a school-home tracker. A *tracker* is a checklist of things needed each day to take to school and to bring home from school. To be successful, you may need to have your child's teacher help with the school-home tracker while at school.
  - Post a morning checklist by the door through which your child leaves the house to go to school, listing the things that need to go with her to school, such as a backpack, shoes, a coat, gloves, and a lunch box.
  - Focus on and praise the effort your child made to do her work and chores, not just the completion of the task.
- **Limit choices.** Help your child learn to make good decisions by giving him only 2 or 3 options at a time.
  - Foster "best outcomes" by creating and encouraging a sense of resilience and participation.
    - Validate your child's positive plans even if you feel some things need to be done differently.
    - Express empathy for concerns and problems.
    - Include your child or teenager in the decision-making process and problem-solving issues whenever possible.

- Encourage involvement in family activity planning and outings.
- Provide sincere praise, even for the small things.
- **Set small, reachable goals.** Aim for systematic step-by-step progress rather than instant results. Be sure that your child understands that she can succeed best by taking small steps and slowly building on those successes.
- **Keep the plan child-centered.** Even though the plan may work well for you, make sure that it works for your child, or it will turn out to be ineffective.

When considering how to structure your child's day-to-day experiences, it may help to picture your growing child as a construction project in progress. The limits, lists, routines, and other measures you are putting in place today are like scaffolding that will provide the necessary support as he develops fully. As he turns these routines into daily habits and becomes more self-directed, some of these supports can be gradually removed while his underlying functioning remains well in place. You may no longer have to create homework checklists with him, for example, because he has learned to make them himself. Far from "babying" your child, helping to structure and organize

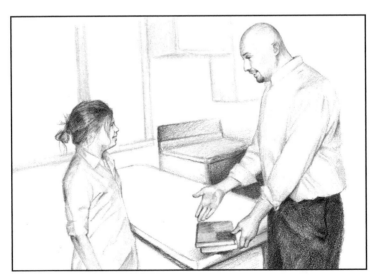

If your child has specific and logical places to keep her schoolwork, toys, and clothes, she is less likely to lose them.

his world allows him to add to his competencies and experience many more small triumphs. So this "scaffolding" structure first helps increase his self-esteem, and then further increases his confidence as the scaffolding is later taken away.

Just as you have observed that your child may feel less overwhelmed when his home life is well organized, so you may find that organizing your own family life as thoroughly as possible will help you feel calmer and more in control. And this might be especially helpful if you also have ADHD. With the number of medical visits, teachers' conferences, and treatment reviews necessary to maintain your child's well-being and continued progress, a family calendar including all scheduled activities can be a big help to many families. Daily lists of tasks to perform and errands to run will help you stay organized just as they help your child. Mobile devices have both calendar and reminder functions. Many parents find it worthwhile to devote a few private minutes before the kids get up in the morning to "regroup"—thinking about everything that must be accomplished that day and arranging tasks in order of priority. Make sure that any plan is realistic and not overwhelming.

Daily Routines and Rhythms

As the parent of a child with ADHD, you may already be aware of certain times of day that are more difficult than others. If your child has begun taking a stimulant medication, you may notice fluctuations in his attention and behavioral control throughout the day as each dose of medication begins to take effect, works well, and then wears off. With stimulant medications, some children will experience *behavioral rebound*, a short period of irritability or moodiness as the medication is wearing off in about 4, 8, or 12 hours (see Chapter 4) that may lead to difficulties at around dinnertime or bedtime that had not generally occurred before. You can help your child adjust to these changes by observing how and when his emotions and behaviors tend to fluctuate each day and arranging his schedule as much as possible to accommodate these ups and downs. If you know, for example, that he is usually somewhat unsettled and irritable for a half an hour after his arrival home from school, offer a healthy snack and schedule his homework for after that time. If his medication suppresses his appetite at certain times during the day, schedule meals to avoid these periods. Take special care to

Tips for Managing Sleep Problems

Many children with attention-deficit/hyperactivity disorder have trouble getting to sleep at night, whether or not they take medication. Good bedtime habits, called *sleep hygiene,* can be a key to good sleep. These include

- Avoid the use of television and media 1 to 2 hours before bedtime. Power media off to avoid disturbing messages, alerts, or "pings."
- Establish bedtime routines. Consider a warning that bedtime is in 15 minutes. Decide together a regular and routine order of toileting, brushing teeth, getting into pajamas, and a short bedtime story or other interaction with a parent.
- Fall asleep with lights off and no television or other media.
- Always falling asleep in their own bed with parents out of the room can play a significant role in children being able to sleep through the night without disrupted sleep.

prepare him for transitions between activities because these are likely to be especially difficult times for him.

Another issue to consider is the way time can feel to a child with ADHD. For a child who struggles with staying focused or behaving for more than a few minutes at a time, tedious, repetitive, or boring activities can seem extra-long and soon become absolutely unbearable. Forcing your child to participate in such an activity, like requiring him to sit still for long periods while you chat with a friend, introducing him to clubs or groups that involve little physical action and too much downtime, or expecting him to pick up all the toys at once in a disorderly room, will probably only lead to failure and the possibly punishment and loss of self-esteem. Even fun activities can be strenuous. For example, baseball, which includes long periods of inactivity while on the field, may not be as good an activity for children with ADHD as soccer, which has a much faster and continuous pace. By avoiding such situations or breaking up activities, including homework, into short chunks of time, you can help your child experience success as he struggles to manage his responses.

It may also help to let your child know ahead of time how long a particular activity will last, and even to place a timer in view to help his awareness of how much time has passed. If he knows he has already been working on his homework or practicing the piano for more than half the allotted time, he may be able, with your support and coaching, to continue to the end. Often, getting started with the first step in an activity is the hardest part. Praise or incentives focused on the start of the routine can go a long way. Over time, your child will get better at getting started and exhibit the ability to work for longer periods.

The First Hour of the Day

The morning routine can be a daunting task for all parents and children. Pressures to get to school and work can feel overwhelming. For a child with ADHD, getting the day started can be especially challenging. To ease the stress on your child, create a consistent and predictable schedule for rising and set up a manageable routine. It may help to put specific steps in writing or pictures, keeping the tasks clear and brief. For example,

alarm rings → wash face → get dressed with clothes laid out the night before → eat breakfast → take medication → brush teeth

Remember to give immediate praise and feedback when your child accomplishes tasks of the morning routine. This will help motivate your child to succeed and encourage independence.

If your child takes medication, your doctor may recommend waking your child up 30 to 45 minutes before the usual wake time to give medication and then let your child "rest" in bed for the next 30 minutes. This rest period allows the medication to begin working so that your child can be better able to participate in the morning routine.

Medication Effects May Vary

- Some children fall asleep more easily if the medication has "worn off" by bedtime. Other children may have a more difficult time, and an evening dose of medication may help.
- Sometimes different preparations of stimulant medication can have different effects on sleep initiation in a given child, and a medication switch may help.
- Medications are sometimes prescribed by physicians if the measures discussed here are not successful and sleep issues are still interfering with day-to-day functioning.

Derived from American Academy of Pediatrics. *ADHD: Caring for Children With ADHD: A Resource Toolkit for Clinicians.* Elk Grove Village, IL: American Academy of Pediatrics; 2005.

Optimizing and Facilitating Communication

Children with ADHD frequently experience difficulty participating in elements of sustained and focused day-to-day conversation. But adapting your own style of communication to your child's needs can help him maintain your connection. When necessary, pause to get your child's attention or call his name before giving a command. Maintain eye contact, and perhaps have him repeat back or explain what you have told him to be sure he has heard and understands. This approach works well not only when issuing commands but also when beginning any sort of conversation with him.

If your child tends to interrupt, help him out by keeping your sentences brief and focusing only on what needs to be said. Avoid interrupting him frequently because he may not be able to stay engaged in this type of interaction. If you sense that his attention is wandering, touch his arm, take his hand, or otherwise make physical contact. Some parents find that conversation flows more smoothly if they are also involved in a physical activity with their child, such as washing dishes or making dinner. Finally, if you are telling your child something that you want him to remember, write it down in simple terms or encourage him to write it down himself.

Introducing concepts such as *rewards, consequences,* and *positive and negative behavior* into the family vocabulary can go a long way to improve communications. Specific behavior therapy language strategies, such as when/then statements like, "*When* you finish your homework, *then* you can go play baseball," may also prove useful when interacting with all your children and can improve communication and morale in the family as a whole. These techniques are common components of parent training in behavior management (as discussed in Chapter 6), which can be very beneficial to children with ADHD and their families.

Educating, Reframing, and Demystifying

Children with ADHD often face a daily struggle with adult disapproval and other negative interactions that result from their behavioral and social difficulties. This experience can easily lead to a loss of confidence and low self-esteem that, if left

Focus on the effort your child made to do a chore, and not just completion of the task.

Tips on Managing Health Care and School Records

■ Create a profile of your child that will follow your child through her years in school as needed.

■ Keep a 3-ring binder with dividers. Each divided section can relate to a section on health care, school records, testing, school educational plans, interventions implemented at school (dated and progress noted), and recorded or documented notes with school personnel.

■ Keep a 2- to 3-page summary of your child's history, testing, and other findings in the front of this binder. These will often be available from major evaluations that your child has undergone, or as part of her medical home. This will help to ensure that you don't need to reinvent this story for every new clinician or treatment resource.

■ Keep a summary page for dates of medications used, doses of medications, and positive and negative responses to the medications. This can be invaluable when changes are needed.

■ Where possible, find out how to access this information in your child's electronic medical record.

unaddressed, can result in even more self-defeating behavior. Designing an effective treatment plan is one way to prevent this negative cycle from occurring with your child because it is likely to lead to more positive feedback and better self-control. You can further increase your child's chances for improvement by taking the following steps:

● **Educate** your child about ADHD and how to manage it.

● **Reframe** any negative attitudes or assumptions and reshape the responses that have developed as a result of these attitudes and assumptions.

● **Demystify** the treatment process and clear up any misunderstandings.

The more fully a child with ADHD can begin to understand and "take ownership" of his own challenges, the more committed he is likely to be to treatment, the more successful he may become at self-management, and the higher his self-esteem is likely to be.

Thus, *educating* your child about the nature of ADHD is a critical part of successful treatment at every stage of development. From very early on, you and your child's pediatrician can begin talking with your child about the nature of ADHD, what it is and what it is not, and how he can learn to manage it. As he grows older, his pediatrician or other pediatric clinician can meet with him alone so that he can feel free to seek any information he needs to become the most active participant in his own care plan. He may also benefit a great deal from your efforts to provide him with developmentally appropriate books and media about ADHD that provide updated information on ADHD and related disorders. Support groups for children and families with ADHD are another source of valuable information, as well as a source of emotional support.

By his teenage years, your child should have had the opportunity to build an informed knowledge base on which to rely when he is making decisions, with your support, about treatment, social and academic pursuits, plans for the future, and so on. Taking control of his own life in this way can be enormously empowering for a child who has struggled with ADHD and can make all the difference in how he views his academic, professional, and personal potential.

As your child grows, keep in mind that he may forget or misinterpret some of what he is told about the nature of ADHD. To minimize his confusion, make sure that you and your child's pediatrician talk with him regularly and repeatedly about ADHD. Ask your child to discuss with you what he understands, listening carefully to his interpretations of what he has learned. Always keep these discussions positive, simple, and brief. The clearer he is about who he is and where he stands in relation to his ADHD, the more competence and confidence he will have in managing his challenges.

Because discouragement is a constant danger for children who face frequent obstacles, be prepared to confront your child's negative ideas and statements and help him *reframe* them in positive ways. "Everyone has attention problems from time to time. I just have them so often that they interfere with my best functioning—but I have learned that there are plenty of things I can do about this." He may begin echoing negative feedback he might get at school or from peers: "I'm different. I can't do anything right." If you hear these comments get out any supportive evidence you have—his report cards, test scores, artwork, or other concrete forms of achievement—to show him the facts so that he can tell that he is making progress.

Celebrate how persistent he was or how much thought, organization, and effort he gave to his work. Help him understand this is even more important than the outcome of simply what grade he was given. Attention-deficit/hyperactivity disorder may commonly involve work production problems. You may also find that it helps to put your child's struggles in context for him. Point out that every child has somethings he's good at (strengths) as well as some challenges to overcome. "I'm so proud of you for working so hard on that report" is an important and powerful comment. Reframing negative attitudes goes a long way in helping a child focus on his strengths rather than his disabilities.

Demystifying the nature and treatment of ADHD is very important if not essential. Children will typically see their diagnosis as a problem and as a stigma. If they don't understand their condition and its management, their treatment plan can be felt like "something done to me by my doctors, teachers, and parents." Help your child understand that he can shift from perceiving himself as a victim of this disorder to recognizing that he can actually learn to master areas of difficulty. To see himself as an active participant in managing his ADHD and to experience his own successes, he needs to appreciate the nature of ADHD—that it has no relation to intelligence, that it is a disorder that can be managed, that many successful adults have this condition. Remind him that many adults in his life, including his teachers and relatives, are supportive and can serve as advocates for his well-being.

For some children and adolescents, the thought of taking medication for ADHD is troubling. Your child may initially feel confused or upset by the prospect of taking medication for a "brain problem." He may worry unnecessarily about other kids' or adults' reactions should they learn he is taking ADHD medications. He may even assume that this treatment decision means there is "something wrong" with him, that he is "stupid," "weird," or "different" from everyone else. Generally, your child's pediatrician or other pediatric clinician will educate your child about how ADHD medications work to demystify, to address concerns or fears, and to help your child feel more positive about treatment.

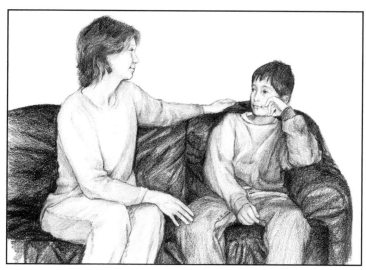

When possible and appropriate, take time to talk about treatment decisions with everyone in your family so you can help to avoid feelings of resentment and stress.

Beyond these steps, you can emphasize to your child that medication is a tool that he can use—like glasses for a person with poor vision who is learning to read, or a hammer for a carpenter building a house. The more you can encourage him to learn how to use and to take advantage of medication, rather than relying on it to "take care of him," the more progress he is likely to make—and the better he is likely to feel about himself as he learns just how well he can do.

Integrating ADHD Management Into Your Family's Life

Successfully managing ADHD takes time and effort on your part, as well as your child's. Sisters, brothers, or other family members without ADHD may resent the time and attention that they feel are taken from them to meet the needs and address the issues of family members who have ADHD. It is no surprise, then, that the pressure to satisfy everyone's demands sometimes becomes overwhelming.

It is also important for you as parents to make sure that you take care of your own health and well-being. It can be a real challenge to implement the activities needed for your child with ADHD while managing the needs of other family members, particularly if you are also working. Make sure to share the effort with spouses, partners, and other family members, including your child's siblings. Structure time for your own and family activities and have family meetings to discuss and monitor family members. Some suggestions are discussed later in this chapter.

Partnering in Your Child's Care Management

Attention-deficit/hyperactivity disorder is a special health care condition, and children and adolescents with ADHD are best cared for in a manner similar to that of other children and youth with special health care needs. Effective ADHD care often requires consultation and communication with many care team members, including the pediatrician or other pediatric clinician, teachers, special educators, therapists, other consultants, and, most importantly, parents.

Practices that conform to the AAP principles of the patient-centered medical home are structured and skilled to provide comprehensive care management for patients with ADHD. The individual pediatrician or practice is unable to address the needs of a child with ADHD and his family alone. It is useful to assemble the multidisciplinary team needed to meet the interdisciplinary needs involved in your child's care. A medical home practice is skilled in providing this comprehensive care.

Your child's medical home can help you develop a team-based, integrated, continuously updated plan of care for managing your child's ADHD. A *shared plan of care*, which can be developed in partnership with your family and multiple care providers, describes your child and his ADHD, notes the family's priorities for his care, and coordinates the care provided by parents, pediatric clinicians, teachers, special educators, therapists, and other consultants. Practice care coordinators, often specially trained nurses in the practice, can serve the important function of helping create and bring together the care team. Subsequently, the care coordinator will facilitate the delivery of chronic care with parents.

Educating Family Members

While you, your child with ADHD, and other adults involved in his care have probably focused a great deal of attention on learning about the nature of his condition, it is important to keep in mind that your other children and relatives are likely to

A Parent's Story

A Support System

"One of the worst aspects of having ADHD for my daughter was the fact that it seemed like no one else in our area had it," writes one mother. "The other kids at school called her 'crazy' all the time, and I think she really believed she would never be OK. Then, when she was about 9, we got her a computer and linked her up to a couple of ADHD websites. She started reading some of the bulletin boards and 'personal stories' and also using some of the 'ask the experts' options. We made sure that the sites she visited were responsible. After a while we saw her attitude really start to change. Not only had she learned a lot of really valuable information about ADHD on the internet, she also began to feel less isolated and more supported. I don't know how she would have gotten through junior high and high school without that computer. Those resources gave her the confidence she needed to get through school."

Mary, Wooster, OH

understand much less. They will need your help in learning how to respond to your child's behavior and to support his efforts to function successfully.

If family members seem to resent or blame your child for his actions, take the time to talk privately with them about the challenges he faces. When appropriate, discuss treatment decisions with your family, explaining the reasons for your choices. If you are implementing behavior therapy techniques in your home, other family caregivers can be a big help if they learn to implement these new techniques as well. Fortunately, all the tools and techniques you will learn through parent training in behavior management apply equally well to other children in the family and can be equally helpful.

Teach other family members to frame ADHD-related challenges positively so that they, too, might work with your child to solve problems. You might ask them to write down any issues they have, such as, "Frances interrupts me all the time!" Then together you can think about how to reframe their distress in ways that may help solve the problem, like perhaps, "I need for Frances to wait until I'm finished talking before she talks." Caring family members can discuss possible solutions, try one out and evaluate it, and move on to another solution if that one does not work (see Chapter 6).

Sometimes family members refuse to cooperate, express chronic resentment, or seem unable to act in positive ways. You might consider locating an ADHD support group in your area or seeking family therapy to help everyone adjust.

Taking Care of Yourself

As difficult as it can be at times, it is vital to do whatever you can to avoid letting all the issues you are dealing with interfere significantly with your own sense of competency and well-being. Temporary resentment and stress are inevitable in any challenging family situation.

Give yourself and your child credit for trying and maintain a sense of humor whenever you can. If you are feeling anxious or depressed, be sure to talk with your pediatric health care professional, psychologist, or other mental health counselor. Think about your own stress management strategies. Consider the reframing approaches that you used to improve your child's understanding of his ADHD—will they help you as well? For example, by reframing, "I handled that situation so poorly. It just goes to show what a terrible parent I am," to "Now that I have had time to think about how I handled today's situation, I realize I can definitely find a better solution," you can transform thoughts that interfere with your parenting into thoughts that facilitate it.

You may also find it stressful at first to carry out some of the behavior management techniques that you will learn in Chapter 6, such as actively ignoring your child's undesirable behavior. Exercise, mental and physical relaxation, or other techniques can help you learn to remove yourself emotionally in healthy ways during these times. For example, if you are about to react to a situation that you know you should really ignore, imagine a virtual podcast telling yourself, "OK, stop. Relax. What are my choices? What is my best response?" Reminding yourself to stop and relax and to think about your response can be very helpful by putting some time and space between your impulse to react and your understanding of why you should ignore that particular behavior. This type of technique takes practice but can soon allow you to make better choices and set an example of sound behavior management for your child.

If you find that the stress of parenting a child with ADHD has caused problems in your relationship with your spouse or partner, you might consider marital or couples counseling to address any ongoing problems. Keep in mind that ignoring problematic issues rarely makes them go away. Your, and your partner's, physical and emotional health must remain top priority—not only for your child's sake but also for your own.

Peer Relationships: Getting Along With Other Children

Social behaviors, like taking turns, may be hard for your child, causing conflict and making it harder to fit in with other kids. Although it can be painful to observe the insensitive ways in which children with ADHD are sometimes treated by their peers, you can do a lot to help your child make friends and work cooperatively with others. Social relationships are critical to address and important to long-term adjustment.

By scheduling playdates for your child with his peers, you might provide structure or "scaffolding" to help him to develop social skills in a comfortable setting. At first keep playdates short and have a parent-supervised agenda, such as baking cookies together or playing a game that you already know is handled well by your child. Consider providing your child with the opportunity to earn a group reward for him and his playmate for demonstrating appropriate social skills, like a treat for them both if he allows his friend to choose an activity 2 or 3 times during the playdate. As time passes and he becomes more successful in relating to peers, you can gradually remove that scaffolding and let him enjoy growing relationships with less of your own involvement. After these kinds of playdates, you may want to sit down with your child and debrief: "I liked it a lot when you decided to let David choose the game. I could see that it made him really happy and you both had so much fun," or "When Jessica started grabbing the Barbies for herself, what do you think are some of the things that you could have done?"

Programs such as special therapeutic summer camps for children with ADHD (see Chapter 7) are particularly effective for teaching social skills and sports competencies that can improve peer relationships.

As your child grows and develops and his social skills improve, your guidance within the context of your child's daily life will continue to be an important tool in helping him improve social relationships. Many of the techniques that parents use with any child can be used in a more focused, deliberate way to help your child with ADHD. While all parents teach acceptable social behavior by modeling it themselves, you may want to be especially sure you are demonstrating certain skills, including using appropriate body language that you hope your child will learn every time you interact with him. Narrating your behavior as you interact with your child can also set a good example: "Here, Joanie, I'll let you have a turn now. We get along better when we take turns." Older children can also benefit from conversations about particular issues and from you interpreting social interactions with them as they happen. *I statements*, like, "I feel scared when you use a loud voice," can be useful in this setting.

Another effective way to boost your child's self-esteem is to encourage him to participate in extracurricular social activities that are set up to foster positive peer relationships (eg, scouts, sports teams, church or community youth groups). The key to your child's success in these extracurricular activities is to have them supervised by adults who are familiar with ADHD and know that this is a concern for your child (see Chapter 6). Parent coaches can be better and more effective soccer coaches for your child and all team members if they use effective behavior management techniques. Becoming part of a small group or team under these conditions can be a great morale booster as your child experiments with making friends in a safe, supervised setting. Such groups can be especially effective if they involve an activity your child especially enjoys or is good at because he can then rely on his skill to help make up for any social weaknesses. Programs that focus on peer relationships and on sports skills can be particularly helpful in this regard. If your child is taking stimulant medication, he may find that the medication helps him considerably in controlling his impulsivity in these types of social situations and allows him to participate more fully. If his daily long-acting medication has worn off by the time his group activity begins, the option of an extra short-term dose half an hour before the meeting begins may help him participate more fully.

Finally, beware of negative social interactions seen on violent television shows or experienced with social media. Limit these experiences when you can, or use them as an opportunity to teach about dangerous behaviors. Violent and inappropriate behaviors in other family members are, of course, a serious concern and can serve as powerful role models for negative and dangerous behaviors.

Seeking Out Other Positive Relationships

Many children with ADHD have difficulty making friends among children their age. If you sense that your child feels lonely and isolated, even after trying some of the social skills techniques outlined previously, consider also the people in your community who might serve as positive role models, supportive mentors, or friends.

An older teenager or adult who shares one or more of your child's interests and understands how his overactivity or impulsivity interfere with his social relationships can make a huge difference in his self-esteem by just listening carefully and offering empathy and advice. Even if your child has a positive, supportive relationship with you, having another adult or older teenager in more of a mentor role can be beneficial, because this is a different kind of relationship with the possibility for unique payoff. Search among your relatives and friends for a responsible person who might be willing to provide this support for your child. If none is available, ask your local ADHD support group for leads or advice. Your religious community, local social service agency, or mentoring organization such as Big Brothers Big Sisters may be another source of help.

Finally, keep in mind that your own presence means a great deal to your child—not just when engaged in practical activities but when both of you are free to just play or hang out together. Remember, handheld media that either of you might use serves to steal this time and miss an opportunity. Your supportive presence, sharing an activity, or just talking lets your child know that you love and like to be with him and can help to balance social disappointment that he may have experienced elsewhere. Sometimes children with ADHD view their parents as the only people consistently in their corner. In addition to providing your child with social and emotional benefits, a close, positive relationship can make you a more effective reinforcer, leading to a decrease in disciplinary problems.

Being Your Child's Best Advocate

As you discover new ways to facilitate positive behaviors, learning, and self-esteem in your child, consider passing these techniques on to the other people in his life—adults in your household, other caregivers, relatives, teachers, and, when appropriate, even empathetic peers or siblings—so that they can help maintain the consistency, structure, and clarity your child needs. If necessary, remind them that ADHD is a neurobehavioral disorder, not the result of poor discipline, and that specific, consistent, positive techniques and attitudes can help to improve a child's ability to manage his own behavior. Show caregivers and close relatives how to implement the techniques you have learned and talk with them periodically about how your child is responding and what, if any, changes they have observed. Remember, all these adults in your child's life can be thought of as part of his team that helps him adjust to and manage his ADHD behaviors and challenges. If they become partners, your child will progress more rapidly than if you are in conflict with teachers, caregivers, and others at every turn. You can read a great deal more about advocacy in Chapter 8.

The symptoms of ADHD can seem so overwhelming at first that many parents fear there is nothing they can do to provide substantial help for their child. Yet while it is true that treating ADHD and managing its symptoms requires time, patience, and a great deal of attention, the benefits can be enormous to family functioning and family relations. Attending treatment review meetings with your child's pediatric clinician, implementing behavior therapy techniques, talking with your child about the challenges he experiences, and providing him with resources may seem like tiny steps on the road to better functioning, but together they really do have a positive effect. Children, who naturally want, most of all, to be like every other child, often tend to resist thinking about or wanting to address the issues that ADHD symptoms impose. Therefore, it is up to you to provide your child with the services he needs, the extras that can so greatly improve his daily life, and the support and education he needs to see them as useful tools for him.

Stay up-to-date on the latest research on ADHD, engage your child's teachers in his evaluation and treatment plan, and do what you can to help your child learn to recognize his own strengths and manage his own targeted problems. With the help and guidance of physicians, nurse practitioners, physician assistants, therapist, counselors, teachers, and other professional advisors, you can make an enormous difference in your child's life. Adults with ADHD successfully attend college, marry, have families, and enjoy fulfilling careers, thanks in large part to the parents who took the time and made the effort to help them navigate their journey.

Q & A

Q: *My 9-year-old son was recently diagnosed with ADHD. He seems to be responding well to treatment and discussions of what ADHD is and how he can work to manage his problems. However, his older sister, who is 13, has responded to the news much more negatively. She resists going anywhere with the family where she might be seen by classmates in the company of her brother. At home, she calls him "weird" and yells at him to stay away from her and her friends. I understand that it can be difficult for an adolescent to deal with anything "different" about her family, but her behavior is rude and is damaging to my son's self-esteem, hard as we are working to build it up. What can we do to persuade our daughter to be more supportive of her brother?*

A: It may help to look at a situation like this as more of an opportunity than a problem because it gives you an opening to work with your daughter on general issues relating to sensitivity to others, respect for family members' rights and feelings, and acceptance of the challenges that each person must face, as well as issues directly related to ADHD. As you are already doing with your son, your daughter needs to be educated on what ADHD is and is not, which of your son's behaviors are typical of children with ADHD and which are just part of normal sibling conflicts, and how her responses can help him achieve better self-control and improve general family functioning. If you have not already spoken directly with your daughter about these issues, be sure to do so; you might do some of this in the context of a "family meeting." Your family may also benefit from one or more sessions with a family therapist or from a support group for families of children with ADHD that may help your daughter understand that the problems that she faces with her brother are common and provide her with positive approaches for interacting with her brother.

Q: *Our 11-year-old daughter, who has been diagnosed with inattentive-type ADHD, has been doing better since she began treatment with stimulant medication. However, we still have* *trouble getting her organized around homework. We have tried setting up an office in her room, taking away all the distractions, keeping the area quiet, and not allowing the television to go on until all her homework is done. We don't seem to be making much progress and, in fact, we are all getting even more frustrated because nothing seems to work. Her teachers still complain that work is not getting turned in, and her grades are still suffering in spite of her teacher always telling us how bright she is.*

A: A common co-occurring condition for children with ADHD is a learning disability. Has your daughter been evaluated for this possibility? In addition, has she been considered for accommodations in school through a Section 504 plan to modify her homework assignments? For what you can do at home, there is no one-size-fits-all solution to the ideal homework setting. Some children with ADHD work inefficiently in an isolated, quiet setting like their room and do better in the midst of some action, like at the kitchen table with a radio playing. You might need to try a few different settings until you find the most efficient one. In addition, you might need to figure out if any other factors are making homework difficult. Think about all the steps involved. Does your child know what all the assignments are? Does she bring the materials home that are necessary for doing the work? Does she have a nightly work plan that fits with her learning style? (She might need to schedule breaks between math and English or between outlining the report and writing the first 3 paragraphs.) Does she have a system to check on whether all the nightly work is done? Is there a system for checking that her completed work gets turned in on the due date? How does she or do you know that work is late? Have you or her teacher set up rewards for progress or consequences for late work? Is there a system for her teacher to communicate with you about late work? Once you have gone through this type of systematic list of questions, you can begin to solve the problem in an organized way—and you might discover some simple and obvious solutions. If she is taking stimulant medication and she does her homework primarily at a time after it has worn off, you could consider a short-acting extended dose of medication for the early evening.

CHAPTER 6

Parent Training in Behavior Management: Parenting Techniques That Work

Many parents discover that their child with attention-deficit/hyperactivity disorder (ADHD) does not respond to parenting efforts that they used successfully with their other children. This failure to follow family rules or expectations can be especially upsetting because it can lead others to assume that a child's behavior is due to poor parenting rather than a diagnosed condition. Your negative experiences with managing your child's behavior may convince you that she is simply unable to understand or to remember your instructions. You wonder if she will ever improve her behavior.

In fact, your child with ADHD is likely as able to understand and remember what you tell her as her siblings are. But because she has difficulties with the ability to control her actions, organize her thoughts, think before she acts, or create a plan of action and follow through, she may not be able to *perform* in a way she knows is appropriate. She may understand, for example, that it is not right to interrupt you repeatedly while you are talking on the phone, or to wander away when you are talking to her, but she might be unable to stop herself. The way she operates may seem more like, "Ready...fire...aim!" She thinks about the rules after she has already broken them instead of before. This is why some of the parenting approaches that worked with your other children may not work for your child with ADHD. It is not that your child does not know what the appropriate behaviors are; it is just hard for her to carry them out.

Parent training in behavior management (PTBM), a form of behavior therapy taught to parents, has been proven to be reliably effective in helping children, including those with ADHD, to use appropriate behavior and function in more positive ways. This form of therapy focuses on helping parents to recognize praise and reward appropriate behaviors and to decrease their child's aggressive, noncompliant, or hyperactive behaviors. It is important to note again that consistent research has shown repeatedly that parenting is not the cause of ADHD, but more enhanced parenting skills are frequently required for parents of children with ADHD to be effective in their parenting, and parents are in the best position to help their children learn new behaviors. The Centers for Disease Control and Prevention has reviewed parent training techniques that lead to better outcomes for families and children, as well as components of programs that are less effective.

Successful methods of helping parents acquire parenting skills and behaviors and emotional communication skills include

- Teaching parents active listening skills, such as reflecting back what the child is saying. This teaches parents to help children recognize their feelings, label their emotions, and appropriately express and deal with emotions. It also sends an important message to their child that they are interested in and accepting of what their child is saying. This may also involve teaching parents to reduce negative communication patterns like sarcasm or criticism and allow children to feel like they are equal contributors to the communication process.
- Teaching parents to interact positively with their child.
- Requiring parents to practice with their child during program sessions.

Successful methods of decreasing children's aggressive, noncompliant, or hyperactive behaviors include

- Teaching parents how to set the stage for better behaviors to occur
- Teaching parents to interact positively with their child and decrease unwanted behaviors by praising positive behaviors and ignoring negative behaviors when possible

- Teaching parents how to use time-outs correctly
- Teaching parents to respond as consistently to their child as possible
- Requiring parents to practice with their child during program sessions
- Teaching parents how to get their child to practice new skills at home

Less effective components of parent training programs include

- Teaching parents how to problem-solve about their child's behaviors
- Teaching parents how to promote their child's academic and cognitive skills
- Including ancillary services, such as social skills training, as part of the parenting program

A Parent's Story

Parenting Approaches

"It was difficult to understand at first why my parenting approach had so little effect with my youngest, Suzanne, who has ADHD," a mother writes. "I treated her the same way I treated all my other kids, but it seemed like every time I figured out how to help her change her behavior in a positive direction she'd fall back into her old habits before the week was up. She was also a lot angrier and more defiant than her older sisters. By the time she was diagnosed with ADHD, I was at my wits' end. Nothing I tried with her—talking, rewarding, punishing—seemed to work. It was only after I went through the parent training instruction recommended by her pediatrician that I started to understand why many of my approaches were not effective and how I could work systematically to shape her behavior."

Gail, Milwaukee, WI

The emphasis of PTBM on ways in which adults can better understand, manage, and shape their child's behavior differs from other approaches, such as traditional psychotherapy, that focus directly on the child and are designed to change the child's emotional status. Cognitive behavior therapy (CBT), which is intended to shape patterns of thinking, while very effective to treat anxiety and depression in older children and adolescents, is also less effective than PTBM. Both psychotherapy and CBT have not been found to consistently help in the treatment of childhood ADHD.

In this chapter, you will be introduced to the principles underlying PTBM for families of children with ADHD. You will learn

- What PTBM consists of, who it is for, and where it is available
- Which specific parenting techniques have been found to be effective in improving children's functioning and how they must be implemented
- How the gains achieved through PTBM techniques can be preserved

Parent training in behavior management techniques are often taught in highly structured 7- to 12-week individual or group parent training sessions by specially trained and certified therapists. Usually there is one session per week. These courses have been shown to be effective for families with ADHD because they allow for weekly feedback, letting parents ask questions and receive helpful advice from the therapist. Sessions provide parents the chance to share their experiences with others in similar situations, and it may not succeed without the help of a trained therapist.

Unfortunately, while PTBM is available in many communities, it may not be in your community, or it may be available but not covered by your insurance plan. If this is the case, by reading the material in this chapter, you should be able to apply many of these principles in your daily interactions with your child. But you will most likely find it more useful to work with a child therapist or your child's pediatric clinician to adapt these techniques to your own unique situation.

What Is Parent Training in Behavior Management, Who Is It for, and Where Is It Available?

Parent training in behavior management consists of a set of practical, tested procedures designed to provide you with the strategies you need to improve family interactions and your child's ability to manage his behavior. Parent training is a program aimed at training you, the parents, to successfully manage and shape your child's behavior. By focusing less on the child's emotional state and more on his actual behaviors, it attempts to turn parents into their child's therapist by teaching them how to encourage and maintain positive behaviors, determine which behaviors can be actively ignored, and know when and how to set and enforce rules. Many of the techniques may be ones which you have used with your other children and tried without success on your child with ADHD. Your child's behavior likely requires more precision and consistency than was required with your other children.

All forms of behavior therapy, including PTBM, share a common set of principles and offer many techniques that can be combined to help increase a child's abilities for self-regulation. A sound PTBM program should help you

- Gain a better understanding of what behaviors are typical for your child.
- Learn to achieve consistent and positive interactions.
- Cut down on negative interactions, such as arguing or constantly having to repeat instructions.
- Provide appropriate consequences for your child's behavior.
- Become more empathetic of your child's viewpoint.
- Assist your child in improving her abilities to manage her own behaviors.
- Avoid problem behavior, when possible, by changing the environment.

Who Benefits Most From Parent Training in Behavior Management?

In most cases, the younger your child is, the more successful a PTBM program is likely to be because it is easier to change negative behaviors that have not been in place for very long. Still, even teenagers can benefit from a sound and consistent behavioral approach, as is described in Chapter 11. Because PTBM requires sufficient verbal skills for your child to understand what you are telling her, it usually is recommended for families when the child is at least 2 years old. Before age 2 it is simply not possible to discuss her behavior patterns and the plan for behavior change. Children who have more serious conduct problems may need additional professional help, or a different type of help, to improve their functioning.

Parent training in behavior management may be most effective in situations when it is used along with stimulant medication that allows the child to be more fully attentive to the techniques being introduced. Combining medication management with PTBM can, in many cases, modestly but significantly increase the chances that parents and teachers will regard a child's behavior as comparable to that of children who do not have ADHD.

For children who have ADHD without coexisting conditions (see Chapter 9), adequate social functioning, and few significant behavioral problems, well-planned and monitored *medication management alone* may be the best treatment option. But for preschoolers, children, and youth who have ADHD complicated by oppositional symptoms, poor social functioning, and behavior problems from less than optimal or negative parenting practices, *a combination of medication management and PTBM* has been found to be the most effective treatment option. For toddlers and preschoolers with oppositional behaviors with or without ADHD, PTBM is the suggested first line of treatment. For school-aged children (6–12 years), medication or PTBM can be started first.

Whether or not your child is taking medication, PTBM may help improve your relationship with her. Parents and children report greater satisfaction when PTBM is included in their overall treatment plan, and in some cases the benefits of PTBM include being able to reduce the dose of stimulant medication needed to achieve targeted behavioral goals. An additional benefit of PTBM is that the principles work well for all children in the family, not just for children with ADHD, and adopting a parenting approach that uses these techniques can lead to better overall family relationships.

Coexisting Conditions and Family Issues

If your child has been diagnosed with ADHD and other coexisting conditions, her pediatrician can help you determine the behavioral treatment priorities for your child based on her individual needs. For example, if your child has been diagnosed with ADHD and also has anxiety, either PTBM or medication management may lead to similar gains. However, children with ADHD and oppositional and defiant or conduct disorders may benefit more from treatment that combines medication and PTBM than medication alone. Although intensive, autism spectrum disorder (ASD)–specific behavioral therapy (Applied Behavioral Analysis) is the first-line and most effective treatment for children with ASD, children who have ADHD symptoms in addition may or may not need medication management for these same symptoms as children who have ADHD alone and may also require other medication. Children with ADHD and severe depression may also require different medication management and a different type of behavioral treatment plan. The kind of PTBM described in this chapter may not be appropriate in these situations.

Ideally, at the time that your child was diagnosed with ADHD, any coexisting disorders were also identified. Keep in mind, though, that certain conditions may escape notice early on or only surface at a later time. If your child exhibits symptoms that make you suspect she has a disruptive behavior disorder, depression, anxiety, or ASD, discuss your concerns with her pediatrician. It may be necessary to reconsider her diagnosis and coexisting conditions and to change her treatment plan accordingly.

Family circumstances may also affect your ability to make gains using PTBM techniques. If communication among members of your family is extremely difficult, if you are experiencing serious marital problems, or if family members are struggling with multiple major issues, parent training may not work for you. Family issues of special concern include any form of family violence and drug or alcohol use. In these circumstances, meeting with a psychotherapist for family therapy may be a more helpful first strategy. Children with ADHD may also have a learning disability or language disorder. It is important to determine if these are problems because the behavior management techniques alone will not address these problems, which also may be contributing to your child's behavior problems.

Where Can I Find a Parent Training in Behavior Management Program?

If PTBM programs exist in your community and are covered by your health insurance, your child's pediatric clinician can often point you toward an appropriate resource. Check to be sure that the behavioral therapist is a qualified mental health counselor or other medical professional. Choose a program that follows a systematic format adapted specifically for parents of children with ADHD. It can be useful to check to see if a particular behavior therapist is certified by the American Board of Professional Psychology. Your own pediatric clinician or mental health resource, a developmental and behavioral pediatrician, or mental health departments at your local children's hospital may be able to help you find a PTBM program. The best programs are evidence based, meaning they have already been proven to be effective through carefully conducted research. While less standardized parent training programs may be available, they are not as likely to be as helpful as PTBM for families dealing with ADHD.

Some schools have been able to fund and train their teachers in the use of behavior therapy techniques and or have a school psychologist or behavior therapist that can advise the teacher about setting up behavior technique. If your child's teacher is able to participate in such courses, she and your child would likely benefit. By participating in parent training with your partner and sharing behavior therapy strategies with your child's teacher and other caregivers, you can help others support your child's efforts to meet the target outcomes that you and the rest of her treatment team have identified.

As you review the information that follows in this chapter, think about the ways in which you may be able to incorporate these practices into your daily life with your child.

Parent Training in Behavior Management : The Specifics of Parent Training

Learning the Basics

As you begin a PTBM program it is important to understand basic information about ADHD and the causes of oppositional and defiant behaviors. As well as reading books such as this and visiting responsible websites, your behavioral therapist will usually include information about these topics as you embark on PTBM instruction.

Setting the Stage for Behavior Change: Learning How to Spend Positive Time or "Hang Out" With Your Child

Parent training in behavior management is not just about a child's behavior. It seeks to improve relationships between a child and her parents and others. It addresses interactions within the family. As a parent, you can take the first step toward improved relationships by understanding how discouraging your child's daily experiences can be to her and by countering that negativity with positive messages and support.

Many parent training programs teach that establishing a positive playtime is a helpful first step in setting the stage for successful outcomes. You can do this by setting aside a short period each day to play with your child, during which you refrain from giving instructions or commands or asking questions and, alternatively, imitate what your child is doing, describing what she is doing, with enthusiasm. During this time, your goal is not to teach your child anything or to shape her behavior. It is to let her know that you are interested in her and want to spend time getting to know her better. This can be accomplished by announcing that from now on you will reserve time during several days each week to be with your child. In a 2-parent household, hopefully both parents can individually find this time on most days.

During positive playtime, allow your child to decide on the activity. Any activity that allows the 2 of you to interact is perfect, like playing with board games or dolls or riding bikes together. Watching television or observing your child as she plays organized sports is not an example of positive play because you are not directly interacting one-on-one. While you are involved in this activity, allow your child to take the lead. Comment occasionally to show you are paying attention and are involved. Provide positive feedback now and then, but do not take over the activity or conversation. Try to select activities that allow you to just enjoy your child's company instead of ones in which you need to provide direction, like a new board game with a lot of rules.

The point is to simply be with your child. Let her be the center of your attention and show you her world. By regularly participating in these activities with your child you are learning to listen and observe while avoiding constantly giving commands or instructions. *These are the first skills necessary to begin reshaping her behavior and changing her relationships within the family.* You are also demonstrating in the most effective way possible that your child does not need to engage in negative behaviors to win your attention. Once she learns she has her parents' interest, she learns she can rely on them to help her figure out how to get along better and develop more positive relationships with others.

Responding Effectively to Your Child's Behavior

Once you and your child have begun to establish a basis of trust and positive support, it is time to look at the ways you hope to improve your interactions with her at home. Parent interactions can be improved, and improved interactions can set the stage for the successful use of PTBM tools and techniques.

One of the first principles of parent training is to expand the notion of the word *discipline*. Many parents assume that the term refers to ways to carry out effective punishment. However, *teaching discipline to a child really means teaching self-control*. This is the broad goal of PTBM. Parent training in behavior management programs take a more positive approach than just constantly devising punishments for breaking rules. As your child's "teacher-coach-therapist," you will learn how to choose the most effective response to any given situation.

In most cases, you will find that you have 3 choices when confronted with a particular behavior in your child: you can *praise* the behavior, deliberately *ignore* it, or *punish* your child for it. Parent training in behavior management programs will help you to decide which response to choose, how to follow up on that decision, and how to become consistent about your choices from one event, and one day, to the next.

It is not always easy to decide whether a behavior deserves to be ignored or punished, and it is not always obvious when and how to provide praise. These and other topics will be discussed in this chapter. In the meantime, it is important to consider that the most powerful tool that parents have in disciplining their child is how they pay attention to behavior. In the heat of the moment ignoring or not paying attention to negative behaviors may go against your instincts or intuition. It may help to think about how much more likely you are to work hard when your supervisor at work recognizes and praises your efforts, as opposed to how poorly motivated and resentful you may feel if she frequently criticizes you. In the same way, your child is more likely to respond positively to your actions if you react positively to her, while a negative comment or response on your part is likely to lead to more negative behavior. This is why in PTBM, parents are encouraged to praise their child's behavior whenever possible, even for neutral behaviors, and ignore it when necessary, as a strong way of shaping behavior while minimizing the need for punishment. This is especially important if the problem behavior your child exhibits is motivated by her desire to obtain your attention, whether negative or positive, by any means possible.

Three Basic Rules

When Responding to Your Child's Behavior

Many parents making use of parent training in behavior management techniques find it helpful to rely on the following simple rules when interacting with their child:

- If you want to see a behavior continue, praise it.
- If you do not like a behavior but it is not dangerous or intolerable, ignore it.
- If you have to stop a behavior that is dangerous or intolerable, like when your child hits a sibling to hurt her, not just to get your attention, punish it.

Giving Clear Commands

The first step in helping your child learn to follow rules, obey your commands, and otherwise manage her own behavior is to make sure that the commands you give her are clear. Some adults often deliver their commands in a variety of ambiguous gestures and phrases. Or many of us tend to react too strongly or impulsively to behavior we consider unacceptable. But *all children need to be told what to do in a clear, straightforward, and nonemotional way if they are to learn to control their actions.* This especially true for your child with ADHD. You can give effective commands by

- **Establishing good eye contact.** You must fully engage your child's attention by making good eye contact if she is going to hear and follow what you say. At first, you may find it helpful to gently touch a younger child's arm or calmly hold her hand before addressing her.

- **Clearly stating the command.** You can make commands clear to your child by first stating what behavior therapists call a *terminating command*—a simple, unemotional statement of what you want your child to do. Try not to raise your voice and use as few words as is possible: "You need to stop pushing your brother."

- If the behavior does not stop immediately, you can then follow up with a *warning* that includes the exact limit and the *consequences. Again, use a calm, soft voice and as few words as is possible:* "If you push your brother one more time, you'll be in time-out. If you stop immediately, the 2 of you can go on playing."

- When stating a command, keep your tone of voice firm and neutral even though that may be difficult at times. Refrain from yelling or looking or sounding angry. It is especially important to monitor your body language because these nonverbal messages are so easy for parents to overlook. State the command as an instruction, not as a question. Instead of "Would you please stop teasing your brother?" or "Stop teasing him, OK?" make a statement: "You need to stop teasing your brother."

- **Observing your child's response.** If you are not sure your child heard the terminating command or warning, ask her to repeat it back to you. Pay attention to whether she carries out your instructions and respond immediately to her behavior.

  - If she responds as you have asked, respond positively with praise, thanks, a thumbs-up, a high five, or other acknowledgment that she has done well.

  - If her response is not exactly what you had hoped for but is in the right direction, offer her immediate praise for the part of your command that she did carry out.

- **Enforcing consequences for negative behavior.** If your child does not start to respond according to the limits you previously announced, invoke the consequences that you have already set, calmly narrating what is happening as you do so: "You did not stop pushing your brother, so you'll have the time-out that we just talked about." Keep in mind that because you have given a warning and a terminating command and spelled out the consequences for complying or disobeying, if she does not follow your instructions you have not "put her in" the time-out—*she* has "chosen" the time-out for herself as an alternative to following your command. But, *if you give your child* *a command, she doesn't comply, and you immediately "put her" in time-out, you have skipped the step of her choosing whether to receive the positive or negative consequence. You have lost an opportunity to teach her self-control.*

Remember the bottom line of what parent discipline is: Does it teach self-control?

If you make a point of following through on the positive or negative consequences of each command, every time, you should soon find that you will not have to repeat your instructions over and over as you probably did before. Your ultimate goal will be to give a command only once for it to be obeyed. Parents are often concerned that "I have to say it 8 times before she does it." Children are thinking, "The first 7 times are free! Then she gets angry and I finally have to do it." The elimination of constant pleading, nagging, or threatening is a great relief to most parents and their children. It goes a long way toward improving their interaction.

If you are tempted to "let it slide" when your child ignores a command, consider how hard it will be to make up for this inconsistency in the future and carry out the promised consequences. If you are going to try to follow up on each command you give, you will need to consider beforehand how important the command you are about to give is. Limiting the number of commands you give will make it easier for you to follow up on each and every one, thus increasing your chances of success.

At first, as you practice giving commands according to these guidelines, you will need to keep things simple. Make sure that all your commands are achievable by your child and wait until she has completed one step of your instructions before giving another. If necessary, break a complex command down into smaller steps, for example "Take off your shoes. Good job! Now take off your socks. Well done!" This can result in your child being able to successfully carry out the command and build on successes. A more complicated command could cause her to fail and can make her feel like she can "never" do what you ask. While your child is carrying out your instructions, avoid distracting her.

Be sure to follow up on each command and stick to commands that you know can be carried out successfully by your child. It is usually best to give a time limit for each command , such as "by the third time" or "in 3 minutes." A time limit helps her focus on accomplishing the task. And it helps both of you define when it has or has not been accomplished.

Keep in mind that children with ADHD often have particular problems with time awareness and time limits. You will need to keep such limits simple and consider using egg timers or other creative clock devices to make these time limits more concrete. By doing so, you can turn commands that have previously ended in failure and frustration, like "Go upstairs and clean your room," into commands that end in success and build on your child's self-esteem, such as, "Put your video game player away by the time this bell goes off in 3 minutes."

Finally, avoid giving commands unless you mean for her to follow them. It is not helpful to tell her to go to bed until it is really time.

Shaping Behaviors Gradually: Small Steps in the Right Direction Add Up

Children with ADHD, like all of us, will probably have particular difficulty changing a complex or long-standing set of behaviors. Expecting your child to make a major behavioral change all at once will most likely result in frustration and failure for you both. You can support your child's efforts to change a complex set of behaviors by breaking the plan down into smaller, achievable steps and tackling one at a time. This is called *shaping* your child's behavior. The idea is to break down tasks to the point at which each step is achievable and ends in praise for success for your child instead of failure and frustration.

Parent training in behavior management will help you learn to do this by having you review your targeted outcomes or specific goals for your child's behavior and develop ways you can help her achieve them. As a parent (or other primary caregiver) you might start by writing down what you see as each step toward completing a task or correcting a complex behavior. Then you may follow up by creating a plan for working on each step, one at a time. You can incorporate your child in the development of each plan at the level that she can appropriately participate. Even minor goals can be broken down in this way. In writing down the steps involved in completing a chore, for example, you might list the steps that your child needs to take in cleaning up his room, such as

- Put dirty clothes in a hamper.
- Put books away.
- Put toys in the drawers under her bed.
- Pull up the covers.

Then you can start with a single command: "You need to start cleaning up your room by putting the dirty clothes in the hamper." Often, getting started with tasks is the hardest part for children with ADHD. When you help with the first step of the task, your child will be more likely to get started too, and once that happens, you can take a step back and focus on praising the behavior. When she has completed this first task successfully, you can praise her: "Good job!"

Once she is praised for placing the clothes in the hamper, she will be more likely to respond to, "Now put your books away." You might respond, "Good progress." This continues until the room has been straightened.

If, on the other hand, you had only said, "You need to clean your room," and she *had* put her clothes in the hamper but not put her books and toys away or pulled up the covers, she would not have been successful. Like most parents, you probably would have ended up making a negative remark or giving a consequence.

After using this new technique for a number of days, if your child is consistently putting the clothes in the hamper when asked, you can add the next step. Now you can start the "clean your room" task with a combined command: "Please put your clothes in the hamper and put your books away." As before, praise her for successful completion. When this is successful you can add the next task, and so on, until the list is complete. In this way you can "shape her behavior" and, at the same time, turn what used to be negative interactions into positive ones that build on her self-esteem and competence.

You might also help your child learn to focus better and accomplish tasks more quickly by timing certain tasks and encouraging her to try to break her own speed record again and again. Small triumphs can mean a great deal to children who have experienced repeated failure or frustration at home or at school. Behavior-shaping techniques also heighten your child's awareness of each successful step, helping her to own her behavioral successes and feel proud about them.

Choosing What to Praise, Ignore, or Punish

The next step in PTBM is learning to recognize behaviors that require positive, ignoring, or punishment responses. You will be encouraged to do your best to "catch your child being good," or even neutral, and praise her for it whenever possible. This allows for positive interaction and enhances her relationship with you as it strengthens her positive behaviors. Praise should be simple, specific, and straightforward: "I like the way you put your clothes away the first time I asked!" Be careful to not spoil the reward by negative references. For example, "Great job! Why can't you always do it like that?" is called *praise spoiling*. In many cases a simple smile, hug, or arm around your child's shoulders is even more effective than words. Immediate positive reinforcement is actually a much stronger way to change behavior than larger, long-term rewards like promising a video game system for maintaining all Bs or staying on the honor roll all semester. For younger children you may still decide to offer your child stickers, points in a token reward system, or other prizes for putting in the effort to help change behaviors you are working on, as long as you know that your child will be successful at achieving these rewards.

Active ignoring is another powerful behavioral tool available to parents but one of the hardest to carry out. Avoid reinforcing negative behaviors by not paying attention to them!

Prior to using active ignoring, you should consider whether there are any changes you can make to the environment that will decrease the likelihood of the problem behavior occurring altogether. For example, if your child tends to argue or fight with her sibling after 30 minutes of play, consider ending sibling play time after 25 minutes, followed by redirection to independent activities. By setting the stage you may prevent some undesirable behaviors before they start.

Once you give a command, you must follow it through to the end if it is going to be effective and meaningful to your child. Many parents are in the habit of giving frequent corrections all through the day that they cannot or do not follow through on many of them. Or they might dole out so many punishments that they become ineffective and set up a negative relationship with their child. Learning how to actively ignore certain situations can lead to many fewer commands and significantly improve this situation.

Parents are often surprised at how effective ignoring a negative behavior can be. This is especially true once your child has grown accustomed to the positive attention she enjoys in your special times together and less frequently demands your attention in negative ways. A child who interrupts your phone conversations over and over is, in most cases, only doing it to get your attention.

If you respond by saying something like, "Sarah, I'm on the phone—wait until I get off!" you may think you are giving a command to stop the behavior, but you are actually rewarding her by giving her the attention she wanted in the first place. If, instead, you ignore her behavior by not looking at her or responding to her in words, her attempts to distract you while you are on the phone will increase at first, while she tries even harder to get the attention that she is used to having. This is what behavior therapists call an *extinction burst*—the behavior gets worse before it gets better. However, if you consistently ignore her even though it doesn't seem to be working, she will gradually learn more functional ways to have her needs met. In this way, ignoring works as a powerful tool for behavior change. A large proportion of behavior problems can be addressed with a combination of praising and ignoring techniques.

As part of a typical PTBM program, you will identify the few behaviors that you consider so dangerous, like running into the street without looking, or intolerable, like hitting other children to hurt them, that they must be met with immediate action or punishment on your part. Your therapist will teach you how to discuss these behaviors with your child ahead of time, figure out the punishments that will follow, and determine possible ways to avoid the same situation in the future. Your therapist will help you understand how much more effective punishment can be if it is limited to only your child's most dangerous or intolerable behaviors.

When punishment occurs too frequently, as it often does for children with ADHD, it is less effective and the child may no longer consistently respond to it. Children can become quite resentful, angry, and negative. Because of this, negative consequences should be reserved for those few instances when parents feel they must do something immediately and not just ignore. Any punishment should be preceded, whenever possible, by a terminating and a warning signal. That way your child will always have the opportunity to exert self-control and avoid the punishment.

It is important for punishments to be appropriate for the infraction or misbehavior. Punishments are most effective when administered as close to the infraction as is possible. The severity does not have to be harsh to be effective. Many studies have proven that less severe punishments that are timely and related to the infraction tend to work better. This is why spanking and other corporal punishments are less effective, can have negative effects, and should never be used.

In addition to setting up a punishment system for dangerous and intolerable behaviors, it can be helpful to have some mild punishments to help children with ADHD understand the one-to-one connection between their behaviors and consequences for those behaviors.

In fact, no matter what your response to your child's behavior, it will be most effective if it takes place immediately. Putting off a discussion until later, or offering a reward at the end of the week for general good behavior, will greatly diminish its effect. In addition, the response you have chosen to a particular behavior should be as consistent as possible. If you responded appropriately to your child's pushing her brother down with a specific punishment yesterday, try to respond in the same way today. Your behavioral therapist will help you decide in advance on the best responses to your child's most frequent behavior issues so you can use these techniques with confidence.

Using Rewards to Motivate Positive Behavior

Praise is a powerful motivator for all children, and many also especially enjoy and respond well to additional, tangible motivators such as reward charts and token economies. *Reward charts*, called contingency charts by behavioral therapists, usually consist of daily calendar sheets listing 4 or 5 achievable chores, behaviors, or other goals on which you and your child have agreed. Before instituting the reward chart with your child, you will have observed her enough to know that she can successfully complete most of the behaviors listed. The description of each behavior needs to be clear, countable, and unambiguous; for example, "is upstairs brushing his teeth within 5 minutes after being told" or "gets out of bed by the third time she's asked." You might have 5 items on a chart, 4 of which are easily achievable by your child with an additional item that may be harder for her and that you are presently working on. Charts can be reviewed daily, and this becomes a time to let your child know how proud you are of her for working on her chores or behavior.

Each time your child accomplishes the goal she receives a sticker, a star, or another mark of achievement on the chart. If too many of the items are not achievable and do not end up with stars or stickers, your child will get easily frustrated and negative about participating. Many younger children are happy enough just to receive the stickers or stars themselves, but some older children may want to accumulate stars or stickers and redeem them for frequent, modest, and prearranged material rewards or privileges. These rewards do not need to be new privileges. What you are trying to do is put some of her everyday privileges under her behavioral control, knowing in advance that she will experience success. Table 6.1 summarizes some of the key concepts described in this section.

Table 6.1. Effective Behavioral Techniques for Children With Attention-Deficit/Hyperactivity Disorder		
Technique	**Description**	**Example**
Positive reinforcement	Providing rewards or privileges dependent on the child's performance	Child completes an assignment and is permitted to play on the computer.
Ignoring behavior	In response to the child's unwanted behavior, parents do not pay attention to it—neither with their body language nor responding in words. They actively ignore it.	When the child recognizes that her negative behavior is not getting the attention she desires, she may first escalate the behavior (extinction burst), but when she sees that it never gets the attention she desires it will stop (extinguish). Extinction bursts are temporary and are often a sign that the behavior is about to go away.
Time-out	Removing access to positive reinforcement because of unwanted or problem behavior	Child hits sibling and, after ignoring the command to stop and being told the choices for complying or not complying, is required to sit for up to 5 minutes in the corner of the room.

(continued)

Table 6.1 (*continued*)		
Technique	**Description**	**Example**
Response cost	Withdrawing rewards or privileges because of the performance of unwanted or problem behavior	Child loses free-time privileges for not completing homework by the indicated deadline.
Token economy	Child earns rewards and privileges because of performing desired behaviors. This type of positive reinforcement can be combined with response cost, where a child can also lose the rewards and privileges based on undesirable behavior.	Child earns stars for completing assignments and loses stars for getting out of seat. The child cashes in the sum of stars at the end of the week for a prize.
Reinforced practice	Using praise or rewards to encourage children to practice skills that are not currently within their reach	Child earns rewards for practicing the steps of getting ready in the morning during the week leading up to a new school year. These scheduled practice sessions can occur at any time of day and serve the purpose of teaching and motivating children to do things they have never done on their own.

Another type of reward system, called a *token economy,* also involves receiving tokens, stars, stickers, or points for behaving appropriately or complying with commands. Token economies are similar to reward charts in that they can often be helpful when praise alone is not enough to motivate a child to complete tasks or stick to routines. The gains from using a token economy approach can often be seen quickly but usually need to continue for some time for the positive effects to become the usual behaviors. Each targeted behavior is given a value (eg, 3 stickers, 4 points), depending on how difficult a challenge it is for your child. You and your child can then create a list of fun activities or treats that she can "buy" with a prearranged number of stickers or points.

This is a reward system to encourage desired behaviors. *Response cost*—the withdrawing of rewards or privileges in response to unwanted or problem behavior—can be added onto this system later if necessary. In that case, your child's failure to accomplish a targeted behavior on her own or after an agreed-on limit results in the same number of stickers or points being deducted from her total. Before response cost is introduced, you need to make sure your child is earning tokens and has accepted and responded to the token economy plan. Make sure that you see it as motivating and that your child sees it as fun. If it will become a frustrating exercise to your child, it will soon become a useless strategy.

Reward charts and token economies are good ways to help motivate children to take responsibility for their own behavioral improvement when praise alone has not been effective enough. They also help parents facilitate these gains in structured, positive, consistent, and objective ways. These techniques work especially well when the rewards for compliance are fairly immediate; give tokens to your child as soon as possible after she complies and go on the earned and agreed-on trip to the beach within a week. Their effectiveness is very much enhanced when your child gets the opportunity to help create the list of goals, the assigned value of each behavior, and the rewards that follow satisfactory compliance. It is best to do what you can to keep point deductions to a minimum. Break tasks up into reasonable steps and don't expect too much too soon, so that your child does not become too discouraged and give up. Some children do not start to warm up to token economies until they have experienced 1 or more of the promised big rewards, so be sure to continue the technique for 1 or more months before deciding whether it is useful for her. To help your child not become too frustrated or resistant, keep her goals achievable and the program positive. This will go a long way toward making this approach successful.

Using Punishment Effectively

No one likes to invoke negative consequences for unacceptable behavior, but doing so calmly and consistently is a necessary part of helping your child learn new ways of functioning. At first it may be difficult to decide when punishment is appropriate because it is easy to attribute much of your child's failure to manage some of her behaviors appropriately to her ADHD. Refusal to obey, even when it occurs along with ADHD, can be greatly reduced with effective parenting techniques.

When parents think about discipline and punishment, they might think about spanking without causing physical injury as a way to reduce or stop undesirable behavior. *Many studies have shown that spanking is a less effective strategy than time-outs or removal of privileges for achieving these goals when those strategies are used properly, and it has been found to have negative effects on a child's health and development.* In addition, spanking models aggressive behavior as a solution to conflict and can lead to agitated or aggressive behavior in your child, physical injury, and resentment toward parents with deterioration of parent-child relationships. Most experts and organizations, including the American Academy of Pediatrics, recommends that children never be spanked or shamed. Spanking when a parent is out of control may be considered child physical abuse.

Time-outs and loss of privileges are the 2 forms of punishment that have been proven effective for children with ADHD. They are appropriate tools for responding to the few behaviors you have identified as intolerable or unacceptable.

Time-out, most often used with younger children, involves sending your child to an area away from you, separating her from you so that you are now able to ignore her negative behavior.

Before instituting time-outs, you must discuss your intention with your child, explaining that there will be the consequences for violating the family's most important rules. Explain that unless behaviors are dangerous and need to be stopped right away, you will always give a terminating command, such as, "Give your brother's toy back." You will also give a warning if the unwanted behavior continues; for example, "If you don't give it back within 1 minute you'll need to be in time-out." Have this conversation before you impose a time-out, at a time you can discuss behavior problems together. It is not a good idea to do this when you are angry or your child is upset, or when your child is hungry, or if either of you are in a rush. Help her understand that you know that she can change her behavior to avoid the problems that you are discussing.

Instruct her that you're going to help her and that time-outs can be avoided. Your child can always choose to avoid time-out by changing her behavior and making a good choice when you remind her. Tell your child that you will use a timer to measure the length of the time-out, and demonstrate to her how the timer works.

Once your child understands how time-outs work, you can begin to implement them when appropriate. When your child displays an unacceptable behavior

- Warn her that a time-out will occur if she does not respond to your warning in a specific amount of time: "Anna, stop pushing your sister. If you haven't stopped by the time I count to 3, you will have a time-out."

- Also state what the good consequences or benefits will be for choosing the appropriate behavior.

- If your child does not comply in the specified time or number of prompts, firmly, but using a calm voice, send her to the time-out setting. Use as few words as is possible, like: "Girls who push their sister need a time-out." Do not give her more time to comply or let her engage you in any distracting interaction. Remember that she has made this choice herself by noncompliance. If you further engage, you are paying attention to—and accidentally rewarding—her negative behavior.

- Tell her how many minutes the time-out will last. A brief time out is sufficient—as little as 2 minutes but almost never more than 5 minutes. Set a timer and leave her alone.

- Avoid negotiating whether she can get out earlier. Sometimes, you might try ending a time-out by waiting until your child self-calms for 2 to 5 seconds. In this manner, the child learns that self-calming is what ends the time-out.

- If she is still distressed or crying at the end of the time-out period, you might say, "Would you like me to cuddle with you and help you calm down?" This way you acknowledge that her distress is not harmful or scary and that she can become calm again.

- When she has completed the time-out process, focus on the future. Avoid lecturing and let the punishment "speak for itself." And make a point of praising her next positive behavior so that the negative "punishment" experience is fully ended.

Be prepared for a great deal of resistance the first few times when time-outs occur. Time-outs teach by repetition, or what is called *conditioning*. Soon your child will learn that you are remaining consistent, so that resisting, arguing, or negotiating no longer work. She will learn that it is better to choose the positive behavior to avoid the time-out altogether. Meanwhile, remember that the goal is for your child to focus on *staying out* of time-outs rather than *getting out* of them. By supporting your child in these positive ways, while sticking to the rules you have created, you are helping your child to learn to control her behavior and respect your fair and consistent requests and commands.

Loss of privileges, a more appropriate negative consequence for older children and teenagers, consists of invoking a "cost" for intolerable behavior. Should your child break a family rule or ignores a command after a pre–agreed-on number of warnings, privileges are removed for a time appropriate to the seriousness of the transgression.

This technique works best if your child has participated in decisions about exactly which behaviors will result in a loss of privileges and agrees to some pre-negotiated penalties. It is important to connect the penalty as closely as possible to the negative behavior. For example, your child's failure to complete her homework may cost her television privileges the next day. Or a teenager's failure to return home after curfew may cause her to lose car privileges for that weekend. Loss of privileges is not likely to work if consequences are perceived as unreasonable or don't make sense to your child. In the previous examples, 3 weeks without driving or television is unreasonable and will probably feel mean. The longer after the inappropriate behavior, the less the learning value—the behavior is forgotten, and the punishment feels unreasonable. Long consequences foster resentment toward parents and become harder and harder to enforce, making them ineffective tools.

If you find that your child continues to strongly resist complying with time-outs or loss of privileges while continuing the negative behaviors, consider the way in which you are implementing these techniques. If you have been giving in to her resistance—allowing her out of the time-out area if she yells and kicks long enough or letting her negotiate her way out of a loss-of-privilege punishment—she will have learned that resistance allows her to have her way. And your continued involvement and attention actually rewards and increased the behavior! If you have been enforcing the rules only sometimes, she may not be able to resist testing your responses again and again to learn what you will do this time.

If you have successfully carried out an effective punishment procedure but neglected to work on fostering a successful, supportive, fun, and well-structured "time-in" home environment, your child may have decided she will never be able to succeed and give up trying. For these reasons it is so very important to remain calm, firm, and consistent while invoking a punishment and to follow up as soon as possible with reassuring praise.

Managing Your Child's Behavior in Public

With training and practice, PTBM techniques can soon become effective at home where a time-out area is clearly identified. At home parents are able to respond immediately to unacceptable behavior. But when intolerable behavior occurs in public it is embarrassing and upsetting. Parents often feel that other adults are negatively judging their child and their parenting skills, but strangers don't know that their child has ADHD. It is also important to establish methods for implementing disciplinary techniques outside the home.

Effective PTBM methods for use in public are the same ones you have developed with your child at home. If she is already familiar with the standard consequences for certain types of behavior, you might quietly and privately remind her of the 2 or 3 main behavior rules she most needs to pay attention to as she enters a new environment. It always helps to let her know what positives will result from her following these rules and, perhaps, what the consequences will be for breaking them.

To help her maintain her efforts to comply, "catch her being good." Praise her positive behaviors during the outing and let her know how much you appreciate how hard she is trying to follow the rules. If she manages to control her behavior throughout the entire period, acknowledge her success and give her special praise. If you have also offered a reward, provide it as soon as possible.

It is helpful if, in advance, you have already decided what the consequence will be. If your child fails to behave acceptably, even after a final warning, you will be prepared to

Before entering a new environment, remind your child which 2 or 3 behavior rules he needs to follow. Praise his positive behaviors during the outing and let him know you appreciate how hard he is trying to follow the rules.

invoke the appropriate negative consequence. To delay responding just because you are in public will probably lead to more misbehavior. You can enforce token economy fines or removal of privileges practically anywhere as long as you keep your conversation private. It may be valuable to talk with your child's behavioral therapist about how you might implement consequences discreetly and effectively at the supermarket, your friend's house, church, or wherever you expect to be.

Your child needs your competent handling of rewards and limits as she practices new behavioral rules in public. She also benefits from your thoughtful planning to help her to successfully maintain her best self-control in these situations. Planning in advance can make all the difference in her ability to control her restlessness and stay focused. Consider the characteristics of where you are going and the length of time it will take.

Whenever you take her along on errands, to a restaurant or friend's house, or even a brief trip, it helps to pack some activities to keep her happily occupied, such as activity books, handheld computer games, and paper and pen. Once you are in public together, involve her in your activity as much as possible. She can help choose items at the store or be helpful making a snack at your friend's house. Keeping the trips short and as kid friendly as possible can help to reduce the possibilities for inappropriate behaviors.

Maintaining the Gains From Parent Training in Behavior Management After the Sessions Are Finished

As your PTBM program is finishing up, your behavioral therapist will want to discuss ways your training will have helped you learn how to recognize when a desired goal has been reasonably achieved and when and how to formulate new targets with your child, her teacher, and the rest of her treatment team. You might also discuss future check-ins with your therapist and the ways you might want to adapt your parenting techniques to your child's future stages of development. Parent training in behavior management programs focus on younger children, and you will want to learn how to move from time-outs to response-cost techniques as your child grows. Ask how to include your child more in discussions about behavioral goals, rewards and punishments, and treatment decisions.

Making the Most Out of Parent Training in Behavior Management Techniques

Clearly, PTBM techniques take a great deal of effort on your part. It is always difficult to change old habits. Altering your parenting approach can be challenging because it has developed from what happened in your own family as you were growing up and from your own childhood experiences. Being able to participate in a formal PTBM program is an excellent way to learn, practice, and get feedback on the techniques discussed in this chapter. You can also work on these principles with your child's pediatric clinician or behavioral therapist in a less formal way. Reading this material gives you a general idea of how PTBM works. However, actually participating in PTBM or working with professionals to learn these techniques helps you to use these methods in your own family situation. You have the chance to try out some of the techniques under expert guidance and get regular feedback on what is and is not working, so that you can adjust and improve your approach. This focused support increases your likelihood of success!

Research has shown that PTBM and classroom behavior interventions have been able to successfully change the behavior of children with ADHD.

If you decide to look further into PTBM, ask your pediatric clinician for a referral. The focus of these parenting programs will be on helping you understand your child's ADHD behaviors and teaching you skills to help improve her behaviors. You'll learn to effectively talk with your child about her behavior and how to reinforce positive actions.

Remember that all behavior therapies, including PTBM, have been shown to be effective only while they are being properly implemented and maintained. *Your child is not likely to keep up her improved behavior if you drop the effective techniques you have learned.* Even during periods when you see little progress, it is important to remain consistent. During those times when you feel exhausted and discouraged and wonder what the point is of trying, consider how hard your child must also work to continue trying to maintain her best self-control. By focusing as much as possible on the positive, thinking creatively, and asking for expert help when needed, you can maintain the supportive structure you have created for your child and eventually see measurable improvement. Most programs also include support to help parents and children maintain the progress that's been made and prevent relapses.

Finally, parents need to take care of themselves if these or any other interventions are going to work well. Some factors that interfere the most with successful PTBM are parental depression and social isolation. Parents who are having difficulty dealing with these issues in their own lives often benefit significantly from getting help for themselves. Your pediatric clinician will want to help.

Additional Approaches

As noted previously, a variety of factors may limit the effectiveness of PTBM in some circumstances. When ADHD is accompanied by oppositional defiant disorder, conduct disorder, and mood and anxiety disorders, these coexisting conditions can compound the behavioral challenges presented by children and adolescents with ADHD. These coexisting conditions can contribute to aggressive behavior, poor tolerance for frustration, inflexibility, poor problem-solving skills, heightened difficulty in complying with parents' instructions, and significant family conflict. When such conditions are present, additional treatment approaches may be useful.

You may hear or read of other behaviorally oriented treatments for ADHD. Some with limited or no evidence of effectiveness include CBT, social skills training, insight-oriented psychotherapy, and play therapy. Cognitive behavior therapy can be valuable for some of the coexisting conditions, especially for adolescents with ADHD.

Other, more alternative therapies, such as vestibular stimulation, biofeedback, relaxation training, electroencephalographic biofeedback, and sensory integration exercises, are costly. They lack the sufficient scientific proof needed to be recommend as effective treatments.

Remember that behavioral treatments, just like medication management, are not curative. Behavioral methods are largely a method of rearranging environments by artificial means to yield improved participation in major life activities.

No matter what approach you ultimately use, seek the guidance of a professional specifically trained to provide effective behavioral therapies. Remember that ADHD is an inherited condition, making it likely that one or both parents may also have some of the same difficulties as their child. Because of that, the successful outcomes for your child may be more difficult to achieve. Behavioral therapy techniques can also be more difficult to use if either parent is depressed, has other emotional or mental health problems, or is under undue stress. This is just a reminder that taking care of yourself and your needs is one of the primary considerations for helping your child.

Q & A

Q: *Our child's pediatrician has recommended PTBM classes for my husband and me as a part of our 5-year-old son's treatment for ADHD. We have read about some of the techniques used in PTBM and they seem much like what we have already implemented with our other children. Anyway, it seems to us that it's our child who needs therapy more than we do, because we are already pretty consistent and predictable in our parenting style. Wouldn't he benefit more from a therapist who could help him work on controlling his behavior and obeying commands?*

A: The parenting techniques taught in PTBM courses designed for families of children with ADHD are noticeably similar to the positive parenting practices used by many parents. However, PTBM provides an opportunity to think about these techniques in the much more structured, detailed, and consistent ways necessary to help with behavior changes with your son, who is posing a much greater behavioral challenge for you than your other children. Parent training in behavior management directly addresses the behaviors that need to be changed and gives you the tools to make those changes. There is generally a lack of literature establishing the effectiveness of treatments other than behavior therapy approaches with ADHD.

Q: *I have implemented a number of behavior therapy techniques, including time-outs, star reward charts, and a token economy, at home with my child. But I find that, while these techniques work well when I first use them, they tend to lose their effectiveness as time passes. Is it necessary to rotate various techniques, phasing in new ones as older ones become less useful?*

A: Many families do find that certain techniques seem less effective over time. This could be because a child grows out of them, like becoming too old for time-outs; certain rewards may become boring; or there may be many other reasons. As with medication or any other part of your child's treatment plan, it is essential to monitor the effects of PTBM techniques on your child's functioning—and to alter the treatment if a particular technique is found not to be working. Your ongoing monitoring of how well your approach supports your child's functioning, and your willingness to change techniques to help your child, will not only help your family work more efficiently but will demonstrate to your child your concern for her well-being and involvement in her life. The principles that you have learned remain sound, although you may need to alter some of the details. Whenever possible, keep your child involved with making sure that the reward process remains fun and the consequences seem fair.

Q: *I have attended a PTBM course designed for parents of children with ADHD and have started using many of the techniques at home with some success. My problem, though, is that my son's father, from whom I'm divorced, refuses to learn about these techniques and use them when my son is with him. How can I maintain a structured life for my son when he is basically on his own every other weekend at his father's house?*

A: Separate households can present quite a challenge to families of children with ADHD because consistency is important for the progress of these children. It is optimal to have your ex-spouse involved as much as possible from the very beginning of the evaluation through developing and carrying out a treatment plan. This will remain in the best interest of your child. Encourage your son's father's buy-in and cooperation with the treatment plan by being sure his opinions have been respected, his questions have been answered, and his input has been sought as the plan develops. If a breakdown in communication remains, your child's pediatrician or pediatric clinician may be able to recommend a family therapist who can help you and your ex-spouse work through some of the issues that are standing in the way of a consistent routine that can be maintained in both households.

If none of these approaches are possible, however, you should still implement and model as many of these PTBM techniques as you can in your own household. They will still work, but it may take a bit longer to see their positive effects.

CHAPTER 7

Your Child at School

School can be particularly challenging for children with attention-deficit/hyperactivity disorder (ADHD), as they may experience poor academic performance, behavior problems, and difficulties with social interaction. Coexisting conditions, such as a learning disability, an anxiety disorder, or disruptive behavior problems, can make it even more difficult for a child to succeed. The situation can be further complicated by the fact that there is no typical, predictable classroom style common to all children with ADHD. Some parents of children with ADHD may receive reports that their child is "not trying hard enough" academically, while others may be told that their child turns in acceptable work but frequently violates classroom rules. As a parent it can be hard to determine how much of any problem identified by a teacher falls into the typical range of child development, how much is due to ADHD, and how much might be due to a coexisting problem (see Chapter 9). Add to these the fact that the focus of your

School can be particularly challenging for children with attention-deficit/hyperactivity disorder.

child's problems may change from year to year—from largely behavioral to academic, from academic to social, and so on. It is small wonder that children with ADHD and their families often find school issues so confusing yet so central to their nonschool concerns. It can also hard for you, the parent, if school was a challenge for you.

The better informed your family is about the many ways in which ADHD may affect your child's school experience, the better prepared you will be to recognize when these issues appear. You can use the information provided in this chapter to help foster your child's academic and social success in school. In the following pages, you will learn

- How to identify your own child's particular areas of concern
- What types of school-related challenges children with ADHD face most often
- Which classroom structures, school policies, teaching styles, and accommodations can best support your child's learning
- What an Individualized Education Program (IEP) and a Section 504 plan are and how to work with your child, his teachers, and the school team to create the best plan for your child
- How to promote school success at home and elsewhere

What Types of Challenges Do Children With ADHD Typically Face at School?

Because ADHD can limit a child's ability to pay attention and control impulses and behavior, it is easy to imagine how problems in these areas can affect many aspects of school life and how such problems can increase if not addressed effectively early on. In general, children with ADHD experience their greatest challenges in the areas of *behavior management, academic progress,* and *social interaction.* Due to changing school demands and changes in your child's symptoms, he may face greater problems in one area at a particular age and that might change as he grows older. It is important to continue observing your child's functioning in each of these areas and to encourage him to gain skills in monitoring his own functioning. That way, you can address together any emerging problems as soon as possible.

Behavior Issues

Disruptive behavior is a common manifestation of children with the hyperactive-impulsive and combined types of ADHD. It can begin to create problems as a child enters kindergarten or elementary school. Because so many of the demands in the early school years involve following rules and settling down, the inability to meet these demands is what frequently leads to questions about whether a child might have ADHD. A teacher may report that a child "talks too much," "acts out constantly," or "doesn't seem to recognize limits." Teachers may suggest that the child's impulsive behavior is alienating the other children or making it difficult to maintain order in the classroom and on the playground. As a child with hyperactive-impulsive– or combined-type ADHD grows, the ADHD symptoms may begin to be expressed more verbally and less in physical terms. The child may interrupt frequently or speak out of turn and perhaps even "mouth off" to authority figures or his classmates.

Other factors not directly attributable to ADHD may increase your child's behavior problems at school. Parents' or teachers' lack of knowledge about how to support or work with a child with ADHD, or a child's past negative preschool or child care experiences, can damage his self-esteem or attitude. This can cause him to give up trying to follow rules or please authority figures, at least temporarily. Coexisting conditions, such as depression, can also intensify a child's difficulties.

Even the typical developmental stages of childhood, such as a sixth grader's testing of boundaries by refusing to do homework, or an adolescent choosing to stop taking his medication to not seem different from his classmates, can have a negative effect on his functioning. Stresses in the home environment—marital conflict, financial difficulties, or other issues—can also affect your child's behavior at school. In addition, it is important to remember the role that general health plays in your child's behavior. A common co-occurring condition that many children with ADHD have is called *oppositional defiant disorder* (ODD). This condition manifests itself by angry, irritable, argumentative, and vindictive behaviors. For a number of children with ADHD and ODD, treating the ADHD also decreases the ODD symptoms. Every child, including children with ADHD, should receive routine medical care and have his vision and hearing tested at certain health supervision (well-child) visits with his pediatric clinician.

Academic Concerns

While improving behavior is often the first school-related issue that children with ADHD experience, academic progress can be or can become an area of increasing concern. Regardless of your child's intellectual abilities, he may find it hard to meet academic expectations because his symptoms can interfere with his ability to learn. Because it is difficult for many children with ADHD to stay on task and work independently for long periods, they often complete less work and, thus, have fewer chances to respond appropriately during the teacher's instruction. Problems with work production (incomplete work, sloppiness, failure to follow instructions) and inconsistency (satisfactory work one day and poor output the next) can become major barriers to school success. This may partially account for the estimates that 60% to 80% of children with ADHD underachieve academically and are identified by their teachers with some school performance problems. About 20% to 40% of children with ADHD have specific learning disabilities, such as a reading, mathematics, writing, or expressive language disorder, that are separate from their ADHD symptoms (see Chapter 9).

It is easy to see how many ADHD-type behaviors can interfere with successful learning in a typical classroom. Your child's distractibility and lack of persistence may prevent him from retaining material taught in class. His impulsivity may cause him to rush through schoolwork and respond spontaneously to questions instead of thinking ideas through. Some children with ADHD can have a poor sense of time, which can make for long homework assignments, difficulty with time-limited tasks, and extremely difficult test-taking. Organizing, planning, and sequencing problems lead to incomplete work, poor note-taking skills, or an inability to follow a work schedule or finish a long assignment. Poor fine motor planning can make the actual writing process difficult. It can limit your child's ability to take notes, complete tests, and write effortlessly. Short-term memory problems can make it difficult to memorize facts. Children with ADHD can also do well in any of these areas one day and poorly the next. Inconsistencies and fluctuations in performance are common.

Around the fourth grade students move from "learning to read" to "reading to learn." This is when there is greater focus on learning more and producing more work, causing children with inattentive- or combined-type ADHD to begin to fall behind academically. Failure to pay attention to classroom lectures and turn in homework are typical symptoms that alert teachers to a child's difficulties.

As children with ADHD enter middle school and high school, they may encounter new challenges due to poor organizational skills, incomplete work, or a failure to turn work in. Children who do not have ADHD may experience some of the same issues to a lesser extent, and your child's teacher may think that these problems are due to lack of motivation, low self-esteem, or other psychological causes. By middle school academic performance can begin to decline if medication schedules are not adjusted to cover lengthening homework time, or if a child's treatment plan fails to meet his changing needs in other ways.

When a child falls behind in learning, a learning disability should be considered. Children with coexisting learning disabilities may experience more long-lasting and serious academic difficulties than those struggling academically on the basis of ADHD alone. Learning disabilities are diagnosed when a child has not developed specific academic skills in spite of adequate intelligence and education. The type of learning disability can be determined by schools or independent school psychologists. Schools need to determine if a child's apparent need will qualify that child for special education services under a disability category, such as a specific learning disability based on the evaluation of their staff or on stats from independent evaluations that you may get from independent psychologists. Federal legislation requires each state to develop its own criteria for determining a specific learning disability. The criteria must be based on scientifically sound research. This is where a teacher will implement some small changes, such as individual help to the student, to see if it can help with the child's problem or to help determine if the child meets the category of specific learning disabilities, which has been defined by the federal government as "a disorder in 1 or more of the basic psychological processes involved in understanding or in using language, spoken or written, which disorder may manifest itself in the imperfect ability to listen, think, speak, read, write, spell, or do mathematical calculations." They may start with what is often called response to intervention (RTI).

The characteristics of a learning disability will vary from child to child. Some children with learning disabilities may have excellent verbal and reading skills but do poorly in math, for example, while others may have the opposite profile. Problems with reading and being able to sound out words is the most common. Keep in mind, however, that ADHD is not itself a learning disorder, that it does not *necessarily* lead to academic difficulties at school, and that neither ADHD nor learning disabilities are signs of low intelligence. In fact, children with ADHD display the same range of intelligence as their classmates. Learning disabilities are recognized in reading, mathematics, and written expression and will be discussed in more detail in Chapter 9. Children with ADHD may also have a problem with using words or language. They may know the words but have difficulty in being able to use them. This disability is called a *pragmatic language disability*, meaning practical use of language. It is helpful to make sure that if your child is evaluated for a learning disability, the possibility of a language disability is also considered, which may require an evaluation by a speech and language clinician.

Social Concerns

For many children with ADHD, interactions with classmates can become difficult. Children with ADHD can be disliked, ignored, or rejected by their peers. Some children with ADHD can be physically or verbally impulsive in social relationships, which can be overwhelming for others. Others may not initiate interactions with their classmates, or they may miss the social cues necessary to establish positive relationships and, thus, become socially isolated. Inattentiveness or impulsivity may decrease a child's success in games, sports, or other group activities that would otherwise enhance popularity. Younger children with hyperactive-impulsive– or combined-type ADHD may frequently experience physical conflicts with their peers, like pushing their way into lines or being "in their face." By middle childhood, a child's hyperactive/impulsive behaviors, discipline problems, perceived "spaciness," or social awkwardness may lead to social rejection. Some adolescents with ADHD may be 1 to 2 years less mature than their classmates, further complicating their social relationships at a time when they are taking on great importance.

Later in this chapter, you will find suggested ways for you and your child's teacher to provide opportunities for your child to improve his social standing and interact more successfully with his peers. Meanwhile, social concerns should be discussed at any meeting aimed at evaluating your child's progress and needs.

Beginning to Identify the Key Areas of Concern

Helping a child with ADHD to better manage his school life is best done in the same way you began to address his functioning in other areas, by

1. Identifying the greatest obstacles to his best functioning

2. Creating a treatment plan to address these concerns

3. Establishing a system of review aimed at measuring the treatment's success and failure and adjusting the plan appropriately

Because problems differ from one child with ADHD to the next, academic, behavioral, and social functioning should all be reviewed carefully. Your greatest ally in arriving at an accurate assessment is your child's teacher. The teacher observes your child every day in the classroom and can compare his functioning to that of his peers. Working together as a team you can help meet your child's needs. This can be an important factor in your child's success and failure in any given year.

The first step in improving your child's experience at school is to arrange a meeting with your child's teacher. Come with a list of questions and concerns to discuss but also listen carefully to the teacher's description of your child's school problems. If at all possible, bring your child with you during parent-teacher conferences so that he can help clarify some of the observations the teacher might provide and also participate by generating ideas for resolving problems. His participation may add important insights about his functioning, and his buy-in to the education program is necessary for success. If you suspect that you may miss or misunderstand important information conveyed by the teacher during this meeting, take a notebook and take notes that you can review later. Bringing a friend or relative to take notes while you listen can also be helpful. Some teachers will also be comfortable if you ask to record the meeting.

The emphasis at these initial meetings should be on describing specific problem behaviors that can be measured, and not on generalities about your child's symptoms, feelings, or intent. If the teacher suggests, for example, that your child does not seem to be trying to succeed academically, ask for specific examples, as in, "Is some of his homework turned in, or none of it?" "Is schoolwork complete one day and incomplete the next, or is it always incomplete?" "Does my child ignore desk work or try but fail to finish it?" "Does my child seem to deliberately try to disrupt the class while others are working?" If the teacher is concerned that your child is having problems getting along with others, ask whether this is due to a tendency to physically overwhelm them, intrude verbally on their conversations, seem isolated or unengaged, or have trouble participating in games due to a lack of coordination, lack of focus, or inability to wait his turn. Ask how frequently each type of conflict happens. These types of specific, quantifiable observations are also necessary as a good baseline for monitoring changes over time. This can also help in identifying necessary modifications in your child's treatment plan. Do not become concerned if your observations of your child differ from his teacher's. This is common and can lead to some good discussions about why behaviors may be seen as differing between home and school.

During the first few meetings, you and his teacher may not be able to precisely define the problems or agree on solutions. What is more important at this early stage is to *establish a cooperative relationship* and to create a plan to gather and analyze observations in the future. Because more and more educators are learning about ADHD and the best ways to manage it at school, each new teacher may show more insight into what is causing your child's problem or suggest some practical responses that have not been tried before. The more clearly you demonstrate your willingness to cooperate and be a member of the "treatment team," the more positive and effective your partnership with the school may become. Problems in the home environment—marital conflict, financial difficulties, discipline problems, or other issues—can affect your child's functioning at school and should be mentioned with discretion in your meetings with his teacher so that you can, together, arrive at an accurate picture of the challenges that your child faces.

Choosing the Most Appropriate Classroom Setting

Because most children with ADHD experience difficulties meeting some of the academic, social, and behavioral expectations of schools, schools need to play a critical role in providing behavioral and academic support for them. Unless your child has especially severe disruptive behaviors accompanying his ADHD or is diagnosed with certain coexisting conditions or disabilities, his needs can probably best be met in a regular classroom with proper treatment and appropriate support in place from you and the teacher. In fact, federal law mandates that children with disabilities, including those with ADHD, must be educated alongside children without disabilities as long as the regular classroom meets their needs and allows them to make educational progress. Still, a number of factors within your child's regular classroom environment, like its physical setup, the sense of community that the students feel, the special resources provided, the educational approach used, the compatibility of your child's and his teacher's personal styles, and, most crucially, the experience and commitment of the teacher and other school personnel, can have a profound effect on your child's progress. If you are in a position to choose the school your child will attend, or at least have input into his teacher for the coming school year, it can make a great deal of difference for you both.

Your Child's Classroom

"My son's first-grade teacher has had a lot of problems with his behavior," writes one parent of a child with ADHD. "He has a hard time sitting still and focusing on desk work. The teacher has been talking with me about ways to help him get better at this skill, but I wonder if my son might be better off in a less-structured classroom where he does not have to sit still as much." Many parents of children with ADHD believe that a more free-flowing classroom environment may allow their children to learn more effectively, in their own way. In some ways, it makes intuitive sense that a child who is not fettered by the constraints of a typically organized classroom will be able to make use of his own unique learning strengths and style at his own pace. In fact, studies have shown that the opposite is usually true: Children with ADHD often make significantly better progress when the classroom is thoughtfully structured—that is, in an organized setting with clear rules and limits; immediate, appropriate enforcement; and predictable routines. Like training wheels on a young child's bicycle, they provide the balance and stability that a child with ADHD may not be able to create on his own. Smaller class size can be another important element that can help prevent sensory overload and allow the teacher to provide the individual support your child needs. The smaller the class the better, in most cases, with no more than a few students who need special educational or behavioral services. Check with your local school district to see if this option is available near you.

Smaller class size can be another important element that can help prevent sensory overload and allow the teacher to provide the individual support your child needs.

The structure in a classroom can affect your child's day-to-day academic and social success. Routine and consistency can be especially important. Few students like surprises in school; they can cause feelings of unease or of being unsafe. This can be especially true for children with ADHD. If frequent social conflicts are a problem during instruction time, it is easy to see how these may be avoided if students are seated facing the teacher instead of one another. If your child has trouble staying seated or remaining quiet when this is required, clear limits and rules can be set with immediate positive feedback for following the rules and some consequences for noncompliance. It may also be possible to make some classroom accommodations.

If your child has difficulty sticking to one task, frequent praise and encouragement when he is persistent may help extend his focus. Of course, just as with the parent training in behavior management (PTBM) techniques you read about in Chapter 6, a structured environment works well only when it is designed to guide and support a child in positive ways rather than focusing on punishment and over-restriction. Positive praise is extremely useful for establishing positive behaviors, especially for children with ADHD. Praise for a specific behavior might sound like

- "Josh, you are doing a great job keeping your head up today."

- "Josh, thank you for raising your hand. Please share your ideas with the class."

- "I am really proud that you have completed your whole Do Now Today list, so I am going to send a note home to tell your mom and dad about it!"

In this manner, your child's teacher will redirect, redirect, and redirect until the behavior is positive and can be praised. These thoughtfully structured routines of the ideal classroom environment may be balanced with a certain amount of variety, flexibility, and humor.

Your Child's Teacher

The most important member of your child's educational team is, of course, the teacher—particularly if your child will spend most of or all his time in a single classroom. The most effective teachers for children with ADHD are those who are generally informed and updated about it and the best ways to manage its related behavioral symptoms. If no such teacher is available, focus on requesting one with whom you feel comfortable and believe will be receptive to learning about ADHD from you, your child's pediatrician, and others. Training in and comfort using behavior management techniques should be a primary consideration. A natural, structured, and consistent teaching style is also a plus. Finally, teachers who speak expressively and who use a variety of different approaches (eg, lectures, class discussion, audiovisual aids, computers) tend to engage the attention of a child with ADHD most successfully. A teacher who is structured and disciplined but also dynamic, fun, and engaging is the best choice for any student, including students with ADHD. If you have a chance to request a teacher for your child, it can help to ask older students and their parents for advice based on their experience. It can also help to make appointments to speak to prospective teachers about your child and your concerns and to get a feel for the teachers' general teaching style and their working knowledge about students with ADHD. It is essential that you and the teacher feel comfortable exchanging ideas and planning strategies. You will spend a substantial amount of time together over the course of the school year. If possible, choose a teacher who is not only capable and knowledgeable but with whom you feel you can connect. As you think about the ideal school environment outlined in this section, it may occur to you that, in many ways, your thoughts are similar to what every parent wants for his or her child.

- Smaller class size

- Regular routines

- A teacher who is engaging, interesting, fun, and exciting; who provides a great deal of structure but can also be flexible; and who is able and willing to use multiple approaches to teaching

It may help to remind yourself as you visit schools and talk with teachers that you are looking for what would be best for any student—but that this environment will be especially important for your child with ADHD.

Special Education Services: Federal Laws

For most children with ADHD, staying in a regular classroom with a trained teacher, who is adept at behavior management, is the preferred situation. This is especially true if any necessary accommodations for your child can be put into place in that setting. Children with ADHD whose academic or behavior struggles cannot be managed effectively in a regular classroom using typical strategies may require special education services. These services may be delivered in a variety of settings, including the regular classroom and separate classrooms for part or all of a school day. The setting is determined by the needs of the eligible child. The federal Individuals With Disabilities Education Act (IDEA) guarantees your child's right to be evaluated for and receive such services if eligible, free of charge. The services should be provided in what they describe as the "least restricted environment," meaning in the regular classroom, if at all possible, or mostly in the regular classroom with a period of individual or group instruction for part of the day.

Individuals With Disabilities Education Act

IDEA was designed to guarantee the provision of special services for children whose disabilities severely affect their educational performance. A child can receive services under IDEA if he has a learning disability or an emotional disturbance or is "other health impaired." Your child may qualify for IDEA coverage if he has been diagnosed with ADHD and his condition has been shown to severely and adversely affect school performance. Note that both conditions must be met: an ADHD diagnosis alone does not guarantee coverage for your child unless it or another disorder interfers with how he performs in school. In most cases, it is a child's coexisting learning disabilities, disruptive behavior disorder, anxiety or mood disorder, or other functional problem, and not the ADHD itself, that qualifies him for IDEA coverage.

IDEA is based on providing services for categories of disability. It includes 13 categories that require coverage "without undue delay." These are

1. Specific learning disability (SLD)

The umbrella term SLD covers a specific group of learning issues. The conditions in this group affect a child's ability to read, write, listen, speak, reason, or do math. Some of the issues that could fall in this group include

- Dyslexia
- Dysgraphia
- Dyscalculia
- Auditory processing disorder
- Nonverbal learning disability

2. Other health impairment

The umbrella term *other health impairment* covers conditions that limit a child's strength, energy, or alertness. One example is an attention issue like ADHD.

3. Autism spectrum disorder (ASD)

Autism spectrum disorder is a developmental disability. It covers a wide range of symptoms and skills but mainly affects a child's social and communication skills. It can also affect behavior.

4. Emotional disturbance

Children covered under the term *emotional disturbance* can have a number of mental disorders. They may include anxiety disorder, schizophrenia, bipolar disorder, obsessive-compulsive disorder, and depression. (Some of these issues may also be covered under *other health impairment*.)

5. Speech or language impairment

The umbrella term *speech or language impairment* covers a number of communication problems. These include stuttering, impaired articulation, language impairment, and voice impairment.

6. Visual impairment, including blindness

A child who has vision problems is considered to have a *visual impairment*. This condition includes partial sight and blindness. If eyewear can correct a vision problem, the child does not qualify.

7. Deafness

Children with a diagnosis of *deafness* have a severe hearing impairment. They aren't able to process language through hearing.

8. Hearing impairment

The term *hearing impairment* refers to a hearing loss not covered by the definition of *deafness*. This type of loss can change or fluctuate over time. Remember that being hard of hearing is not the same thing as having auditory processing disorder.

9. Deaf-blindness

Children with a diagnosis of *deaf-blindness* have hearing and visual impairments. Their communication and other needs are so great that programs for the deaf or blind can't meet them.

10. Orthopedic impairment

Any impairment to a child's body, no matter what the cause, is considered an *orthopedic impairment*.

11. Intellectual disability

Children with this type of disability have below-average intellectual ability. They may also have poor communication, self-care, and social skills. Down syndrome is one example of an intellectual disability.

12. Traumatic brain injury

This is a brain injury is caused by an accident or some kind of physical force.

13. Multiple disabilities

A child with multiple disabilities has more than one condition covered by IDEA. Having multiple issues creates educational needs that can't be met in a program for any one condition.

Under this law, schools are responsible for identifying and evaluating children who are suspected of having disabilities and who may need special education services. Depending on his diagnoses and assessment, your child's disability may be categorized as *specific learning disability*, *serious emotional disturbance*, or *other health impairment*. After these needs are evaluated and documented and your child's eligibility is determined, an IEP can be created to detail the special education services that are necessary.

Specific Learning Disabilities

The IDEA criteria for specific learning disabilities can vary from state to state. Children qualify for learning disabilities under this law if they have significant needs in the areas of

- Oral expression
- Listening comprehension
- Written expression
- Basic reading skills
- Reading comprehension
- Mathematics calculation
- Mathematics reasoning

Testing for learning disabilities generally includes assessment by the school psychologist.

In addition to learning disabilities, children with ADHD and significant emotional problems can also receive services through IDEA. To receive these services, a child's *educational performance* needs to be adversely affected by emotional and behavioral concerns.

- An inability to learn that can be best explained on a behavioral basis
- An inability to build or maintain relationships with peers and teachers
- Inappropriate types of behavior or feelings
- A persistent mood of unhappiness or depression
- A tendency to develop physical symptoms or fears associated with personal or school problems

Other Health Impaired

Children with severe ADHD usually qualify under this category. To qualify for services under *other health impaired*, a child with ADHD needs to be documented as showing "limited strength, vitality, or alertness" that results in limited alertness in the educational environment, which adversely affects the child's educational performance. Attention-deficit/hyperactivity disorder is listed as one of the "chronic or acute health problems" that may lead to other health impairment eligibility.

Individualized Education Program (IEP)

You, as a parent, can initiate a referral process if your child is doing poorly in academic, behavioral, or social functioning. The request has to come from you. A letter alone from your child's pediatrician will not start the process. The best way to make a referral is to write a letter to the principal outlining your concerns and requesting an evaluation. Send copies to your child's pediatrician as well as the school system's director of special education. The school will set up a meeting that must include you, the parents, to discuss the referral. Parents must always be included and involved in the identification and evaluation planning for their children. You are entitled to bring along a friend or consultant for support. There may be a support organization in your community that can provide advice and may be able to provide a knowledgeable person to go with you to the meeting. This group may plan the comprehensive evaluation at this meeting. Or this group may decide to try some accommodations or modifications in the regular education classroom before recommending a more comprehensive evaluation. Sometimes called *pre-referral interventions*, this may include the RTI methods mentioned earlier.

The law states that a group of professionals from different disciplines must take part in the evaluation and that it needs to be comprehensive and objective. Typical evaluations include

- Assessing your child using reliable, valid, individually administered tests that take into account any disability the child has and what the child's primary language is
- Reviewing teachers' and parents' written observations
- Comparing your child's progress to that of others his age
- Interviewing you, the child, his teacher, and others who know or have worked with him

As a parent, you need to give informed consent before any evaluation is done. Keep in mind that the team is not required to accept a diagnosis that is made by an outside pediatrician or psychologist, and they may find a child ineligible for services. The decision must be justified by an evaluation, and not just someone's opinion. You have the right to dispute the decision. Particularly by middle school and high school, it is helpful to have your child attend these meetings and provide input into the plan.

An IEP That Meets Your Child's Unique Needs

After the evaluation has been completed, you must receive a written copy of the results, and you should meet with the evaluation team to discuss the results in detail. If the team determines that your child is eligible for special services under IDEA, the team will develop an IEP. The IEP needs to meet your child's unique educational needs in the academic, behavioral, or social areas and will go into effect once you sign it and agree to the program. The material and conference need to be provided in the parent's primary language if you do not speak English, and you are entitled to bring along a friend, relative, or consultant. The IEP will

- Address your child's present academic achievement and functional performance and how his disability affects his involvement and progress in the general curriculum.
- State all the supports to be provided, including special education, related services (eg, counseling, occupational therapy), and any modifications.
- Set yearly measurable goals.
- Describe how and how often your child's progress on the goals will be measured.
- Explain any exceptions to a child participating with children in his regular class and in other school activities.
- Describe any necessary test-taking accommodations.
- Describe in detail when, where, and how often services will be provided.

Your child is entitled to an IEP that meets his unique educational needs. His IEP may call for adjustments within the regular classroom, such as a structured learning environment, individualized test-taking conditions, the use of a recording device or computer, modified textbooks, individualized homework assignments, modifications during nonacademic times such as lunchtime or recess, or other accommodations. It may call for the use of a classroom aide or note-taker, a trained tutor, or psychological or speech and language services. If your child's educational needs cannot be met through a regular classroom with these special supports, a self-contained special education classroom for part or all of a day may be proposed. After an IEP is written, the special education team, which includes the parents, will meet at least once a year to see if the IEP needs to be modified. The team can meet more often if the program requires changes based on how well or poorly certain approaches work for your child. If the school no longer thinks that he needs these services, the team needs to reevaluate your child to see if he still requires special education services. If his IEP is still in place during his high school years, the team will also create a transition program to help with college, career, and/or daily living skills planning.

If you and the school district disagree at any point in the process about the request for an evaluation, the evaluation itself, or the resulting determination of the services needed, a variety of methods for dispute resolution are available in each state. As a parent, you can always contact your state's department of education for more details on this. Schools are also required to provide information about the process, including what is called *due process* and *parent rights*.

Section 504 Services

If your child does not qualify for services under IDEA, he may still qualify for services under Section 504 of the Rehabilitation Act, which prohibits discrimination against any person with a disability. Section 504, a civil rights law, applies to all public and private schools that receive federal financial assistance and is aimed at preventing discrimination against students with disabilities.

An important aspect of Section 504 is its emphasis on accommodating students with disabilities in *the regular classroom* whenever possible. This is done to help ensure that students with disabilities receive the same education as those without disabilities, while benefiting from whatever in-class accommodations are deemed necessary. Under Section 504 students may receive accommodations such as

- Reduced class size
- Preferential seating
- Modifications in homework and classroom assignments
- Extended time for testing
- Written instructions to supplement teachers' verbal instructions
- Behavior management strategies
- Help with organizing
- Note-takers

Children With Disabilities

Criteria for Section 504 Eligibility

Students with disabilities are defined in Section 504 as those who have a physical or mental impairment that substantially limits one or more "major life activities."

Because learning is considered a major life activity, children who have been diagnosed with attention-deficit/hyperactivity disorder and who have significant difficulty learning in school are considered disabled under this law.

An evaluation is required to determine eligibility under Section 504. An eligible child may receive accommodations or modifications that are not available to nondisabled children. Children eligible for services under the Individuals With Disabilities Education Act (IDEA) are also covered under Section 504, but the reverse is not true. Children covered by IDEA have a right to receive "educational benefit," while those covered under Section 504 are only protected from discrimination based on their disability. They have a right to access the same education as all children.

IDEA or Section 504: Which Is Most Appropriate for Your Child?

The laws and regulations relating to attention-deficit/hyperactivity disorder (ADHD) can be confusing, and parents often aren't sure which is more beneficial for their child: to receive an Individualized Education Program (IEP) under the Individuals With Disabilities Education Act (IDEA) or a Section 504 accommodation plan. It is the school district's evaluation that determines if a student is eligible under IDEA or Section 504 for any such services or supports.

To qualify under IDEA, it must be determined that the disability is causing an adverse effect on the child's educational performance to the extent that special education is needed. If your child with ADHD has significant school difficulties, the provisions under IDEA have the following advantages:

- They provide for an IEP tailored to meet the unique needs of the student.
- A wide range of program options, services, and supports is available.
- They set out specific, measurable goals that are regularly monitored for progress.
- They provide funding for programs and services (Section 504 does not).

■ They provide more protections with regard to the evaluation, how often reviews are done, parent participation, disciplinary actions, and other factors.

Section 504 plans serve many students well. For those students who qualify for a Section 504 plan, it is a faster and easier procedure for obtaining accommodations and supports (which may include some services). It may be more appropriate for

■ Students with milder impairments who do not need special education

■ Students whose educational needs can be addressed through adjustments, modifications, and accommodations in the general curriculum and classroom

The pediatrician's diagnosis of ADHD, in most cases, is adequate in making a student eligible for the plan.

Modified from Rief SF. *The ADD/ADHD Checklist: A Practical Reference for Parents and Teachers.* 2nd ed. San Francisco, CA: Jossey-Bass; 2008. This material is used by permission of Jossey-Bass, a Wiley Imprint.

In most cases, you will find that as a parent you are the driving force behind the evaluation process, and you may need to actively advocate for your child if he is to receive the services he needs. Parent support associations have made a great deal of progress in persuading states to follow federal guidelines, but cost considerations and lack of understanding of ADHD can limit a district's response. To learn about the federal, state, and local district guidelines for the services available to your child, contact your school district and your local chapter of CHADD: The National Resource on ADHD at www.chadd.org.

What Can Schools Do?

General Classroom Supports

Earlier in this chapter you learned that certain aspects of your child's school environment, such as a structured routine and a traditional seating arrangement with clear rules, can affect his ability to function. Other environment-related strategies shown to help children with ADHD include seating the child near the teacher and away

A simple routine, such as silently counting to 5 while taking a drink from the water fountain, may keep your child from getting distracted and playing.

from distractions, such as the windows, hallway, or pencil sharpener, and surrounding him with students who focus well on their own work. The teacher may even decide to create a "buddy system" for your child, or for the class as a whole, in which children remind one another of academic, behavioral, or social goals and where the class as a whole earns points or tokens that can be traded in for privileges, like a class party. The less distracting your child's teacher can make your child's environment, the more likely it is that he will focus better on the task at hand. This way of preventing negative behavior from occurring in the first place is far preferable to trying to "fix" it later.

Helpful Teacher Supports for Students With ADHD

Keeping Things Simple and Doable

- Break down complicated instructions into doable steps.
- Adjust the length of assignments to fit a student's attention span.
- Keep the more academic subjects in the morning, when children are fresher and more alert.

Keeping Things Interesting

- Teach with enthusiasm and invite class participation.
- Vary lectures with hands-on experiences and physical activities.
- Supplement lectures with drills and computer games that teach the same materials to keep things novel, engaging, and motivating.

Keeping Things Organized

- Clearly state, repeat, and post the classroom rules. It is important for teachers to reinforce following classroom rules by regularly praising students who are complying.
- Preview the school day with a morning class meeting.
- Write things down for students who may miss verbal instructions or may have trouble copying from the board or finding them on the computer.
- Encourage the use of simple daily planners that do not overwhelm students.

Your teacher will benefit from keeping the following mantra in mind as she works with your child in the classroom: *Keep things simple and doable, keep them interesting, and keep them well structured and organized. Emphasize the positive things that students are doing.*

As you have seen, most methods your child's teacher can implement are likely to benefit all her students, not just your child. Nearly all children, by nature, are distractible and have problems with organization and staying focused at one time or another, and your child's peers will profit from the teacher's efforts to overcome this.

Schools and Behavior

Teachers, who must constantly deal with behavior problems in their classrooms, are generally encouraged to try prevention first, rewards for positive behavior second, and discipline measures only as a final resort when managing problem behaviors in any student. When teachers take this approach there is usually a dramatic improvement in how well the classroom functions and a noticeable reduction in how much classroom time is taken up with disciplinary measures. For children with ADHD and behavior concerns, IDEA actually mandates that the IEP team includes positive behavior approaches in the child's educational program.

Functional Behavior Assessments and Individual Behavior Plans

If the positive behavioral approaches described previously have proven unsuccessful, your child's teacher will often seek the input and support of the special educators at your child's school. A special education counselor may be asked to observe your child in multiple school settings and take low inference notes. These notes are simply observations that might catalogue

- Is the student more on task in one class than others? Why?
- What time of the day is it?
- Where is the student sitting?
- What are the established routines in that class that set the student up for success?

With such data a *functional behavior assessment* can be completed and a plan developed. Functional assessments include a description of the behavior problems, direct observations of your child in different settings, and positive strategies to gradually decrease the specified behavior and increase other behaviors that are appropriate. Functional assessments are generally done by the school behavior specialist, who analyzes the triggers for specific problem behaviors, the behaviors that arise, and the consequences that are in place when those behaviors occur. The information is then used to try to understand the function of the behavior. For example, if a student gets out of his seat frequently and this disrupts the class, a functional analysis can help to pinpoint the reason: Is it to avoid finishing an assignment or otherwise escape a situation? To get attention? To get something he needs? To create some self-stimulation in a quiet classroom? Each of these reasons may have different solutions, and a one-size-fits-all approach is inappropriate. The value of a functional analysis is that it can lead to a specific plan for your child's individual needs. Once this analysis is done, this type of positive individualized plan can be created. A typical plan may include instituting preventive measures, teaching the child new behavior strategies, and using behavior therapy techniques to help him improve his functioning.

Preventive measures include changes that the teacher can make in the classroom environment to help students with ADHD avoid targeted behaviors. These include changing the seating arrangement in the classroom, altering classroom routines, posting the 5 most important classroom behavior rules on the board, or allowing frequent breaks during long assignments.

When Discipline Is an Issue

Many parents of children with attention-deficit/hyperactivity disorder (ADHD) feel that disciplinary actions tend to target their children due to a lack of understanding of ADHD-type behavior and reluctance to make appropriate accommodations and allowances. Children with serious behavior problems, such as extreme impulsiveness or a conduct disorder, may find themselves suspended from school again and again while their behavior goes untreated.

Children covered under the Individuals With Disabilities Education Act (IDEA) are protected to a large degree from such nonproductive disciplinary actions. Under the IDEA provisions, any child who has been identified as having a disability, who has demonstrated a need for services, or whose parents or teacher have expressed concern in writing or requested an evaluation, may not be suspended or expelled for more than 10 consecutive days for behavior that is related to his disability. To determine whether the disability is a factor, the student's evaluation team, which includes his parents, must determine whether the conduct in question was caused by or had a direct relation to the child's disability or if the conduct was a direct result of the school's failure to implement the Individualized Education Program (IEP). If the student's disability is determined to have been a factor or the IEP was not appropriately implemented, the child cannot be held to the same standards and arbitrarily suspended or reassigned to another program. Instead, the child must be returned to his placement and a functional behavior assessment conducted or the current behavior plan modified to prevent similar behavior problems in the future.

Children covered under Section 504 are not as well protected. Section 504 does not require the school to keep the child in school or in ongoing programs while a reassessment takes place.

Students with ADHD can also be taught new strategies to replace their problem behaviors. For example, if your child disrupts the class during long assignments, a teacher might arrange a "secret signal" that he can use to let her know that he needs a break. When the teacher sees the signal she can respond by asking him to do a task that involves getting up and walking around.

The plan can also include teachers using PTBM principles. Techniques that have been found to be most successful in the classroom include

- Clearly conveying and consistently enforcing class rules
- Giving clear, doable commands
- Establishing daily goals for the child and for the class as a whole
- Praising students for positive behaviors and ignoring negative behaviors that are not intolerable
- Using rewards to encourage appropriate behavior, including using token economies (point, sticker, and poker chip reward systems) and response-cost systems (losing tokens for inappropriate behaviors)
- Using appropriate nonphysical punishments, such as time-out, to cut back on unacceptable behaviors
- Using behavior report cards to motivate children and enhance parent-teacher communication

The use of these techniques can not only help your child but all the children in the classroom as well. Regular communication between parents and teachers is essential to make some of these measures as effective as possible. A good working relationship with your child's teacher and the development of mutual respect will set a good tone for a team approach. For example, tokens earned in the classroom can be converted into rewards at home if there is good communication between parents and teachers.

Ideally, your child's teacher has received training in classroom behavior therapy techniques. In some, but not all, areas of the country, more teachers are trained in behavior therapy now than ever before. If your child's teacher has not received training, you may be able to advocate for teacher training funds, especially if you have requested services for your child under IDEA or Section 504 legislation. However, limited funding and support for such training means that your child's teacher may have to seek some of this information on his/her own. If you have participated in PTBM, you and your behavioral therapist may be valuable resources. You may want to share any teaching materials and workbooks you used. There are also self-monitoring and self-evaluation strategies that children and adolescents can use. The CHADD website (www.chadd.org) and books that specifically address classroom intervention and school behavior therapy training programs are other good sources of information for teachers. Local ADHD support groups and other community resources may be helpful as well.

ADHD and Academics

Even if your child does not have a learning disability, the academic side of school can be difficult for students with ADHD. Some common concerns and practical suggestions are listed in Table 7.1.

The Social Side of School

Social difficulties are an aspect of school life that can become especially painful for a child with ADHD. Your child may have difficulty forming friendships due to a tendency to act before thinking, disruptiveness, failure to make plans, or acting inappropriately in spite of knowing what he is supposed to do. Children with inattentive-type ADHD can be socially isolated or withdrawn. If you are concerned about your child's social experiences at school, talk with his teacher about ways to bolster his social confidence, increase his status, and help him improve his skills. If improvement in specific social skills is already part of your child's IEP or other education program, you and the teacher may brainstorm about behavior therapy techniques to reinforce and build on his skills in this area. Sound behavior management and medication approaches can go a long way toward improving the social functioning of children with ADHD. You might also suggest to the teacher such actions as casually but publicly praising your child for his talents or choosing him for classroom duties in front of other children. This allows other children to see him in a positive light and can enhance his self-esteem and sense of acceptance. You can also ask his teacher to intervene in tactful ways when your child begins to fall into social difficulty. His teacher may be able to find ways to set social skills goals, monitor his progress, and set up a system of rewards and privileges to recognize him for meeting these goals. The entire class can benefit from group discussions about how we all manage our feelings, the value of diversity, and the importance of respect. It is surprising how effective a well-timed word or action can be.

Table 7.1. Attention-Deficit/Hyperactivity Disorder and Academics	
Area of Academic Difficulty	**Suggestions**
Written Expression *Difficulty with* ■ Fine motor skills ■ Attending to all aspects of written language at the same time ■ Following multiple or sequential steps (as in spelling) ■ Writing (considers it boring)	■ Stimulant medications can sometimes markedly help fine motor paper and pencil skills. ■ Students with ADHD can start instruction in word processing by third grade and be permitted to complete assignments by computer. ■ Consultation with an occupational therapist can help set up exercises to improve handwriting.
Note-taking *Difficulty with* Listening and taking notes at the same time	■ Teachers can provide students with lecture outlines or notes. ■ Students can listen to lectures and borrow a classmate's notes to study. ■ Students can record lectures, but this can become tedious and time-consuming.
Rote Memorization Tasks Requires sustained attention to tasks that are frequently boring	Computer software can be a helpful and motivating way to memorize material like math facts.
Variations in Performance Can occur from day to day or one grading period to the next	Token economies and reward systems can help with motivation.

(continued)

Table 7.1 (*continued*)	
Area of Academic Difficulty	**Suggestions**
Incomplete Assignments *Can occur from* ■ Problems in following multiple directions ■ Becoming bored with an assignment	■ The use of study cubicles has not been found to be helpful in increasing attention or concentration. ■ Computer-assisted instruction may be more stimulating and interesting; thus, children may be more likely to complete an assignment that is computer based, particularly in the context of educational game software (eg, Math Blaster). ■ Classroom seating next to a positive peer model can lead to fewer off-task behaviors and greater work productivity. ■ Peer tutoring can also be effective in helping students to practice academic skills. ■ In-school solutions should be found for incomplete classroom work, and teachers should avoid sending it home.
Organizational and Study Skills ■ Lost books ■ Assignments not turned in even if they have been completed ■ Messy and illegible papers	■ Step-by-step tutoring on how to complete daily assignments and long-term projects ■ Extra set of books at home ■ Setting of homework time limits ■ Modifications in homework assignments
Reading Comprehension Tuning out or getting distracted while reading	■ Brief exercise breaks. ■ Parent reads part of the material while the child listens. ■ Parent and child discuss the material before, during, and after the material is read. ■ Older students preview the questions at the end of the chapter before reading the chapter so that they can focus on the most important points.

Abbreviation: ADHD, attention-deficit/hyperactivity disorder.

Modified from Hannah JN. The role of schools in attention-deficit/hyperactivity disorder. *Pediatr Ann.* 2002;31(8):507–513. Originally printed in Hannah JN. *Parenting a Child With Attention Deficit Hyperactivity Disorder.* Austin, TX: Pro-ed; 1999. Used with permission.

If your school offers social-skills training groups, consider enrolling your child. Although effective social-skills treatments have been difficult to develop, programs in school with the classmates that your child interacts with every day are more likely to be successful than those run in clinics or other settings outside of school. Some of the most effective programs involve parents and teachers, help children to be aware of and understand verbal and nonverbal social cues, and use the same types of well-thought-out reward and response-cost systems that you read about in Chapter 6. They teach skills like good sportsmanship, problem-solving, accepting consequences, being assertive without being aggressive, ignoring classmates when they are provocative, and recognizing and dealing with feelings. In the better programs children are coached and receive feedback. Techniques are taught by role-playing real-life situations and modeling by coaches and teachers, and children receive reinforcement in real-world settings that they have learned as part of training. These types of programs can be incorporated into IEPs and behavior plans. With the increase in the use of social media everywhere, it is important to teach children about social media etiquette and how to deal with bullying on social media too.

Closing the Gap Between Home and School

Daily Communication and Reports

Constant feedback for your child and frequent communication between you and your child's teacher are necessary components in keeping your child on track. Working together, you can make an enormous difference in how quickly positive results are seen. Both of these aims can be accomplished through daily communication between teachers and parents. With today's classroom technologies and messaging and communication options, this process can often be easily established. Some families will wish to simply use an occasional text message or email with a teacher. If this is chosen, families may want to consider using secure text and email platforms. New information-sharing software may also be available in some school systems to allow easy school-to-home and home-to-school communications.

For schools fortunate to have electronic tablets for each student, assignments are easily listed. Some students will email themselves their homework and use a system like Google Docs. Now every child, and not just those with ADHD, will have the convenience and support of always having their assignments with them. No longer will we hear, "The dog ate my homework!" In the past, report cards filled out by teachers and/or a journal for teachers' and parents' comments were common paper solutions for communication. The child with ADHD kept this in his school backpack. Unfortunately, papers and journals were still lost, and children were often embarrassed by the journals. It is also difficult for a teacher to keep up with daily notes during class time when there are so many demands in the teacher's busy day.

Such daily communication can be especially effective because it identifies daily goals for your child, lets him see almost immediately how effectively he has met them, and motivates him to try harder to meet his goals as he receives agreed-on rewards for good reports. You and your child's teacher may find that it is best for you to provide some of these rewards at home because providing them in class takes up valuable class time, and some of the most effective rewards (eg, telephone or television time) or negative consequences (eg, restriction of privileges) may not be possible at school. Your willingness to respond appropriately at home can ease the teacher's workload and increase the teacher's willingness to work more closely with your child. Home-based reinforcements also highlight for your child the link between behavior at school and at home.

Ideally, this system of continuous communication will foster a positive working relationship between you and your child's teacher that will also help your child achieve his goals. You may find, however, that you disagree with the teacher's approach. If you have tried and failed to work productively as a team with the teacher, consider asking your partner, the school principal or counselor, or even your child's pediatrician or mental health provider to mediate. Some local parent advocacy groups provide staff members to accompany parents to school and help advocate for services. Your child's pediatrician or other pediatric clinician may be able to help you locate this type of support. However, you will need to weigh the potential benefits of these types of actions against the possibility that the teacher may begin to see you as an adversary rather than a teammate—a position that may diminish your ability to advocate for your child. To help avoid such conflicts before they happen, be sure to express support for the teacher. If you are pleased with some aspects of the teacher's work, make sure to tell the teacher and the principal. Your positive attention to the teacher will usually translate into positive attention to your child.

Homework

"I can't wait for summer to come!" writes the mother of a seventh grader. "Suddenly the gloom lifts, the arguing stops, we relax, and we remember how much fun our family can have together." Dealing with issues around homework can be one of the most stressful and time-consuming elements of parenting in the family of a child with ADHD. Successfully dealing with homework production involves developing skills in time management, organization, and study habits; using behavior management techniques; and understanding your child's limits and frustration tolerance. Some hints are included in the Homework Tips for Parents box.

Homework Tips for Parents

- Establish a homework routine (a specific time and place) and adhere to this agreed-on schedule as closely as possible. Try not to have your child wait until the evening to get started. If he is on stimulant medication, it is preferable to schedule it for when he still has the effects of the medication.
- Limit distractions in the home during homework hours (eg, reduce background noise; turn off the television and phones).
- Assist your child in dividing assignments into smaller parts or segments that are more manageable and less overwhelming.
- Assist your child in getting started on assignments (eg, read the directions together; do the first items together; observe as your child does the next problem on her own). Then get up and leave.
- Monitor and give feedback without doing all the work together. You want your child to attempt as much as possible independently.
- Praise and compliment your child in a supportive, noncritical manner when she puts forth good effort and completes tasks.
- It is appropriate to gently point out some errors and make some corrections on your child's homework.
- It is not your responsibility to correct all your child's errors on homework or make her complete and turn in a perfect paper.

- Remind your child to do homework and offer incentives: "When you finish your homework, you can...."

- A contract for a larger incentive may be worked out as part of a plan to motivate your child to follow through with homework: "If you have no missing or late homework assignments this next week, you will earn...."

- Let the teacher know your child's frustration and tolerance levels while doing homework in the evening. The teacher needs to be aware of the amount of time it takes your child to complete tasks and what efforts you are making to help at home.

- Help your child study for tests. Quiz your child in a variety of formats.

- If your child struggles with reading, help by reading the material together.

- Work a certain amount of time and then stop working on homework. Do not force your child to spend an excessive and inappropriate amount of time on homework. If you feel your child worked enough for one night, write a note to the teacher and attach it to the homework.

- It is very common for students with attention-deficit/hyperactivity disorder to fail to turn in their finished work. It is very frustrating to know your child struggled to do the work but then never gets credit for the work because it wasn't turned in. Watch as your child puts her homework in a folder and then into her backpack for school. You may want to arrange with the teacher a system for collecting the work immediately on arrival at school. Emailing homework to the teacher can also be beneficial.

- Many parents find it very difficult to help their own child with schoolwork. Consider hiring a tutor! Often a junior or senior high school student is ideal, depending on the needs and age of your child.

- Make sure your child has the phone number of a study buddy—at least one responsible classmate to call for clarification of homework assignments.

- Parents, the biggest struggle is keeping on top of those dreaded long-range homework assignments (eg, reports, projects). This is something you will need to be vigilant about. Ask for a copy of the project requirements. Post the list at home and go over it together with your child. Write the due date on a master calendar. Then plan how to break down the project into manageable parts, scheduling steps along the way. Get started *at once* with going to the library, gathering resources, beginning the reading, and so forth.

Modified from Rief S. *The ADD/ADHD Checklist: A Practical Reference for Parents and Teachers.* 2nd ed. San Francisco, CA: Jossey-Bass; 2008. This material used by permission of Jossey-Bass, a Wiley Imprint.

Summer Schools and Camps

Many families have found it useful to supplement home- and school-based behavioral training techniques with a specially designed summer school or camp program for children with attention-deficit/hyperactivity disorder and their parents. The best of these programs focus on improving learning and academic achievement: developing children's abilities to follow through with instructions, complete tasks that they commonly fail to finish, and comply with adults' requests. They also help children develop problem-solving skills, social skills, and the social awareness needed to get along better with other children. Parents, meanwhile, are taught how to develop, reinforce, and maintain these positive changes. Summer programs also provide an excellent environment in which to carefully monitor and adjust doses of stimulant medication. However, these programs are typically expensive and the generalization and maintenance of benefits into the regular school setting may be limited.

Medication Management

In addition to implementing behavioral training techniques that can help your child function successfully at school, your child's teacher is an essential resource in successfully managing medication issues. Your child's teacher can help provide information that can help your child's treatment team decide whether to initiate medication, adjust the dosage, and so on. Your child's pediatrician should be in close contact with your child's teacher, calling the teacher before each follow-up visit or reviewing the teacher's current written narrative or rating scales that reflect your child's academic, behavioral, and social functioning at school. Teachers need to be aware of what medications can and cannot be expected to do, as well as the possible adverse effects of any given medication. Your child's pediatrician may be able to provide the teacher with handouts explaining approaches to medication management as well as positive effects and side effects. As a parent, you can play a key case management role by encouraging this communication between your child's teacher and pediatrician to ensure they each get the information they need.

In most states, medications must be administered to students by a licensed medical provider, most often the school nurse or designated school personnel, particularly because stimulant medications are legally considered controlled substances (see Chapter 4). Because many of the stimulant medications have "street value," it is usually not appropriate (or legal) for your child or adolescent to take them to school or to self-administer them, even if a particular school may be lenient in its policies. If medications are to be taken during the school day, make sure that you have filled out the appropriate consent forms for medication administration and that school personnel are informed immediately about any changes in dose or in the timing of doses. Keep in mind that several longer-acting medications are available that eliminate the need to take medications during the school day (see Chapter 4), allowing your child to avoid the embarrassment and compliance issues associated with the administration of medication at school.

A Personal Coach/Trainer

If parents and teachers can be said to share one goal regarding children with ADHD, it is to help them learn to manage their own behavior and academic life so that they can enjoy an independent, happy adulthood. At first, most children with ADHD require a great deal of external monitoring because they are unable to provide it themselves. Gradually, with support and encouragement, they will begin to internalize this role. The concept of *coaching* has been developed over the past several years. The technique involves identifying a single person to serve as the child's daily monitor—briefly chatting with him each day, asking him what his most important tasks are for that day and how he plans to accomplish them, and praising him for working toward his goals. While parents have such conversations with their children as a matter of routine, a nonparent like a school employee, neighbor, friend's parent, responsible classmate, or even a hired college student can sometimes have a greater effect simply because of that person's outsider status. The daily conversation between your child and his coach is brief and can take place by telephone. It might take place in the morning before the school day begins, in the evening before the child starts his homework, or at any other time that your child feels is best. This practical assistance can be effective for your child because of the emotional support as well as the consistency and reliability of this person's presence in the child's life. While this brief, daily form of coaching does not replace the role of a parent, psychologist, pediatrician, or medication, it may make a substantive difference in a child's functioning at school. It can also take some of the tension out of day-to-day parent-child interactions when a more neutral party is helping to facilitate charged issues like homework flow. When meeting with your child's teacher, consider asking the teacher to recommend someone who would work well with your child.

Support at Home

There is no denying that children with ADHD can make teaching, learning, and even playing more difficult at times. There is also no question that children with ADHD often have a special type of intensity, energy, and enthusiasm that can enhance everyone's daily experience. As you support your child through his academic career, make a point of focusing on these positive qualities and asking others to do so as well. Your child has much to contribute to his classroom and school. Do what you can to help improve his chance for success in this challenging but potentially rewarding environment.

By the time they enter college, many students with ADHD have grown accustomed to seeking outside support, when necessary, such as special tutoring, coaching, and altered testing conditions, and tailoring their medication schedule to the demands of each semester's academic schedule. As these students demonstrate, the presence of

ADHD does not spell the end of academic success but will likely require careful planning in a well-informed and positive way.

Q & A

Q: *My 6-year-old was recently diagnosed with hyperactive-impulsive–type ADHD. He had a great deal of difficulty with behavioral issues in kindergarten, and now his first-grade teacher has suggested that he might benefit from being held back a year before starting second grade. My son doesn't seem to be experiencing any academic problems so far. Is it a good idea to hold him back to allow him to learn to deal with behavioral issues?*

A: Parents of young children with ADHD—particularly kindergartners and first graders—are frequently advised to allow their child to be held back a year to "catch up" on social skills or "grow out of" unsatisfactory behaviors. However, research does not support the notion that most children with ADHD will advance significantly in these areas as a result of being held back. In fact, repeating a grade can sometimes worsen behavior as boredom increases, prevent a child from receiving necessary special services because his performance resembles that of his younger classmates, and lead to self-esteem issues. For these reasons, most experts recommend advancing the child to the next grade while providing him with the support services he needs, including medications. These services might include behavior modification techniques, tutoring services, social-skills training within the school setting, or placement in a smaller classroom. Kindergartners may also benefit from moving into a kindergarten–first-grade transitional program combining kindergarten and first grade.

Q: *If it is determined that my child is eligible for Section 504 coverage, will she be automatically eligible for IDEA services as well?*

A: No. The 2 programs differ in their eligibility requirements and in their assessment and implementation processes. Your best plan would be to determine as best you can ahead of time which program is best suited to your child and request an evaluation under that program first. In general, a child with ADHD who requires special education services and who has a coexisting disability or who experiences serious and frequent behavior problems at school is best suited for IDEA coverage. A child whose needs are less severe may find suitable coverage under the less stringent and more inclusive requirements of Section 504.

Q: *Does my child have to be failing to qualify for special education services?*

A: No. Failing grades are a red flag for seeking extra help or special education services, but they are not a prerequisite for obtaining special services. The RTI services discussed in this chapter may be a road to securing valuable education services that may derail failure before it occurs.

CHAPTER 8

Advocating for Your Child and Others

An *advocate* can be broadly defined as someone who speaks up to make things better. Advocates can speak up for themselves or others. You advocate for your own child each time you speak to teachers, physicians, nurses, social workers, and others. You are, in fact, the most important advocate for your child. You will also advocate for people with attention-deficit/hyperactivity disorder (ADHD) when you speak knowledgeably about your family's experience. When you combine your commitment to your child with effective advocacy skills, your child can become as independent and productive as possible.

Learning the skills needed to be an effective advocate can empower you as you help your child navigate life. As you advocate for your child to receive services and supports, remember that you are the expert on your child. Professionals have knowledge and expertise in specific areas, but your experience and long-term connection with your child is unique and invaluable. Professionals will pass in and out of your child's life, but you will always be her parent. Your knowledge can be used to improve her life and the lives of many other families and children.

As your child's advocate, you work to change "systems" that affect your child. Every day, families of children with ADHD are affected by a variety of systems and how they operate: the school system, the health care system, government, and others. Most of the time these systems are helpful, but sometimes they may not adequately meet the needs of your child and other children. You may see the need to advocate for a system to change.

This chapter outlines how to be an effective advocate for your child and provides information on system advocacy. In the following pages you will learn about

- The 6 skills of an effective advocate
- Advocacy at school and with the health care system
- Advocacy for systems change

Six Skills of an Effective Advocate

Supporter, backer, believer, promoter, coach, cheerleader—you are all of these when you advocate for your child. By using the 6 advocacy skills, you can become even more effective at promoting the interests of children with ADHD.

1. Understand your child's disability.

Understand all you can about your child's specific ADHD diagnosis. The knowledge you gather will allow you to ask educated, informed questions of your child's teachers and pediatric clinicians. Also, as well as reading this book, you may consider joining support groups or specific organizations focused on ADHD, such as CHADD: The National Resource on ADHD (www.chadd.org). Becoming acquainted with adults who have ADHD can also be helpful. Their past experiences and current lives can provide you with great insights on your child's potential. The more you understand your child's specific diagnoses, the more you will be able to know if the services provided are appropriate to meet her needs. The knowledge you gather will also allow you to ask educated, informed questions.

2. Know the key players.

To influence someone to make a change you think is necessary for your child, it is essential to know the appropriate person to contact. Who has the authority to make decisions that could lead to a change? Is it the Individualized Education Program (IEP) special educator, the social service case manager, a school administrator, a patient representative, or a city council member? If one person can't or won't help you, ask that person who else might be able to help you or ask to speak to a person with more authority. To find the key players, ask at school for contact information or check your school department's website. You might also ask staff at your local parent advocacy or resource center for ideas.

3. *Know your rights and responsibilities.*

Knowing who is in charge is not enough. It also helps to know the "rules," which allows you to participate from a position of knowledge. Each agency, service provider, or school has guidelines and protocols for how it works. Each one has certain procedures, forms, policies, and, sometimes, even laws and regulations that you will need to understand. See what you can learn by reading the agency's or service's website; ask where you can find policies and procedures in writing, if available. Because there is a direct link between how an agency or service is funded and what your specific rights and responsibilities are, it's also important to find the funding source. If the service is funded by the public, it is required to follow certain laws, not just policies. Publicly funded systems are supported by taxes and include public schools and all levels of government.

4. *Become well organized.*

Most agencies and services require documents, data, and other records. It's important to organize the information and documents that you have and to be prepared by using the following tips:

- Separate your records by service or agency.
- Keep written correspondence, including printed emails, from schools, county services, medical professionals, or any other system.
- Keep a list of names and contact numbers for each system related to your concern.
- When you attend a meeting, bring the pertinent records from your file or folder.
- Keep records in order by date so you can easily find what you need.

It is always best to have as many things in writing as possible. This includes copies of any letters or emails you send yourself. People who have experience with advocacy have a saying: "If it's not in writing, it doesn't exist."

If someone tells you something on the phone or in a hallway conversation that you feel is important, try to document it in writing. To do so, you might write a letter or email saying, "Thank you for talking to me today. I think what you said was…, and that you will…. Unless I hear from you in writing by next week, I will assume you understood the conversation the same way as I did."

It may also be helpful to keep a phone log and meeting notebook. Include the date, name of the person you talked with, a summary of what was said or decided, and brief notes of the issues that were discussed. If there were any specific things that you or the other person agreed to do, highlight them in your log so you can check on progress later. Schedule follow-ups and other action steps in your planner. If organization is not one of your strengths, you may wish to ask a family member or friend to help you organize these records.

5. Use clear and effective communication.

The way you talk to others has a direct relationship to how they interact with you and perhaps how they will serve your child. That's why it's important to make sure that your communication style is helping and not hindering your efforts. It's always important to have a positive attitude and tone of voice, even if that is hard. You have good ideas and valid requests. If you sound angry, others might respond to your anger in a negative way, and your child may not receive the help you were hoping for.

How would you define your communication attitude?

- Are you *passive?* If you are, you might feel that "the professionals know more than I do; they won't listen, so there is no need to speak up; I feel powerless and controlled by others."

- Are you *aggressive?* Be careful! It is risky to believe that "I know more than anyone else; I will make others fear me so I can achieve my goal; I don't care if I violate the rights of others."

- Are you *assertive?* Try advocating this way: "I will share what I know; I will express my child's needs clearly; I will listen as others share what they know."

Strive to become an assertive communicator. To do that, you must first define your goals and then keep your eyes on the prize: effective services for your child. The focus should primarily be on your child and what your child needs, although you also need to keep your needs and the rest of the family's needs in mind. Second, listen and ask questions. Listening gives you information that you will need and helps you engage others to be on your child's team. Whether you agree or not, try to understand what others are saying as you listen. To make sure you understand what the other person is saying, you might ask: "I think I heard you say.... Is that correct?" or "Tell me more so I'm sure I understand what you are suggesting."

Asking questions is also important. If someone says, "Your child is disruptive," ask detailed questions about what that person means. What are those specific disruptive behaviors? When, and how often? Is there a pattern to the time of day the disruptive behaviors occur? What precipitates these disruptions? Knowing the answers to these questions will help determine a solution to the problem.

Effective communicators and advocates are as clear and direct as possible. They also turn negatives into positives. This technique allows you to take a negative comment made about your child and turn it into a positive. For example, if you are told, "He's always fighting," you might respond by suggesting, "I hope we can plan together to help my child to learn social skills."

At the end of a conversation it's important to clarify and summarize what you and others have said. Ask if you've misinterpreted or misunderstood anything, and ask to be corrected if you have. Ask if someone is writing down what was discussed; request a copy. Remember that good communicators focus on a goal, show respect and expect it from others, ask questions, rephrase what is said for clarification, and say "thank you."

6. *Know how to resolve disagreements.*

As a parent, you may agree or disagree with the decisions made by an agency or service provider. Because of this, it's important to know how disagreements are settled within a specific organization. Each agency or service provider has formal or informal guidelines on how it works; each one has procedures, forms, policies, and, sometimes, laws and regulations. Ask if a given agency has a dispute resolution procedure and where you can find it in writing.

There are many ways to resolve disagreements. It's usually best to use informal means if possible. Start your efforts at the level closest to the problem. Talk to people, such as the teacher, case manager, or service provider, about your differences and be clear about why you do not agree. This often is the easiest way to solve a problem. Often, a compromise or "trial solution" can be worked out. Sometimes, more formal means are necessary to clear up disagreements. Among the options may be

- **Mediation:** Agencies and service providers sometimes provide mediation. The parties who disagree meet with a neutral mediator and the mediator guides the discussion so that all sides and options can be heard.
- **Filing complaints:** Some agencies and service providers have a formal means of filing a grievance or complaint.
- **Filing appeals:** Some agencies and service providers have a written process for filing an appeal of a decision made by the agency or provider. All government agencies must have an appeals process. In addition, insurance companies also have appeal processes if a claim or procedure is denied.

At times, you may need to be "the squeaky wheel." Parents and guardians who are persistent often receive the services their child or family needs.

Personal Advocacy at School

Advocating for your child at school usually involves attending meetings. Effective advocates prepare for these meetings, effectively communicate during the meetings, and try to end the meeting on a positive note.

When you attend a meeting, be sure to bring important records from your file. To help prepare, make a list of questions in advance of the meeting.

Preparing for Meetings, Conferences, and Conversations

To be prepared, read your child's current evaluation, IEP, and IEP goal progress reports. If you find it hard to understand the IEP reports, find someone—a teacher, a counselor, or another knowledgeable parent—to help you understand the report. Think about what the issues are and be ready to state them clearly. Consider ideas for a solution and find specific facts to support your position. You will also want to make a list of your priorities and concerns before a meeting and be sure that they are listed on the meeting's agenda. Keep in mind that you may need to narrow your list because you may not be able to cover every issue at one meeting. You may wish to share your priority list with your child's case manager. To properly prepare, you can also write a list of questions and concerns, keeping in mind who will be at a meeting and what their roles will be. Make sure you know the purpose(s) of the meeting, and consider inviting someone to go with you to a meeting to take notes and to help you understand and remember the details of the discussion accurately. It's wise to inform the case manager if you invite someone.

Beginning a Meeting

To set the stage for an effective meeting

- Learn who will be the chair or moderator of the meeting. It might be helpful to have a brief phone call with the moderator to learn about how he or she feels the meeting might be most effective.

- Arrive early enough to sit where you will feel most comfortable and effective. Consider the advisability of bringing your child to the meeting. Older children who are interested should be encouraged to be included.

- Establish rapport. Consider starting with a brief family update about your child and his strengths.

- Make sure there is an agenda and that it includes your items.

- Find out how much time has been scheduled for this meeting. Is it enough?

During the Meeting

- Take notepaper or a laptop with you.

- Identify and focus on your goal. How will you hold yourself accountable?

- Show respect, expect it from others, and remain calm.

- Be specific and clear. Instead of, "He follows directions at home," you may want to say, "At home he follows directions better when I give him 2-step directions with one reminder."

- Acknowledge that you understand that teachers have multiple and complex roles.

- Ask questions if unfamiliar terms are used or unfamiliar district policies are mentioned.

- Don't interrupt. Allow the speaker to finish; don't assume you know what the speaker will say. Listen intently. If you also have ADHD, try to manage your own impulse to interrupt by taking or typing notes or repeating what your heard.

- You may ask for pauses so that you can record your thoughts.

- Rephrase what you hear to be sure that you understood correctly.

- Use praise and say "thank you" whenever possible.

Ending a Meeting

The moderator will end your meeting by summarizing its results. This is your opportunity to make sure you understood everything correctly and can clarify who will do what by when.

End on a positive note whenever possible. Even if you've disagreed, you may be able to say, "I think we understand each other's perspectives more clearly now."

Other Tips for Effective School Meetings

Use "This will..." instead of "I think...."

For example: "Seating Jimmy in the front row and away from the window will help him focus on his work," versus, "I think Jimmy needs to sit somewhere else." The first statement offers a concrete reason to consider your suggestion, while the second statement is an opinion.

Use "You could..." or "Could you..." rather than "You should...."

For example: "Instead of sending Tara to the office, you could call the social worker," versus, "You should never send Tara to the office." Or, "Jon's progress in learning to read seems very slow; could we look at other methods?" versus, "You should use a different method for teaching reading." The first statements suggest an option that's open to discussion and flexibility. The second statements imply that you are ordering someone to do something.

Ask "What other options would be helpful?"

- This is a meeting of adults who want your child to succeed. It's an opportunity to problem-solve together.
- As a group, systematically analyze the pros and cons of each option suggested so that everyone may feel that their participation is of value.

Choose your pronouns.

- *Use "I" statements.* Here are some examples: "I would like to talk about what my daughter is learning"; "I feel like I'm not being heard"; "I didn't understand that—I'd like to stop and go back."
- *Leave out the word "you."* Using the word "you" in a sentence can cause other people to feel defensive. Defensive people don't listen because they are busy thinking of ways to defend themselves. This accomplishes nothing positive for the child. For example: "You are not helping my daughter," versus, "My daughter is not getting the help she needs."

Phrases that may improve communication include

- "Tell me more about...."
- "That term (or acronym) is unfamiliar to me. Would you please define it?"
- "Please explain...."
- "Would you please rephrase that so I can understand?"
- "How will I know this plan is working?"
- "What will the school propose to do about...?"
- "What do you suggest we do about...?"
- "I think I heard you say.... Is that correct?"
- "How was that progress you mentioned measured?"
- "That is interesting. Tell me more so I'm sure I understand your view."
- "How long will we need to use this intervention to determine if it is successful?"

Working as a Team

Communicating at a Meeting

Team meetings, sometimes called *care coordination meetings,* are generally an effective process to share information, note strengths, problem-solve, plot progress, and answer questions. These meetings might be convened by your pediatric clinician, school special educator, or you as parents. Unfortunately, they are difficult to organize because of the time demands placed on most care providers and teachers.

You can problem-solve with professionals to find solutions using the following steps:

- Describe the problem clearly. Prepared an outline of your thoughts.
- Encourage input from all members of the team.
- Brainstorm without evaluating the ideas.

- Choose a solution by consensus.
- Develop a plan. Define who is responsible for an action and when it will be done.
- Put that plan in writing.
- Make sure that each item of the plan is clear and measurable so that you can track future progress.
- Create a timeline and criteria to evaluate success.
- Follow up to make sure the plan is implemented.

Written Communication

Clear written communication is an important tool of effective advocates. Letters or emails may be sent for many reasons, such as making a request, asking for clarification, recording what you said, asking for a decision, and documenting a verbal discussion. You might even write simply to say, "Thank you!"

Use the following checklist when you write a letter or email and remember to keep a copy for yourself. Letters should

- Be sent to a person who can make a change.
- Be dated and signed.
- Focus on 1 or 2 issues.
- Be no longer than one page.
- Set a deadline if a reply is requested.
- Give your contact information.

Personal Advocacy Within the Health Care System

The first step in advocating for your child in the health care system is making sure you have a positive relationship with a compassionate and qualified pediatric clinician, such as a pediatrician, an advanced practice registered nurse, a physician assistant, a family medicine physician, or a mental health clinician such as a child psychiatrist or a psychologist. Consider whether your child's pediatric clinician meets the following basic expectations:

Does the pediatric clinician

- Show respect for you and your child?
- Show a willingness to listen patiently?
- Take your concerns seriously?
- Have courteous office staff?
- Support your goals for your child?

Throughout your relationship with the pediatric clinician, you should think about whether these basic expectations are being met. As a parent, you must also do your part to ensure a good relationship and good communication with your child's pediatric clinician. As you work with your child's clinician, keep the following things in mind:

- Remain realistic about what you can expect of your child's pediatric clinician. Remember that one visit with one clinician cannot solve all your child's issues or answer all your questions.
- In the medical home model, you are part of the health care team, participating in decision-making about your child's care. This means that you have responsibilities for communicating effectively with your child's pediatric clinician, keeping records, and following up.

Advocating for good health care and communicating well with your child's pediatric clinician is easier if you are prepared and organized.

Before an Appointment

- Write down your observations of behavior, reactions to medications, sleep patterns, eating habits, or anything else that your pediatric clinician may need to know.
- Keep medical records. You have the right to copies of your child's medical records. You may wish to keep your own records of tests and procedures and their results. You can do this by dividing a 3-ring binder into relevant sections, such as current

care plan, providers' names, health history, current and past medications, addresses and phone numbers, bills, referrals, insurance information, and appointment logs. Premade medical record systems are also available, as well as online medical organizers.

● Write out questions. Do not hesitate to ask questions and do not be embarrassed to ask for clarification when you don't understand something the pediatric clinician says.

● Prepare your child. Tell your child who you will be seeing, why, and what tests may be done. If appropriate, let your child know that blood tests and shots are not part of this visit. Take comfort items along on the appointment.

During the Appointment

Make an effort to understand the pediatric clinician—listen and take notes. Ask the clinician to explain anything you do not understand in the treatment plan. You may ask the clinician to write out the treatment plan and then repeat the plan back to the clinician as you understand it. Ask questions.

After the Appointment

Your child's pediatric clinician will most often schedule a recheck in about 2 to 4 weeks after starting any new medicines. If your child is starting a stimulant medication, the clinician may ask you to call back in a week because effects with those medications are seen more quickly. Otherwise, children with ADHD will be seen for their annual health supervision (well-child) visit, as well as any additional ADHD recheck visits that you and your pediatric clinician decide together are necessary.

If you feel it is needed, you may ask for a second opinion from another clinician. If you are uncertain or uncomfortable about a diagnosis or treatment, follow your instincts and talk more with the clinician about your concern. You may feel it's necessary to change clinicians. Some reasons for selecting another pediatric clinician are if your current clinician is not responsive to your concerns, is not listening to you and your child, is not communicating with specialists, or is not helping you coordinate your child's care.

Personal Advocacy With Your Health Insurance Company: Appealing Health Plan Decisions

To be an effective advocate for your child's needs within the guidelines of your health insurance plan, you will need to understand the plan.

Review your health plan policy, certificate of coverage, health benefits handbook, or other documents that explain your plan's benefits, as well as its coverage limits. Note which services are and are not covered. You may need to read the "definitions" section of your plan so you understand unfamiliar terms. If you have coverage questions, call the health plan's customer service line; the number can be found on the back of your member card and in your benefit handbook. You may want to ask

- Do I need a referral from my child's pediatrician or pediatric clinician to see a specialist?
- Must I use a preferred list of network health care professionals?
- What if I want to see someone outside that network?
- Is there an annual deductible? If there is, what is it?
- Are there limits on the number of visits?
- Does the plan exclude certain diagnoses or preexisting conditions?
- Is there a lifetime dollar limit?
- What is my prescription coverage? Particularly with stimulant medications, newer forms of extended-release stimulant medications vary in how many hours they are effective per day and in cost. It is helpful to determine which of the new medications are covered by your insurance and how much your co-pay is.

As with other areas of advocacy, it's important to keep good records. Record the date, time, and name of the person you spoke with on any calls to or from your health plan. Take notes on the conversation and the information you were given. You can then verify that the information provided over the phone agrees with what your policy appears to say.

Developing a strong relationship with your child's medical home is also beneficial when dealing with insurance coverage and any appeals process. The health care professionals that make up your child's medical home can likely help with referrals and even appeals; these are components of a medical home's coordination of care. This will ensure smooth delivery of services and good communication. Be sure that requests, referrals, or orders for services come from a medical clinician. Requests from a therapist or licensed psychologist may not be accepted by health plans.

Denial of Insurance Claims

If coverage for services for your child is denied, first determine the reason for the denial. Compare the reason stated in the denial letter to your certificate of coverage. You should also make certain that any denials are in writing, not in person or over the phone.

If services are denied because they're not covered under your plan, explore whether the plan is clear about its exclusions and whether any exceptions are allowed. If services are denied because they're not considered medically necessary, file an appeal based on factual reasons why the services are necessary for your child. Don't hesitate to challenge any denial of services. Those in your child's medical home can help you with this information.

Appealing Health Plan Decisions

Your insurer will send you a letter that explains why your request has been denied. Read the reasons carefully so you can prepare a strong appeal. To successfully appeal a decision of your health plan, you will need to understand the appeal process and give the health plan as much information as possible to support your claim.

All health plans are required by law to have an appeals process. You will find information about your plan's appeals process by reading your policy or certificate of coverage, consulting the insurance company's website, or contacting your health plan and asking for a written copy of the appeals process. Many states require that the appeals process be included with a denial of care letter.

In most cases, to start the appeals process you must submit your appeal in writing. Use these guidelines to organize your letter.

- **Purpose:** State your purpose for writing.
- **Diagnosis:** Explain your child's diagnosis and how it affects your child.
- **Reasons:** Give specific reasons why your child needs the service.

- **Documentation:** Mention the supporting documentation you are including.

- **Action:** Close by requesting a written reply.

Strengthen your appeal by including written support from your child's pediatrician or pediatric clinician explaining why your child needs the services requested. Ask for letters of support from one or more doctors familiar with your child's case. It is also helpful to create a paper trail by organizing your policy, copies of denial letters, copies of any correspondence with your health plan, detailed notes of conversations (date and time of call, name of person you spoke with, what was discussed), and copies of any correspondence between your pediatric clinician and the health plan concerning your problem. Finally, send copies of all correspondence with your plan to all interested persons. For example, you may send copies to your pediatric clinician and anyone else you have contacted about your situation. Indicate that they have been sent copies by noting each name at the bottom of the letter.

Should your appeal be denied, request a higher-level review. When all appeals to the insurer have failed, consider contacting your state commissioner of insurance for assistance or for an additional appeal.

Systems Advocacy: Taking a Step Further

Strengthening your advocacy skills will benefit your child now and in the future and will help you secure needed supports and services for your child. Some parents take advocacy a step further and use their personal stories, skills, and knowledge to push for changes that will improve the lives of other children with ADHD.

Often families begin the journey from personal advocacy toward systems advocacy after they are faced with payment limitations and regulations that limit services and supports for their child. Because they have the "lived experience" of parenting a child with ADHD, they know what works and what doesn't work in a system. They see a need to change a "system," including the policies, laws, or rules that determine how services will be provided to families of children with disabilities, including ADHD.

Unhappy with the way the health care system or public school system has responded to their needs, families may seek new ways to change the system to address the needs of not just their own child but all children, adolescents, and adults with ADHD.

They begin working with others, including national support groups and advocacy organizations, to make large-scale improvements. As an advocate for systems change, you speak up to improve services for all children with ADHD and their families. You can learn to advocate for meaningful changes that may affect thousands of children in your community or state or throughout the country.

Many systems affect the families of children with disabilities. Each system has a certain way of operating, whether it's a school, a hospital, a health insurance company, a community center, a faith-based organization, or a city, county, state, or federal government. To change how a system operates, parents need to understand how it works. This is not always easy, especially within the public policy arena. Working for change within the US intergovernmental system of national, state, and local governments can be daunting. That's why most advocates for systems change turn to *allies*—those in a similar position who are dealing with the same issue, like, for example, the differing ways the health care system and the public school system treat individuals with disabilities.

Individuals have stepped forward, joined together, and made changes at the system level that now provide basic educational and civil rights for people with disabilities. If you choose to follow in their footsteps and work for systems change, follow these first important steps:

- **Link with others and build relationships.** Who in your school, family, neighborhood, or faith community is facing similar limitations and frustrations? Seek them out. It's particularly effective to connect with families who are already involved in health, education, and disability advocacy—they can teach you.

- **Connect to organizations doing public policy work.** Many groups that focus on particular disabilities and work to change public policy for the benefit of children and adults with disabilities have public policy advocacy specialists and are a natural place to go for support and to become involved. For ADHD, CHADD (www.chadd.org) is one such group. There are parent training and information centers and community parent resource centers throughout the United States that provide information and support for families of children with disabilities, as well as advocacy support. Talk with your child's pediatrician or pediatric clinician if you have any questions.

- **Learn public policy facts.** Public policy is a complex arena, but it is one you can work in. Support groups can offer a wealth of factual information, particularly those physically located in Washington, DC, and in state capitals. In addition to support and family advocacy groups, professional and trade associations may be a good source of information should their agenda match your own. Although you may not always agree with your school principal, school psychologist, and health insurance plan, their professional and trade associations have much information.

Legislative Advocacy

Laws in the United States are written by legislative bodies. To advocate for a change in the law, you must work with the people in those bodies, which include the US Congress, state legislatures, county councils, city councils, and school boards. Most legislative bodies have their own websites, and you can use them to research the existing laws governing health care, public education, and disability services. Support and advocacy groups also have information on legislation and legislative bodies.

To advocate for change, you will need to convey your message to the appropriate legislators. Because US legislative members represent geographic areas, legislators respond best to their *constituents* (the voters from their own area). If you are a constituent, remember that constituents carry influence. Your first task is to determine which legislators represent your area.

Once you know who your legislators are, ask to meet with them or a senior staff member and tell them your personal story. Legislators need to know how a particular public program is affecting or limiting the welfare and needs of your family. If possible, relate your personal story to the personal stories of others and work in coalitions and partnerships. Keep it short. When advocating, don't forget to ask yourself: Who is it I want to persuade? What seems important to them? How can my personal story relate to that person I want to persuade? Educating legislative members about health, education, and disability by telling your personal story is important.

Dos and Don'ts for Dealing With Your Legislators

Do

- Be concise and clear. Legislators are busy and hear from many people. Can you tell your story in 5 minutes?
- Stick to one issue. What is the one takeaway they should remember?
- Provide a handout to help deliver the message. The "leave behind" document is important. Try to limit the length to no more than one sheet (front and back).
- Send them an email or a thank-you letter and stay in contact with their office.
- Join coalitions. Many other people will be contacting their legislators, frequently on the same issue. Being part of an organization and having your organization working in coalitions builds numbers and increases information. Consistency of message is more likely to garner a legislator's support. Mention to legislators the other organizations, coalitions, and constituents that you are working with. Legislators want to know that you are not alone—that other constituents are concerned with the same issues and likely have the same advocacy positions.

Don't

- Mix causes and messages. Don't share your views on a wide variety of issues and concerns.
- Threaten, offend, preach, or write off anyone. You will meet legislators and their staff who aren't supportive or interested. State your case and be polite. Try to be a good listener regarding what they care about and why.
- Be late for appointments. This may be a particular challenge for many people with attention-deficit/hyperactivity disorder.
- Guess about answers. If you don't know something when they ask, say you don't know and will get back to them.

Advocating in the Health Care System

The US health care system, which, in 2015, was close to 17.5% of the US economy, is extremely complex. Trying to figure out who pays can be difficult. Many Americans are enrolled in more than one health care program. Each program has its own legal and regulatory requirements and limitations. The largest and most important health care payment programs and the number of Americans they insure are

- Employer-paid health insurance: 165 million Americans; 51.6% of the US population
- Federal employee health benefits program: 8 million federal employees, retirees, former employees, and their families; 2.5% of the US population
- Other private insurance (non-employer paid): 22.6 million Americans; 7.1% of the US population
- Medicare: 57 million Americans; 17.5% of the US population
- Medicaid: 67 million Americans; 20.5% of the US population
- Children's Health Insurance Program (commonly known as CHIP): 6.5 million Americans; 2.0% of the US population
- Veterans Health Administration: 9 million Americans; 2.8% of the US population

Note: Coverage types are not mutually exclusive; individuals may have more than one type of coverage. Sources include the Centers for Medicare & Medicaid Services, State Health Access Data Assistance Center, US Office of Personnel Management, US Department of Veteran Affairs, and the US Census Bureau.

Additionally, there are specialized health care delivery programs such as Tricare (www.tricare.mil) for active duty military personnel and their families, federally qualified health centers for medically underserved populations, and state mental health authorities serving the most severely disabled by mental illness and children with mental health challenges.

It is easier to influence public sector health programs, which are provided by the government, than private sector health programs, which are private insurance plans purchased by employers.

Public programs are authorized by federal and state law and sometimes complemented by county governments. Government agencies issue regulations governing these programs. Typically, there is a public comment period on proposed regulations, which allows advocates to share their viewpoints. Increasingly, contracts between government agencies and health plans are available to the public, which helps advocates be informed. Most states have consumer protections and consumer rights laws and regulations, including internal and external appeals procedures that can allow advocates to work for change.

A fundamental barrier to receiving needed health services is the definition of *medical necessity.* The definition is frequently held "confidential" to the health plan decision-makers but can be challenged by mental health and pediatric clinicians on behalf of patients and their families. Another quasi-public barrier is medication formularies. These are often challenged by pediatric clinicians on behalf of consumers and their families but typically with limited success.

In the private sector, one way you may advocate for change is through state law. Many states have laws providing consumer grievance procedures against health plans in the private sector. In this area, a helpful consumer organization is the National Alliance on Mental Illness (www.nami.org).

A major systems advocacy objective of the American Academy of Pediatrics, actively supported by CHADD, is establishing family-centered medical homes. A *medical home* is a single medical practice taking ownership and responsibility to coordinate interventions for children with special needs. The medical home is further discussed in Chapter 5.

A Success Story

The Mental Health Parity and Addiction Equity Act of 2008 requires health insurance companies to treat mental illnesses and disorders on an equal basis with physical illnesses and disorders, when polices cover both. Prior to this legislation most health insurance plans in the United States treated mental disorders separately and differently from physical disorders. For example, prior to the act, insurance plans typically authorized unlimited hospitalization for physical disorders but limited hospitalization for mental health disorders to 30 days per calendar year. Then insurers authorized a broad array of outpatient services for physical conditions but limited outpatient mental health services and required significantly higher out-of-pocket co-payments for mental than for physical health problems. These forms of discrimination have been abolished in most health insurance plans.

This important legislative success was the product of many national organizations working in coalition over many years with the same public policy objective. Families can change systems and laws if they unite and persevere in their efforts.

Advocacy Makes a Difference

You can be an advocate for systems change while continuing to personally advocate for your family member. Whether you are learning how to be a better advocate for your child or delving into systems advocacy, know that advocacy of all types is an art—the art of persuasion.

Being knowledgeable, honest, polite, and persistent are important tools in being persuasive. Patience is required for systems change, as is collaboration with others for common objectives. Remember, you are not alone in your desire to make positive changes for your child and others.

Public policy advocacy can be a frustrating experience, but many find it to be an exciting, dynamic activity. When you engage in systems advocacy, you'll find people who share your interest in promoting public welfare and helping other families overcome their challenges. Children with disabilities receive services today based on the past advocacy work of parents like you who worked together with committed professionals. You can add your important voice to improve the services for children and families today and tomorrow.

CHAPTER 9

When It Is Not Just ADHD: Identifying Coexisting Conditions

Attention-deficit/hyperactivity disorder (ADHD) often occurs with other problems or diagnoses, called *coexisting conditions*. Fifty percent to 60% of children with ADHD have at least one coexisting condition. More than 10% of children with ADHD have 3 or more coexisting conditions. Disruptive behavior disorders, which involve behavior and conduct problems, anxiety and depressive disorders, learning disabilities, and language impairments, are the most common.

Coexisting conditions may share many of the same symptoms or mimic the symptoms of ADHD. Coexisting conditions in young children with ADHD are particularly hard to identify correctly because children's behavior changes quickly and certain conditions can only be diagnosed later because the age of onset of some diagnoses present later than ADHD. What seemed at 4 years of age to be a developing mood disorder may turn out to be symptoms of ADHD.

In addition to diagnosed disorders, many children with ADHD experience coexisting "problems"—functioning difficulties that are not formally defined as disabilities but that still require special attention. For example, up to 60% of children with ADHD experience some form of academic problem in school subjects, like reading, math, or social studies; skills, such as handwriting or motor planning; or productivity (completing assignments accurately and on time). Most of these children do not have learning disorders.

A learning problem that impedes school performance is a coexisting condition or problem that may affect your child's functioning in ways that require changes in his education or treatment plan. Sometimes the symptoms of the coexisting condition may be more problematic than those of the ADHD and must be treated first, even if the ADHD was the original cause of your child's referral for treatment. This certainly may be the case with a coexisting major depressive disorder (MDD).

In addition, a child's environment usually plays an important role. The behavior of a child with ADHD may *cause* stress within the family or may *reflect* stress within the family. Both may result in greater severity of the child's symptoms. Some conditions, such as conduct disorder (CD), which involves extreme defiance and flaunting of rules, increase the risks for substance use, criminal behavior, or other difficulties later in life. *These risks may be diminished or even avoided if the condition is identified early and treated.*

For all these reasons, it is always necessary to consider whether any coexisting conditions are present when your child is being evaluated for ADHD. A comprehensive evaluation at the time of diagnosis is needed to diagnose any additional conditions and problems that can accompany ADHD. Continued and ongoing monitoring is vital throughout childhood and adolescence. Some coexisting conditions may develop long after the original ADHD diagnosis, while others may diminish over time. In this chapter you will find information on how best to recognize and treat the types of coexisting conditions that most commonly accompany ADHD, including

- **Disruptive behavior disorders,** including oppositional defiant disorder (ODD) and CD
- **Anxiety disorders,** such as generalized anxiety disorder, separation anxiety disorder, and phobias
- **Mood disorders,** including major depression, dysthymia, disruptive mood dysregulation (DMD), substance/medication-induced depression, and bipolar and related disorders
- **Motor disorders,** such as tics, Tourette syndrome, and obsessive-compulsive disorder (OCD)
- **Learning, motor skills, and communication disorders,** including developmental coordination disorder
- **Intellectual disability** (formerly called mental retardation), including autism spectrum disorder (ASD)
- **Trauma- and stress-related disorders,** such as posttraumatic stress disorder (PTSD)
- **Sleep disorders,** such as restless legs syndrome and obstructive apnea
- **Coexisting problems** that do not reaching the severity required for a specific diagnosis but may still significantly stand in the way of your child's progress

There are other problems that might either look very similar to ADHD or make the symptoms of ADHD stand out more. These include

- Sensory deficits, such as hearing or vision problems

- Sleep deprivation

- Bereavement

- Certain physical illnesses (eg, thyroid disease, hypoglycemia, hyperglycemia, side effects of medications, endocrine tumors)

- Substance use or withdrawal from substances

- Exposure to adverse childhood experiences

When viewed all together, this list of disorders may seem daunting and even frightening. Keep in mind, however, that although coexisting conditions occur in most children and adolescents with ADHD, no child has all these conditions, and most are treatable. With early identification and a systematic evidence-based treatment program, you and your child may be able to avoid or minimize many of the effects of disorders that do appear. Furthermore, the strengths of your child and family are important factors in increasing the likelihood that he will function well despite these conditions.

What Else Is Going On? Recognizing and Diagnosing Coexisting Conditions

Your child may frequently seem defiant and uncooperative for many reasons. Identifying a coexisting condition can be difficult. Sadness, anxiety, frequent rule breaking, or other behaviors might indicate another problem but could also be ADHD related. Behavior problems can also be responses to conflict at home or at school, or just a normal part of the process of growing up.

As with ADHD, there are no medical tests to determine the reason for your child's behavior. An accurate diagnosis involves thorough assessment, including a review of your observations of your child's behavior, an interview with your child, regular discussions among all members of his treatment and education teams, a review of your family's medical history, and the use of other tests or standardized rating scales. Even with these aids, categorizing your child's cluster of behaviors as ADHD alone, as ADHD plus a coexisting condition, or even as a separate condition without ADHD may require observation and review over time.

If your child has already been diagnosed with ADHD but has shown little or no response to careful trials of medication and behavior therapy techniques, he may have one or more coexisting conditions or problems in addition to ADHD. If your child was very young when he was diagnosed with ADHD, it may even turn out that he has another disorder and not ADHD. If you are beginning to question whether your child has a different or coexisting condition and he is not just functioning poorly due to stresses or frustrations directly related to ADHD, ask yourself

- **How long has the troublesome behavior lasted?** Has defiant or oppositional behavior been going on for longer than about 6 months? Particularly in younger children, troublesome behavior can normally come and go quickly. But if your child's difficulties persist beyond half a year, he may need assessment for a coexisting condition. In the case of depression or anxiety symptoms, an even shorter observation period of only weeks or a month is recommended.

- **Is the behavior typical of his age group?** Troublesome behavior occurs in all children during various stages of development. Assessment may be necessary, however, if your child's problems develop or persist long past the age when others his age have outgrown such behavior.

- **How intense is the behavior?** All children test boundaries, act fearful, or are depressed now and then, but children with a diagnosable condition act in more prolonged and intense ways than others their age.

- **How much of a problem is it causing in his day-to-day functioning?** Is the behavior significantly interfering with your child's academic progress, social relationships, or other important aspects of daily life? If so, a coexisting condition may be the cause.

- **Do you see any developmental delays?** Particularly during your child's preschool and early school years, keep track of whether he reaches the standard developmental milestones listed on child development charts at or around the ages indicated. Your child's pediatric clinician will be checking on these during your health supervision (well-child) visits. Watch especially for any significant delays in language development, social skills, motor skills, or academic progress (Table 9.1).

Table 9.1. Developmental Milestones for Developmental Surveillance at Health Supervision Visits			
Age	Social Language and Self-help	Verbal Language (Expressive and Receptive)	Gross Motor	Fine Motor
3 y	Enters bathroom and urinates by self Plays in cooperation and shares Puts on coat, jacket, or shirt by self Engages in beginning imaginative play Eats independently	Uses 3-word sentences Uses words that are 75% intelligible to strangers Understands simple prepositions (eg, *on*, *under*)	Pedals tricycle Climbs on and off couch or chair Jumps forward	Draws a single circle Draws a person with head and 1 other body part Cuts with child scissors
4 y	Enters bathroom and has bowel movement by self Brushes teeth Dresses and undresses without much help Engages in well-developed imaginative play	Uses 4-word sentences Uses words that are 100% intelligible to strangers	Climbs stairs alternating feet without support Skips on 1 foot	Draws a person with at least 3 body parts Draws simple cross Unbuttons and buttons medium-sized buttons Grasps pencil with thumb and fingers instead of fist

Reprinted from American Academy of Pediatrics. *Bright Futures: Guidelines for Health Supervision of Infants, Children, and Adolescents.* Hagan JF, Shaw JS, Duncan PM, eds. 4th ed. Elk Grove Village, IL: American Academy of Pediatrics; 2017:86–87.

- **Do others in your child's family have ADHD or one or more coexisting conditions?** Many coexisting conditions run in families. A child with ADHD and a close relative with conditions such as an anxiety disorder, depression, learning disorders, oppositional behavior, or a more serious CD may have greater chance of having ADHD and/or a coexisting condition himself.

If your answers to any of these questions have left you with doubts or even questions about your child's functioning, be sure to discuss your observations with your child's pediatric clinician and other professionals involved with your child's care. If the diagnosis of ADHD has been made, your child's pediatrician probably evaluated your child for any coexisting conditions at the time of diagnosis. Coexisting conditions may require additional or different treatment.

In many cases, treatment of the ADHD itself may actually resolve the coexisting condition. But the types of behaviors described in this chapter are likely to suggest a coexisting condition. Changes in treatment may be necessary to address the coexisting condition along with ADHD.

Disruptive Behavior Disorders

Disruptive behavior disorders are among the easiest to identify of all coexisting conditions because they involve behaviors that are readily seen: temper tantrums, physical aggression like attacking other children, excessive arguing, stealing, or other forms of defiance of authority. These disorders, which include ODD, CD, and DMD, often first attract notice when they interfere with school performance or family and peer relationships, and they frequently intensify over time.

Behaviors typical of disruptive behavior disorders can closely resemble ADHD—particularly where impulsivity and hyperactivity are involved—but ADHD, ODD, and CD are considered separate conditions that can occur independently. About one-third of all children with ADHD have coexisting ODD, and up to one-quarter have coexisting CD. Children with both conditions tend to have more difficult lives than those with only ADHD because their defiant behavior leads to regular conflicts with adults and others with whom they interact. Early identification and treatment may, however, increase the chances that your child can learn to control these behaviors.

Disruptive mood dysregulation is a new condition that is suggested by severe temper outbursts in a child whose mood is mostly irritable or angry. Disruptive mood dysregulation and ODD cannot exist at the same time. Disruptive mood dysregulation management will almost always involve a referral to a mental health specialist.

Oppositional Defiant Disorder

Many children with ADHD display oppositional behaviors at times. Oppositional defiant disorder is defined in the American Psychiatric Association *Diagnostic and Statistical Manual of Mental Disorders,* Fifth Edition (*DSM-5*) and includes persisting symptoms of "negativistic, defiant, disobedient, and hostile behaviors toward authority figures." A child with ODD may argue frequently with adults, lose his temper easily, refuse to follow rules, blame others for his own mistakes, deliberately annoy others, and otherwise behave in angry, resentful, and vindictive ways. A child with ODD is likely to encounter frequent social conflicts and require disciplinary situations at school. Without early diagnosis and treatment ODD symptoms tend to worsen over time. Many mental health specialists believe that ODD sometimes becomes so severe enough that it evolves into CD.

Conduct Disorder

Conduct disorder is a more extreme condition than ODD. The *DSM-5* describes CD as "a repetitive and persistent pattern of behavior in which the basic rights of others or major age-appropriate social rules are violated." Conduct disorder may involve serious aggression toward people, hurting animals, deliberately destroying property or vandalism, stealing, running away from home, skipping school, or otherwise trying to break rules without getting caught.

As noted, many children with CD were or could have been diagnosed with ODD at an earlier age, especially those who were physically aggressive when they were younger. As the CD symptoms become evident, these children usually retain their ODD symptoms, such as argumentativeness or resisting authority, as well.

This cluster of behaviors, combined with the impulsiveness and hyperactivity of ADHD, may cause these children to be suspended from school and have more police contact than children and adolescents with ADHD alone or ADHD with ODD and not CD. Children with ADHD whose CD symptoms started at an early age also tend to fare more poorly in adulthood than those with ADHD alone or ADHD with ODD, particularly in the areas of delinquency, illegal behavior, and substance use.

Early and effective treatment can prevent later problems of delinquency, illegal behavior, and substance use. Treatment frequently requires even greater coordination among parents, schools, primary care and mental health caregivers, human services, and, in some cases, law enforcement.

Oppositional Defiant Disorder and Conduct Disorder: What to Look For

A child with ADHD and a coexisting disruptive behavior disorder is likely to be similar to a child with ADHD alone in terms of intelligence, medical history, and neurologic development. He may be no more impulsive than children with ADHD alone. But if he has CD, his teachers or other adults may misinterpret his aggressive behavior as ADHD-type impulsiveness. This is not correct. The behavior of children with ADHD does not typically involve this level of aggression.

A child with ADHD and CD does have a greater chance of experiencing learning disabilities, such as reading disorders and verbal impairment. But what distinguishes children with ODD and CD most from children with ADHD alone is their defiant, resistant, and, in the case of CD, aggressive, cruel, or delinquent behavior.

Other indicators to look for include

- **Relatives with ADHD/ODD, ADHD/CD, depressive disorder, or anxiety disorder.** A child with family members with ADHD/ODD or ADHD/CD should be watched for ADHD/CD as well. Chances of developing CD are also greater if family members have experienced depressive, anxiety, or learning disorders.
- **Stress or conflict in the family.** Divorce, separation, substance use, parental criminal activity, or serious conflicts within the family are common among children

with ADHD and coexisting ODD or CD. Traumatic experiences resulting in PTSD can also contribute to the child's behavior.

- **Poor or no positive response to the behavior therapy techniques at home and at school.** If your child defies your instructions, violates time-out procedures, and otherwise refuses to cooperate with your use of appropriate behavior therapy techniques, and his aggressive behavior continues, he should be evaluated for coexisting ODD or CD.

Disruptive Mood Dysregulation

Disruptive mood dysregulation is a newly defined disorder with severe recurring temper outbursts characterized by verbal anger and rage and physical aggression with persistent irritability. It is diagnosed in children between 6 and 10 years of age and, although it has behaviors such as anger and aggression that are seen in children with ODD or CD, it is considered a disorder of mood and is not felt to occur with ODD.

Treatment

Children with ADHD and disruptive behavior disorders often benefit from special behavioral techniques that are implemented at home and at school. These approaches typically include methods for teaching your child to become more aware of his own anger cues and using these cues as signals to initiate various coping strategies, such as, "Take 5 deep breaths and think about the 3 best choices for how to respond before lashing out at a teacher." In addition, it is important to teach him how to provide himself with positive reinforcement for successful self-control; for example, telling himself, "Good job, you felt the signal and used your strategies!"

You and your child's teachers, meanwhile, can learn to better manage ODD- or CD-type behavior through negotiating, compromising, and problem-solving with your child. Anticipating and avoiding potentially explosive situations is useful. Learning to prioritize goals is also important so that less important problems can be ignored until the more concerning issues have been successfully addressed. These highly specific techniques can be taught by behavior therapists or other mental health professionals recommended by your child's pediatric clinician, school psychologist, or other professionals involved with your family.

If your child has been diagnosed with coexisting ODD or CD, schools are mandated to educate your child in a mainstream classroom if possible. Special educators will then regularly review your child's education plan and reassess the appropriateness of his placement. It is very advisable, if possible, to keep your child in an environment where appropriate behaviors are being modeled every day, rather than a special classroom where inappropriate behaviors may be more frequent. However, should well-planned classroom behavioral techniques in his regular classroom not be helpful, it may be important to consider placement in a special classroom at school that is set up for more intensive behavior management.

There is growing evidence that the same stimulant medications that improve the core ADHD symptoms may also help with coexisting ODD and CD. Stimulants have been shown to help decrease verbal and physical aggression, negative peer interactions, stealing, and vandalism. Although stimulant medications do not teach children new skills, such as helping them identify and respond appropriately to others' social signals, they may decrease the aggression that stands in the way of forming relationships with others their age. For this reason, stimulants are usually the first choice in a medication treatment approach for children with ADHD and a coexisting disruptive behavior disorder.

It is of value to introduce stimulants early to treat coexisting ODD or CD. By treating these behaviors in elementary school or even earlier, you may have a better chance of preventing your child from creating a negative self-identity. Untreated, he may start to identify with others who experience discipline problems. By adolescence, he may resist treatment that could help him change his behavior and make him less popular among these friends. He will have grown accustomed to his defiant self and may feel uncomfortable and not like himself when stimulants help keep his reckless, authority-flaunting style in check.

If your child has been treated with 2 or more types of stimulants and his aggressive symptoms are the same or worse, his pediatrician may choose to reevaluate the situation and replace the stimulants with other medications. If stimulant medication alone led to some but not enough improvement, his pediatrician may continue to pre-scribe stimulants in combination with one of these other agents. Finding and learning behavioral management methods that work, however, is always a central approach for an overall treatment plan. More intense services, including a child psychiatrist and child psychologist, may be needed. Disruptive mood dysregulation may need treatment with medications used for anxiety or depression if behavioral intervention is not sufficient.

Measures Parents Can Take for Oppositional Defiance and Conduct Problems

Promote daily positive messages to your child.

- Praise compliant behavior—"catch them being good."
- Encourage praise and rewards for specific, agreed on, desired or target behaviors.

Focus on prevention in the following ways:

- When possible, reorganize your child's day to prevent trouble by avoiding situations in which he cannot control himself. Examples include asking a neighbor to look after your child while you go shopping, ensuring that activities are available for long car journeys, and arranging activities in separate rooms for siblings who are prone to fight.
- Monitor the whereabouts of adolescents. Telephone the parents of friends whom they say they are visiting. Find ways to limit contact with friends who have behavior problems and promote contact with friends who are a positive influence.
- Talk to the school and ask that similar principles are applied. Request that the school watch for learning problems if you suspect this is a possibility. The frustration experienced by the child with a learning problem may be intolerable for him.

Be calm and consistent.

- Set clear house rules and give short, specific commands about the desired behavior, not prohibitions about undesired behavior. "Please walk slowly," is more likely to be effective than "Don't run."

- Provide consistent, appropriate, and calm consequences for poor behavioral choices. Try to maintain a calm tone of voice.
- When enforcing a rule, avoid getting into arguments or explanations because this merely provides additional attention for the inappropriate behavior.

Create a safety and emergency plan.

- Develop a list of telephone numbers to call in the event that the child's behavior causes a threat to his own safety or the safety of others.
- Remove weapons from the home before there is any chance of a problem.
- Watch for situations that trigger outbursts and avoid them if possible.
- Gather the telephone numbers for hotlines, on-call telephone numbers for your pediatric clinician's practice, or area mental health crisis response team contact information.

Modified from American Academy of Pediatrics Task Force on Mental Health. *Addressing Mental Health Concerns in Primary Care: A Clinician's Toolkit* [CD-ROM]. Elk Grove Village, IL: American Academy of Pediatrics; 2010.

Anxiety Disorders

There is also a great deal of overlap between anxiety disorders and ADHD. About one-fourth of children with ADHD also have an anxiety disorder. Likewise, about one-fourth of children with anxiety disorders have ADHD. This includes all types of anxiety disorders—generalized anxiety disorder, OCD, separation anxiety, and phobias including social anxiety. Younger children who are generally overanxious or have great anxiety when separated from family or friends are more likely to also have ADHD.

Anxiety disorders are often more difficult to recognize than disruptive behavior disorders because anxious symptoms are *internalized*. *Anxiety* often exist within the mind of the child rather than in outward or *externalized* behaviors, like verbal outbursts or pushing others to be first in line. An anxious child may be experiencing guilt, fear, or even irritability and yet not be noticed by a parent, teacher, or pediatric clinician. Only when his symptoms are expressed in actual behavior, such as sleeplessness or refusal to attend school, will he attract the attention he needs. It is important to ask your child's pediatric clinician or psychologist to talk with your child directly if you suspect the presence of persistent anxiety in addition to his ADHD.

Anxiety Disorders: What to Look For

Identifying an anxiety disorder in your child can be difficult not only because his symptoms may be internal but also because certain signs of anxiety may be misinterpreted as symptoms of ADHD. This is especially the case for symptoms of restlessness and poor concentration. With only ADHD, there is usually a general lack of focus or a restless response to boredom. For children with an anxiety disorder, anxiety and worry usually focuses on specific situations or thoughts. They may seem tense, irritable, tired, or stressed out. They may not sleep well and may even experience brief panic attacks—involving a pounding heart, difficulty breathing, nausea, shaking, and intense fears—that occur for no apparent reason. Many times, anxiety shows up as physical complaints of stomachache or headache.

While their school performance may be similar to that of children with ADHD alone, they tend to experience a wider variety of social difficulties and have more problems at school than children with ADHD alone. At the same time, they may behave in less disruptive ways than children with ADHD alone because their anxiety may inhibit spontaneous or impulsive behavior. Instead, they may tend to seem inefficient or distracted and have a great deal of difficulty remembering facts or processing concepts or ideas.

Your child can be an important source of information that may lead to a diagnosis of anxiety disorder. However, many children are anxiously reluctant to admit to any symptoms even if they are quite significant. If the possibility of an anxiety disorder concerns you, be sure to discuss with your child any fears or worries he has and listen carefully to his response. Report his comments to his pediatric clinician or psychologist. Encourage him to speak directly with these professionals. In the meantime, ask yourself

- **Did frightening or stressful experiences occur earlier in his life?** Experiences such as loss of a loved one or exposure to violence can later cause emotional distress, including PTSD. Symptoms may resemble symptoms of ADHD.

- **Does he seem excessively worried or anxious about a number of situations or activities, such as peer relationships or school performance?** Are his fears largely irrational, overly exaggerated, or unrealistic? Or are they realistic worries about punishment for negative behavior? Does he find it difficult to control his worrying?

- **Does his anxiety lead to restlessness, fatigue, difficulty concentrating, irritability, tense muscles, or sleep disturbance?**

- **Does his anxiety or its outward symptoms significantly impair his social, academic, or other functioning?**

- **Does his anxiety occur more days than not and continue for a significant duration?** Have his anxiety symptoms lasted for at least 6 months? Do his bouts of anxiety occur at least 3 to 5 times per week and last for at least an hour?

- **Is his anxiety caused by another disorder, substance abuse disorder, or other identifiable cause?** A child who is distressed over a life event, who is abusing drugs, or whose family is in conflict may exhibit symptoms of anxiety disorder. It is important to consider these other causes as the reason for anxiety. Anxious symptoms can be a reaction to a life event rather than be caused by an actual anxiety disorder.

- **As a young child, did he experience developmental delays or severe anxiety at being separated from a parent, express frequent or numerous fears, or experience unusual stress?** Children with ADHD and a coexisting anxiety disorder are more likely to have experienced developmental delays in early childhood or more stressful life events such as parental divorce or separation.

- **Have others in his family been diagnosed with anxiety disorders?** Anxiety disorders tend to run in families. A careful review of your family's medical history may provide insight into your child's condition.

These are some symptoms of anxiety disorders, and their presence may indicate a need to have your child evaluated by his pediatric or mental health clinician. Proper and effective treatment of anxiety allows your child to improve his functioning and balance in his daily life.

Treatment

Treatment for children with ADHD and an anxiety disorder relies on a combination of approaches geared to each child's specific situation. Comprehensive anxiety treatment begins with educating the child and his family about the condition. Behavior therapy is initiated, including cognitive behavior techniques, and family therapy is sometimes also necessary. Antianxiety medications may be considered. Ongoing input from school personnel is valuable.

Behavior therapies, like cognitive behavior therapy (CBT), are among the most proven and effective non-medication treatments for anxiety disorders. The effectiveness of traditional psychotherapy has been less well studied. Behavior therapies target *changing the child's behaviors* caused by the anxiety rather than focusing on the child's internal conflicts as in psychotherapy. Cognitive behavior therapy techniques help children *restructure their thoughts* into a more positive framework so that they can become more assertive and increase their level of positive functioning. For example, a child can learn to identify anxious feelings and thoughts, recognize how his body feels when it responds to anxiety, and devise a plan to mentally cut down on these symptoms when they appear. Other behavioral techniques that can be used for treating anxiety include modeling appropriate behaviors, role-playing, relaxation techniques, and gradual desensitization to the specific experiences that make a given child anxious.

Decisions about medication treatment for ADHD and a coexisting anxiety disorder depend largely on the relative difficulty of each condition. In the Multimodal Treatment of Attention Deficit Hyperactivity Disorder Study of large numbers of children with ADHD and various coexisting conditions, behavioral treatments were equally as effective as medication treatment for children with ADHD and parent-reported anxiety symptoms. It was not known, however, how many of these children had true anxiety disorders.

In general, if your child's ADHD symptoms interfere with his functioning more than the anxiety does, and a medication is needed, his pediatric clinician may choose to begin treating him with a stimulant. As the clinician adjusts your child's dosage for maximal effect, the clinician will monitor your child for side effects, such as jitteriness or overfocusing, which can be undesired responses to stimulants among children with ADHD and an anxiety disorder. If your child begins taking stimulant medication, his coexisting anxiety symptoms may often decrease, while at the same time there is improvement in the ADHD itself. The anxious symptoms may have actually stemmed from the ADHD-related behavior and not be a sign of an anxiety disorder. On the other hand, if the ADHD symptoms improve but your child's anxiety remains, his pediatric clinician may decide to add another type of medication. These medications are often in the class known as selective serotonin reuptake inhibitors (SSRIs).

Measures That Parents Can Take for Their Child's Anxiety

- Identify your child's worries and fears. Help your child set goals for reducing symptoms.
  - Learn strategies to improve coping skills, like deep breathing, muscle relaxation, positive self-talk, anxious thought stopping, or thinking of a safe place.
  - Ask your pediatric clinician to recommend informational materials that might be helpful.
- One of the best-validated approaches to anxiety and phobias is to *gradually increase exposure* to the feared objects or experiences. The eventual goal is to master rather than avoid feared things.
  - Start out with brief exposure to the feared object or activity and gradually make it longer.
- Imagine or talk about the feared object or activity or look at pictures.
- Learn to tolerate a short exposure.
- Tolerate a longer exposure in a group or with a coach.
- Tolerate the feared activity alone but with a chance to get help if needed.
  - During these trials you need to stay as calm and confident as possible. Otherwise, you will cue for your child to become distressed.
  - For some children who are vulnerable to anxiety disorder, it is necessary to promptly return them to the anxiety-producing situation. School phobia is an example.
- Make sure that this avoidance is not due to bullying, trauma, learning difficulties, or medical conditions that may be contributing to stress and fear.
- Partner with school personnel to manage your child's return to school.
- Gently but firmly insist that your child attend school, coupled with positive feedback and calm support.
- If you are uncomfortable with any of these recommendations, seek help from your pediatric clinician or a mental health specialist.

- Work with your child to give the fear a name, like "the worry bully." Teach your child that the worry bully is not the boss; help him learn to "boss it back!"
- Reward brave behavior. Give positive feedback or small rewards for displaying brave behavior.
- Pay attention to your own parenting style.
  - You probably don't always have to remind an anxious child to be careful when playing.
  - Be sure that you or the other parent controls his or her own anxiety and stays calm while helping the anxious child.
  - Children can become anxious if parents are inconsistent about rules and expectations.
  - Try to eliminate factors that increase anxiety, like, "I know Dad will get angry if I bring home a bad grade."
  - Be aware of and correct your child's unrealistic thinking, such as, "I know that the only reason Mom and Dad work hard is so I can go to a better school, so I'm afraid that if I don't do well...."

Modified from American Academy of Pediatrics Task Force on Mental Health. *Addressing Mental Health Concerns in Primary Care: A Clinician's Toolkit* [CD-ROM]. Elk Grove Village, IL: American Academy of Pediatrics; 2010.

Mood Disorders

Like anxiety disorders, depressive and other mood disorders may be subtle, with internal symptoms that can be difficult to recognize until seen in outward behavior. Mood disorders occur in 15% to 20% of children with ADHD. Children with ADHD often have difficulty with irritability, moodiness, and emotional immaturity and tend to overreact to disappointments or frustration. However, these problems can also be seen with depression. If symptoms are severe or interfere with functioning, evaluation for a mood disorder is recommended.

Types of Mood Disorders

The mood disorders most likely to be experienced by children with ADHD include dysthymic disorder, MDD, and, rarely, bipolar disorder. Dysthymic disorder is a chronic low-grade depression, with persistent irritability, feeling demoralized, and low self-esteem. Major depressive disorder is a more extreme form of depression. It often comes on suddenly. It is seen in children with ADHD and even more frequently among adults with ADHD. Dysthymic disorder and MDD typically develop several years after a child is diagnosed with ADHD and, if left untreated, may worsen over time.

Bipolar disorder is a much less common and severe disorder that does not usually show up until late adolescence or adulthood. Disruptive mood dysregulation, discussed previously with the disruptive behavior disorders, is also considered a mood disorder. Many children with bipolar disorder also qualify for a diagnosis of ADHD.

What to Look For

Every child feels discouraged or acts irritable once in a while. Children with ADHD, who so often must deal with extra challenges at school and with peers, may exhibit these behaviors more than most. However, if your child feels depressed or seems irritable or sad *a large portion of each day, more days than not,* he may have a coexisting dysthymic disorder. To be diagnosed with dysthymic disorder, a child must also have at least 2 of the following symptoms:

- Poor appetite or overeating
- Insomnia or excessive sleeping
- Low energy or fatigue
- Low self-esteem
- Poor concentration or difficulty making decisions
- Feelings of hopelessness

For dysthymic disorder to be diagnosed, children must have had these symptoms for a year or longer, although symptoms may have improved for up to 2 months at a time within that year. And with dysthymic disorder, the symptoms must not be caused by another mood disorder, a medical condition, or substance abuse disorder. If low self-esteem stemming from poor functioning in school is the cause of the sadness, the problem is likely related to ADHD itself rather than dysthymic disorder. Finally, the symptoms must be shown to significantly impair your child's social, academic, or other areas of functioning in daily life. Your child's pediatrician or mental health professional can help consider this diagnosis.

In contrast with dysthymic disorder, MDD is marked by a *nearly constant* depressed or irritable mood or a marked loss of interest or pleasure in *all or nearly all* daily activities. Children may look happy at times and be able to play but may still be experiencing symptoms. In addition to the symptoms listed previously for dysthymic disorder, a child with MDD may cry daily or withdraw from others and become extremely self-critical. He might talk about dying or even think about, plan, or carry out a suicide attempt.

Unlike the brief outbursts of temper exhibited by a child with ODD who does not get his way, the irritability of a child with depression may be nearly constant and will not appear to have any clear cause. His inability to concentrate differs from ADHD-type inattention in that it is accompanied by other symptoms of depression, such as loss of appetite or loss of interest in favorite activities. Finally, the depression itself stems from no apparent cause, as opposed to becoming depressed in response to parental divorce or any other stressful situation. Research has shown that the composition of a child's family and its socioeconomic status have little or no effect on whether a child develops MDD.

While children with ADHD and CD alone are not at higher than normal risk for attempting suicide, children with ADHD and CD who also have an MDD are more likely to make a suicide attempt and should be carefully watched. Substance use further increases risk. Being impulsive increases the risk of suicide. **If your child speaks of suicide, even if you are not sure if it is serious, remove guns from your home.** The most effective way to prevent unintentional gun injuries, suicide, and homicide to children and adolescents, research shows, is the absence of guns from homes and communities. The American Academy of Pediatrics advises that the safest home for a child is one without guns. If there is a suicide attempt, self-injury, any violent behavior, or severe withdrawal, this should be considered an emergency that requires the urgent attention of your child's pediatric clinician, mental health professional, or local hospital.

A child with depression may admit to feeling guilty or sad, or he may deny having any problems. Many depressed children refuse to admit to their feelings, and parents can easily miss the subtle behaviors that signal a mood disorder. Keep your child in close contact with his teacher and therapist, if he has one; bring him to each of his treatment reviews with his pediatric clinician; and include him in all discussions of his treatment that are appropriate for his age. In this way, he will have more opportunities to talk about his feelings and his pediatric clinician or mental health professional might detect signs of a developing depression.

A child with bipolar disorder and ADHD is prone to explosive outbursts and extreme mood swings of high, low, or mixed mood. Severe behavioral problems, chronic irritability, and grandiose thinking or actions can be the most prominent features. A child with bipolar disorder is often highly impulsive and aggressive. His prolonged outbursts typically come out of nowhere or in response to trivial frustrations. He may have a history of anxiety. He may also have an extremely high energy level and may experience racing thoughts with inflated self-esteem or grandiose thinking, extreme talkativeness, physical and emotional agitation, overly sexualized behavior, or a reduced need for sleep. These symptoms can alternate with periods of depression or irritability, during which his behavior resembles that of a child with MDD. A child with ADHD and bipolar disorder usually also has poor social skills. Family relationships can be very strained because of the child's extremely unpredictable, aggressive, or defiant behavior. Early on the symptoms may only occur at home, but, as the child gets older, they may occur in other settings as well.

Bipolar disorder is a serious psychiatric disorder that can sometimes include psychotic symptoms of delusions and hallucinations. Self-injurious behavior, such as cutting, suicidal thoughts and impulses, and substance use, are also common. Many children with bipolar disorder have a family history of bipolar disorder, mood disorder, ADHD, or substance abuse disorder. Children with ADHD and bipolar disorder are at higher risk than those with ADHD alone for substance abuse disorder and other serious problems during adolescence.

If your child has ADHD with coexisting bipolar disorder, his pediatric clinician may refer him to a child psychiatrist for further assessment, diagnosis, and recommendations for treatment.

Treatment

Helping a child with ADHD and depression requires a broad approach. Treatment approaches will include CBT. Traditional psychotherapy to help with self-understanding, identification of feelings, improving self-esteem, changing patterns of behavior, interpersonal interactions, and coping with conflicts, or perhaps interpersonal therapy focusing on areas of grief, interpersonal relationships, disputes, life transitions, and personal difficulties, might also be recommended. Family therapy may also be needed.

Medication management again begins with treating the most disabling condition first. If your child's ADHD-related symptoms are causing most of his functioning problems, or the signs of depression are not completely clear, your child's pediatric clinician is likely to start with stimulant medication to treat the ADHD. As depressive symptoms often stem from poor functioning due to ADHD and not to a depressive disorder, stimulants may diminish the symptoms of sad mood as the ADHD symptoms improve. If this is the case treatment might be continued with stimulant treatment alone.

If your child's ADHD symptoms improve but his depression remains the same, even after a reasonable trial of the psychotherapies described previously, his pediatric clinician may add an antidepressant medication, most commonly an SSRI. This class of medications includes fluoxetine (eg, Prozac), sertraline (eg, Zoloft), and others. If this approach is unsuccessful, you may be referred to a developmental-behavioral pediatrician or a psychiatrist, who may try other classes of medications.

Recent experience in treating children and adolescents with depression includes a third component: lifestyle. Regular exercise, attention to sleep habits, and a healthy—or, at least, healthier—diet all help reduce symptoms. Alcohol and drugs, especially marijuana, make depressive symptoms worse. Focus on strengths and consider mindfulness meditation. Those with depression can be helped to realize that taking care of yourself really works.

Depression

Measures That Parents Can Take

Consider the Environment

- **Think about whether there are grief and loss issues in your child and/or other family members.** Grief and loss are common childhood experiences. Children vary widely in their reactions to these events, depending on their developmental level, temperament, prior state of mental health, coping mechanisms, parents' responses, and support system. Seek supportive counseling if grief does not seem to be resolving appropriately.

- **Reduce stress.** Your family can work to try to reduce stresses and increase support for your child or adolescent. This may involve reasonable and short-term changes in demands and responsibilities for your child, including negotiating extensions for assignment due dates or other ways of reducing stress at school. It may also include seeking help for others in the family who are distressed.

  If you as a parent are grieving a loss or manifesting symptoms of depression, it is particularly important that you address your own needs as you find additional support for your child and other family members.

- **Guns and other weapons should be removed from the home, and medications, over-the-counter drugs (including acetaminophen or Tylenol), and alcohol should be removed from the home, destroyed, or secured.**

Educate Your Family

- Your child is not making the symptoms up.
- What looks like laziness or crossness can be symptoms of depression.
- There is often a family history of depression; talking about this may reduce stigma and increase empathy in other family members.
- Depression is very common and not the result of lack of coping ability or personal strength.
- The hopelessness of depression is a symptom, not an accurate reflection of reality. However, this negative view of the world and of future possibilities can be hard to penetrate.

■ Treatment works, though it can take several weeks for improvement, and the affected individual is often the last person to recognize that it has taken place.

Help Your Child to Develop Cognitive and Coping Skills

■ Many negative thoughts can be empathetically challenged and looked at from another perspective.

■ Relaxation techniques and visualization, like practicing relaxing cued by a pleasant memory or imagining being in a pleasant place, can be helpful for sleep and for anxiety-provoking situations.

■ Take advantage of what your child already does to feel better or relax and, if appropriate, encourage more of that (behavioral activation). Encourage a focus on strengths rather than weaknesses. Encourage doing more of what the teen is good at.

Help Your Child to Develop Problem-solving Skills

■ Determine what small, achievable steps would help your child feel that he is on the way to overcoming his problems.

■ You might suggest that your child begin to list out difficulties, prioritize them, and concentrate efforts on one issue one small step at a time.

Rehearse Behavior and Social Skills

■ Reactions to particular situations or people may often seem to trigger or maintain low mood. If these triggers can be identified, try to assist your child in developing and practicing alternative responses to try to prevent reacting with sadness.

■ Encourage your child to practice doing things and thinking thoughts that improve mood.

Create a Safety and Emergency Plan

■ Develop a list of telephone numbers to call in the event of a sudden increase in distress.

■ Remove weapons and other potentially lethal products from your home.

■ Watch for risk factors for suicide, such as increased agitation, stressors, loss of rational thinking, and expressed wishes to die.

■ If your child is starting a medication for depression, develop a monitoring schedule with his pediatric clinician.

■ Post a list of contact numbers for suicide or depression hotlines, on-call telephone numbers for your pediatric clinician, and contact information for the area mental health crisis response team.

Modified from American Academy of Pediatrics Task Force on Mental Health. *Addressing Mental Health Concerns in Primary Care: A Clinician's Toolkit* [CD-ROM]. Elk Grove Village, IL: American Academy of Pediatrics; 2010.

Motor Disorders: Tics, Tourette Syndrome, and Obsessive-Compulsive Disorder

Tics are rapid, repetitive movements or vocal utterances. They may be motor, like excessive eye blinking, or vocal, such as a habitual cough or chronic repetitive throat-clearing noises. Chronic tics continue throughout childhood; transient tics last less than 1 to 2 years. In children who eventually develop tic disorders and ADHD, the ADHD usually develops 2 to 3 years before the tics.

Tourette syndrome, which is quite rare, is a more severe form of tic disorder that involves *both* motor and vocal tics that occur many times per day and cause dysfunction. The average age at which the tics associated with Tourette syndrome appear is 7 years, and they usually diminish after puberty. While most of the children with Tourette syndrome may develop ADHD, the 2 disorders are separate and independent conditions. Attention-deficit/hyperactivity disorder is not a variant of Tourette syndrome, and Tourette syndrome is not just a variety of ADHD. Research has shown that chronic tic disorders, Tourette syndrome, and OCD may stem from some common factors, and a child with any of these conditions is quite likely to also have ADHD.

Obsessive-compulsive disorder involves such symptoms as obsessive thoughts (eg, a highly exaggerated fear of germs) and compulsive behaviors (eg, excessive handwashing in an attempt to reduce the fear of germs). In this disorder the child is unable to control or limit the obsessions and compulsions. In this sense, OCD is similar to tic disorders and Tourette syndrome and creates additional functioning problems for children with ADHD. Many children and teens with OCD recognize that these thoughts are weird or silly but are still forced to have to ask or do them.

What to Look For

Tics tend to resemble certain ADHD-related symptoms—fidgeting and making random noises in particular—and may occasionally be mistaken for signs of ADHD. True tics, however, differ from ADHD-type fidgetiness or hyperactivity in that they almost always involve rapid, repeated, identical movements of the face or shoulders, or vocal sounds or phrases that may cause a child to become socially isolated. The diagnosis of Tourette syndrome is made only when the tics developed before 18 years of age include motor and vocal tics, occur many times each day, and continue for at least 1 year. Individuals can control the tics for brief periods. Although the intensity of the tics may increase or decrease periodically, a child with active Tourette syndrome is rarely completely tic-free for more than 3 months at a time. Tourette syndrome may also resolve by itself, without any explanation.

While tic disorders and Tourette syndrome involve outbursts of simple movements or vocalizations, OCD consists of obsessive thoughts and compulsive behaviors. In contrast with the common childhood "obsessions" with computer games or television, OCD-type obsessive thoughts and behaviors provide no pleasure and stem from no rational desire or motivation. Rather, they occur because the child is unable to stop them, even when he realizes that they are inappropriate—and they can interfere with his functioning for literally hours a day.

Treatment

Mild or transient tics may not need to be treated with any medication. Stimulant medications do not cause Tourette syndrome or even increase tics in most children with ADHD. In the past, stimulant medications were not recommended for children with ADHD and a coexisting tic disorder because the stimulant medications were thought to be a possible cause of Tourette syndrome. Actually, stimulant medications may result in improvements in the tics in some cases.

It is recognized that stimulant medications *at high doses* may bring out or exaggerate tics in a child with ADHD. Research has shown that these children would have eventually developed tics even without stimulant medications. The potential disadvantage of mildly increased tics is often outweighed by the positive effects of stimulant medications in treating the symptoms of ADHD. Lowering the stimulant medication dose or switching to a different medication can sometimes decrease or eliminate some tics altogether. If your child's tics are especially severe or socially disruptive, a combination of stimulant medication and clonidine, guanfacine, or other medications may also be considered. Possible side effects must be taken into account when using any of these medications.

Learning, Motor Skills, and Communication Disorders

Most learning problems encountered by children with ADHD are not due to learning disabilities. About 40% of children with ADHD experience learning challenges, such as work production problems and organizational difficulties, that are categorized as learning "problems," not disabilities. Learning disabilities are generally thought of as a child's failure to develop specific academic skills at the expected level, in spite of adequate intelligence and education. Attention-deficit/hyperactivity disorder itself is not a learning disorder; with proper treatment and support, many children with ADHD can perform as well as their peers academically. The true incidence of coexisting learning disabilities is not clear because of discrepancies in how they are defined, and estimates vary widely.

Although there is increasing controversy about how learning differences and disorders should be defined, they have been defined in the past by showing that there is a significant discrepancy between a child's cognitive abilities, as measured by standard measures of intellectual function or IQ tests, and his actual learning, which is assessed with specific testing of achievement in reading, math, and written expression. With learning disabilities, the child's skills lag behind what his intelligence predicted he would be able to accomplish. There are problems with this "discrepancy" model. Few characteristics differentiate poor readers whose skills differ from those predicted by their IQ scores and would be labeled learning disabled from those children whose reading skills match their IQ scores. In addition, the amount of difference between IQ scores and measured achievement in reading is not necessarily related to the severity of the learning disability. It also does not predict the potential for gain from reading interventions, the reading level of a child over time, or how a child will respond to any given reading program. Using a discrepancy model, children with low average IQs and commensurate low average achievement would not qualify for services, in spite of the evidence that they would benefit.

Since 2004 school districts are no longer required to use the discrepancy model to show that a student has a specific learning disability. Schools can now use measures that are more relevant to the instruction students receive in the classroom. School districts can determine if a student responds to scientifically based interventions as a part of the evaluation procedures. Response to intervention (RTI) is an example of this kind of process. In RTI, students who show signs of learning difficulties are provided with a series of increasingly intensive, individualized instructional or behavioral interventions.

Disorders That Interfere With Academic Functioning

Specific Learning Disorders

1. Difficulty reading, eg, inaccurate, slow, and only with much effort
2. Difficulty understanding the meaning of what is read
3. Difficulty with spelling
4. Difficulty with written expression, eg, problems with grammar, punctuation, or organization
5. Difficulty understanding number concepts, number facts, or calculation
6. Difficulty with mathematical reasoning, eg, applying math concepts or solving math problems

Specific learning disorders can vary in severity.

- **Mild:** Some difficulties with learning in 1 or 2 academic areas but may be able to compensate
- **Moderate:** Significant difficulties with learning, requiring some specialized teaching and some accommodations or supportive services
- **Severe:** Severe difficulties with learning, affecting several academic areas and requiring ongoing intensive specialized teaching

Motor Skills Disorder
Developmental coordination disorder

Communication Disorders
- Expressive language disorders, eg, difficulties with using language to express oneself, including having a limited amount of speech, limited range of vocabulary, difficulty acquiring new words, using appropriate grammar, etc
- Mixed receptive-expressive language disorders, eg, difficulty understanding and using language, words, sentences, or specific types of words
- Phonologic disorders, eg, difficulty with pronunciation or articulation of speech sounds
- Stuttering

Medical Disorders
- Hearing deficits
- Vision deficits
- Chronic illnesses

Derived from American Psychiatric Association. *Diagnostic and Statistical Manual of Mental Disorders.* 5th ed. Washington, DC: American Psychiatric Association; 2013.

Learning Disorders

Reading Disorders

Reading disorders are the most common and best studied of the learning disabilities that account for 80% of all children diagnosed as learning disabled. Children with reading disorders are able to visualize letters and words but have difficulty recognizing that letters and combinations of letters represent different sounds. Most reading disorders involve difficulties with recognizing single words rather than with reading comprehension. The cause often lies in the area of the child's *phonologic awareness,* or difficulty perceiving how sounds make up words. Reading disorders—even including letter reversals—have little to do with vision. These problems make it quite difficult for children to add new words to their reading repertoire and become good readers. While their listening and speaking skills may be adequate, they may have trouble naming objects, such as quickly coming up with the word for "computer" or "backpack" or remembering verbal sequences like, "The boy saw the man who was driving the red car." A smaller group of children also have reading disabilities that involve comprehension. These children tend to also have poor receptive language skills; that is, difficulty understanding language even when it is spoken to them. A reading disorder, depending on how it is defined, is not necessarily a lifelong condition, but these problems do persist into adulthood in at least 40% of children.

Like all other learning disabilities, reading disorders cannot be detected through neurologic tests, such as special examinations, electroencephalograms or brain wave tests, or brain scans like computed tomography and magnetic resonance imaging. They are identified when a child's reading level or language achievement scores are significantly lower than those of his classmates. In assessing reading disabilities, it is important to identify each component of your child's problem so that specific treatment measures can be given. It is also important to address the attentional and behavioral aspects of the ADHD so that your child can make optimal progress at school.

Mathematics Disorder

Mathematics disorder is a type of learning disability in which spoken language is not affected but computational math is. Children with mathematics disorder also may have difficulties with motor and spatial, organizational, and social skills. Children with coexisting ADHD, or even ADHD alone, can have problems in math without a mathematics disorder. Attention-deficit/hyperactivity disorder can involve delays in committing math facts to memory, making impulsive or careless math errors, rushing through problems and impulsively putting down the wrong answers or not showing work, or making errors because columns were misaligned during addition or long division.

Although math disabilities are about as common as reading disabilities, they are not well studied. It is generally agreed on that children with mathematics disability have trouble recalling math facts. Accurate and fluent recall of single-digit math facts is believed to be important in freeing up higher brain areas for learning and applying more complex tasks. Children with both reading and math disabilities struggle particularly with word problem-solving.

Written Expression Disorder

Children with written expression disorder can have difficulty composing sentences and paragraphs. They have trouble organizing paragraphs and using correct grammar, punctuation, and spelling in their written work. Writing legibly can be a struggle. Children with spoken-language problems can develop problems with written language as well as math.

Children with ADHD can also have difficulty with taking the mental time to plan their writing, and their handwriting can be immature and sometimes unreadable without

Being in touch with your child's learning abilities will allow you to provide the support she needs to succeed in the classroom.

necessarily having a written expression disorder. When handwriting problems are more a function of ADHD than a written expression or motor skills disorder, they sometimes improve rapidly and dramatically with appropriate stimulant medication treatment.

Nonverbal Learning Disability

Nonverbal learning disability (NLD) is a condition that is not yet formally categorized as a disorder but that has been the subject of increasing interest. It is particularly important to consider in children with ADHD because it relates to attentional functioning. It is often difficult to decide whether a child with ADHD has a coexisting NLD or whether he just has an NLD that mimics ADHD, especially the inattentive symptoms.

Nonverbal learning disability consists of a cluster of deficits, including poor visuospatial skills, problems with social skills, and impaired math ability. In some cases this makes children with NLD difficult to differentiate from children with high-functioning ASD. Problems with disorganization, inconsistent school performance, and social problems may lead to an evaluation for ADHD.

General functioning in children with NLD who are younger than 4 years can be relatively typical or only involve mild deficits. Following this period, children with NLD can develop disruptive behavior and may develop hyperactivity and inattention. They are frequently thought of as acting out and hyperactive and are commonly identified by their teachers as overtalkative, troublemakers, or behavior problems. As they grow older, their high activity level can disappear. By older childhood and early adolescence, problems can tend to be more internal, characterized by withdrawal, anxiety, depression, unusual behaviors, and social skills problems. Interactions with other children may become more difficult, and their faces can seem unexpressive. These behaviors can be accompanied by deficits in how they judge social situations, judgment, and interaction skills.

Children with NLD are particularly prone to emotional problems over the course of their development, more so than children with other learning disabilities. They frequently develop symptoms of depression and anxiety.

Nonverbal learning disabilities are less prevalent than language-based learning disorders. Where it is estimated that about 4% to 20% of the general population have identifiable learning disabilities, it is thought that only 1% to 10% of those individuals would be found to have NLD. Nonverbal learning disability is often not identified until late elementary school or middle school, when peer problems increase and academic tasks become more complicated.

Academic Problems

As was pointed out earlier in this chapter, children with ADHD frequently experience significant challenges at school and elsewhere that cannot be formally categorized as disabilities or formal disorders. As many as 40% of children with ADHD, for example, who do not qualify for a diagnosis of learning disability still experience learning problems that can lead to underachievement at school. These learning problems may include

- Inattention and distractibility
- Lack of persistence and inconsistent performance
- A tendency to become easily bored or to rush through or not complete work
- Impulsive responses and careless errors
- Difficulty self-correcting mistakes
- A limited ability to sit still and listen
- Difficulty with time-limited tasks and test taking
- Problems with planning, homework flow, and work completion
- Difficulty taking notes or performing other forms of multitasking
- Difficulty memorizing facts
- Difficulty organizing and producing written work
- Immature and slow handwriting that can also create obstacles in expressive writing
- Difficulty with reading comprehension

Stimulant medications that improve your child's ADHD symptoms are likely to help him address many of these problems. Behavior therapy techniques aimed at increasing or decreasing specific behaviors at home and in school can also prove beneficial for learning. As discussed in chapters 5 and 7, completion of assignments or other specific behavioral goals can be addressed by understanding your child's individual strengths and weaknesses and collaborating with school staff. Helpful supports may include using positive reinforcement, appropriate behavioral techniques, daily report cards, and ongoing monitoring.

Motor Skills Disorder

Motor skills disorder, also known as developmental coordination disorder, is diagnosed when motor skill problems significantly interfere with academic achievement or activities of daily living. It is frequently overlooked in children with ADHD due to its nonspecific cluster of symptoms, yet it can affect children's lives by interfering with writing and other academic activities. It may also make it hard for children to participate at their classmates' level in sports and in play. Children with ADHD and other learning disabilities may also have motor skills disorder as well.

Motor skills disorder involves a developmental delay of movement and posture that leaves children with coordination substantially below that of others of their age and intelligence level. These children seem so clumsy and awkward they are rarely picked for teams at school. As the years pass, they tend to fall further behind in terms of motor skills, and their confidence diminishes. By adolescence, most children with motor skills disorder not only perform poorly in physical education classes but may also have a poor physical self-image and perform below expectations academically.

Motor skills disorder may be first identified when a preschooler or kindergartner is unable to perform age-appropriate skills, such as buttoning buttons and catching a ball, or when an elementary school child struggles with writing or sports activities. A child with motor skills disorder may have difficulty with the mechanics of writing, with planning motor actions, or with memorizing motor patterns. While many young children with ADHD but no motor skills disorder may seem clumsy in their younger years, their awkwardness is related more to inattentiveness or impulsivity than to poor motor control and is frequently outgrown. However, a child with ADHD and coexisting motor skills disorder may not outgrow his clumsiness.

If your child is diagnosed with developmental coordination disorder, he may be referred to a pediatric occupational therapist for individualized therapy and, particularly if his deficits negatively affect his academic performance or daily skills, be recommended for special gym activities at school to promote hand-eye coordination and motor development and improve specific skills. It also helps to direct him to individual physical activities that can be less competitive, such as martial arts, swimming, running, or bike riding.

Communication Disorders

Communication disorders are conditions that interfere with communications with others in everyday life. They involve not only the ability to appreciate language sounds (phonologic awareness) but also to acquire, recall, and use vocabulary (semantics) and to deal with word order and appropriately form or comprehend sentences (syntax). Subcategories of these disorders have been identified, including expressive language disorder, mixed receptive-expressive disorder, phonologic disorder, articulation (word pronunciation) disorder, and stuttering.

Because there is such a close association between communication and social relationships, these language deficits are often accompanied by social skill difficulties. Children with ADHD without a language disorder may also have difficulties in using language, particularly in social situations. You may notice that your child has problems with excessive talking, frequent interruption, not listening to what is said, blurting out answers before questions are finished, and having disorganized conversations.

Treatment

Treatments for learning disabilities that lead to strong outcomes include learning (cognitive) strategies; changing learning behaviors, which is a cognitive-behavioral approach; and breaking down tasks into smaller teachable units, known as task analytic methods.

Cognitive strategies target processes that are directly linked to academic skills and encourage academic strategies. Cognitive models target information-processing abilities, such as using memory, as well as developing skills directly linked to academics, such as awareness of how words are constructed (phonologic awareness). *Cognitive-behavioral approaches* combine these approaches with behavioral principles used during teacher-directed instruction. Cognitive-behavioral strategies help students with self-regulation by forming positive attitudes about themselves and their academic capabilities. In this manner children with learning differences also master strategies that form the basis for their own effective academic performance. *Task analytic methods* teach effective direct instruction methods and emphasize providing a student with well-specified learning objectives and detailed sequences of instructional steps.

However, if too much class time is spent dealing with behaviors and self-regulation issues, little academic learning will occur because there is no time to teach the academic content. When students are pulled out for special education academic instruction, this might pose problems when returning to the classroom if the student does not understand what the class is doing. Therefore, it is important to carefully balance out-of-classroom activities with the need to acquire the academic content being taught in the classroom.

Children with a learning, motor skills, or communication disability may require tutoring, an in-class aide or other classroom support, an altered curriculum, special education classes, speech-language therapy, occupational therapy, or adaptive physical education. Many children with ADHD benefit from a positive behavior management plan. As described in Chapter 7, many of these services must be provided free of charge by your school district if your child qualifies for coverage by the Individuals With Disabilities Education Act or Section 504. Your child's pediatric clinician can also refer your child to private sources for evaluation and help.

While stimulant medication does not improve the academic achievement of children with learning disabilities alone, it can help children who have both learning disabilities and ADHD improve their reading performance and work completion by helping them improve their attention and focus during these tasks. This is most likely due to stimulant medications' positive effect on children's attentiveness, which allows them to benefit more from special tutoring and other forms of therapy. Thus, use of stimulant medications to treat ADHD symptoms is often recommended as an important part of treatment for ADHD with coexisting learning disabilities.

Intellectual Disability

Most forms of intellectual disability (no longer called mental retardation) are recognized early in a child's life with failure to achieve standard developmental milestones at appropriate ages. However, at early ages, developmental delays do not necessarily predict that intellectual disabilities will be present when a child reaches school age. A given child's predicted abilities (IQ) cannot be measured until school age. An average IQ is 100; intellectual disabilities are diagnosed in the 2% to 3% of children who score the lowest on a standard IQ test and are delayed to the same extent in such life skills as self-care, self-direction, and the use of academic skills. Eighty-five percent of children with intellectual disability fall into the mild range, with IQ scores from 70 to 55. Intellectual disabilities are often suspected within the first few years after birth if children are experiencing lags in the rate of their development in social, self-help, motor skills, and language development. Children with milder forms of intellectual disability may escape detection until their school years, when parents or teachers begin to wonder if their difficulties in learning signal the presence of ADHD or learning disabilities and parents bring them to a pediatric clinician for evaluation. In the past, physicians did not believe that ADHD occurred in children with intellectual disabilities. As a result, treatments for ADHD, including stimulant medications, were rarely used to treat children who actually had ADHD and coexisting intellectual disabilities. However, as many as 25% to 40% of children with intellectual disability also have ADHD, significantly more than in the general population.

Treatment for children with intellectual disability includes

- Family support
- Family education and counseling
- Special educational programs
- Paying attention to transitional needs and educational rights
- Identifying community supports and support groups
- Paying close attention to your child's strengths and abilities

Autism Spectrum Disorder

Autism spectrum disorder is characterized by significant deficits in social understanding, delays in communication and unusual use of language, and unusual restricted and repetitive interests or behaviors. The latest estimate of prevalence of ASD is 1 child in 59. Schools can designate children as qualifying for services under the category of ASD, although a significant number of children identified for these services do not have an ASD diagnosis by strict diagnostic standards. About half of children with ASD also have intellectual disabilities.

The number of children with ASD and ADHD is difficult to determine because children with ASD alone often have elements of attention problems, impulsiveness, and hyperactivity. A child with ASD may also have intellectual disability, but even if he does not, his challenges associated with ASD are likely to prevent him from participating fully socially and in many school and home activities. The most severe form of ASD, autistic disorder or autism, involves severe language and social impairment and abnormal, repetitive, and unusual patterns of behavior. Autistic disorder usually becomes manifest by age 2 to 3 years. Children with ASD are unable to form typical social relationships with others. Coexisting ADHD can add a significant overlay of aggressive, impulsive, or hyperactive symptoms to the behavior of a child with ASD, although it is not always easy to separate the ADHD behaviors from those related to ASD itself.

There are some children with ASD who are of average to above-average intelligence and are able to function adequately in many aspects of daily life. They do not have a history of language delays but have difficulty making conversation and using polite manners and may have an unusual tone of voice. They experience significant disabilities in social interaction with peers and display unusually intense and narrow interests or obsessions. This was previously described as Asperger syndrome but is now referred to as high-functioning ASD. Many of these children will have coexisting ADHD.

Treatment

Individualized educational programming, behavior therapy, and family support are essential elements in the treatment of children with ASD. Identifying children with ASD early is critical because intensive early interventions of 20 hours per week or more have been demonstrated to lead to very significant gains in connecting with the social world and developing language, communication, and cognitive skills. Medication may be helpful for specific symptoms. Stimulant medications can be used to treat ADHD symptoms in children with combined ASD and ADHD, although the rates of side effects and nonresponse are somewhat greater than in those with ADHD alone. Most children with ASD and coexisting ADHD may need special education–related services, such as speech-language therapy, occupational therapy, and behavior management programs. You can further support your child's progress by educating yourself about his condition, monitoring the latest research on his areas of disability, and advocating for his rights and appropriate services within the public school system. See Chapter 7 for descriptions of resources and laws relating to student disabilities.

Coexisting Problems

Children with ADHD may have problems in some of the areas described previously even though they fall short of receiving formal diagnoses in these areas. You should not hesitate to confer with your child's pediatric clinician, teachers, mental health professionals, and community support agencies to seek help even if your child falls short of receiving a formal diagnosis. Not having a formal diagnosis certainly does not mean that no help is needed.

Recognizing Coexisting Strengths

Finally, but *most* importantly, don't forget to pay attention to your child's coexisting strengths. The main focus should always be on your child, and not on his challenges, disabilities, and coexisting conditions. Children with ADHD frequently meet with disapproval, social rejection, and other forms of discouragement. However, if encouraged to grow up aware of and invested in their own talents, strengths, positive energy, and achievements, they can mature with a healthy and balanced perspective and better self-esteem as they head toward productive and successful adult lives.

CHAPTER 10

Complementary and Alternative Treatments for ADHD

In this book you have been introduced to the treatment approaches that have been proven most effective for children with attention-deficit/hyperactivity disorder (ADHD). You are also likely to read or hear about complementary and alternative treatments. In this chapter we will define and discuss these treatments.

Complementary treatments are meant to be used in conjunction with the multimodal treatments already discussed in this book. They are added to the usual effective medication and/or sound psychosocial or behavioral treatments. They are often used by parents for children who have not experienced sufficient improvement despite standard treatments or who have symptoms not addressed by the primary treatments, such as irritability or mood swings. They are also used by parents who want to enhance their child's overall health and well-being while they are treating the child for ADHD.

Alternative treatments are those that claim to be as effective, or more effective, than prescription medications and the scientifically sound psychosocial/behavioral treatments for the core symptoms of ADHD that you have read about. These types of treatments are often used by parents for children who have not experienced sufficient improvement in spite of standard treatments, who are uncomfortable with the idea of daily medication use, or who want to explore all possible avenues of treatment for their child. Some of these treatments have the additional attraction of being proposed as "cures" or "natural treatments." The theories on which they are based may make a great deal of intuitive sense as well; for example, when they target a child's diet to treat hyperactivity or his hearing to help attention. The question with these treatments, as with more traditional treatments, is whether they have been shown to reliably produce positive and sustained effects for most children with ADHD. Some have actually been proven ineffective or even harmful. Others may or may not eventually be demonstrated to have a positive effect but have not yet been studied sufficiently for their use to be recommended at this time.

Because the claims for ADHD treatments are so vast and so varied, it is important to subject any report of a new or an unconventional treatment approach to the same scrutiny and consideration you would apply to any major decision affecting your family: by considering the source of the information, the reasonableness of its claims, and the scientific evidence that backs them up, and by discussing the treatment with experts in the field, such as your child's pediatrician or psychologist. In this chapter you will learn how to consider the validity of claims for ADHD treatments by

- Knowing what target behaviors the proposed treatment claims to address
- Understanding how a proposed treatment is scientifically evaluated and what steps must be taken to prove that a treatment is sound
- Reviewing the evidence for and against proposed ADHD treatments, such as dietary changes; visual, auditory, and sensory integration approaches; hypnotherapy; biofeedback; applied kinesiology; homeopathy; and various other methods
- Considering the types of questions you should ask, and the steps you should take, before committing effort, time, and money to a new form of treatment, however promising it may seem

As part of your consideration of any measure, you might see if evidence is available on a given treatment from the National Center for Complementary and Integrative Health at the National Institutes of Health. Some of this information is contained on its website at https://nccih.nih.gov. You might also want to inquire whether a particular treatment will be paid for through your health insurance.

How Treatments Are Proven Effective

You may have noticed that the media seem to report on a new treatment for ADHD frequently. If so, you may wonder why so many alternative treatments exist for ADHD, and why they so easily gain credibility with the general public. One reason is that, as opposed to such medical conditions as diabetes, the results of a given treatment for ADHD are difficult to measure objectively; that is, there is no blood, urine, or other laboratory test that can prove conclusively that the treatment has worked. Instead, as you will see, the effectiveness of treatments for ADHD are judged through rigorous studies of groups undergoing the treatment compared with those who are not. Because effects of these treatments are determined through relatively subjective methods, such as changes in teachers' and parents' observations, and ratings of behaviors over time— not by objective blood, urine, or magnetic resonance imaging studies—it is often more difficult, even with careful statistical analysis, to clearly establish that any proposed standard or alternative treatment for ADHD is well-founded. If a treatment cannot quickly and objectively be proven effective, it is easier for its proponents to just claim that it works. Thus, claims for a particular approach can be greatly exaggerated and widely disseminated long before it has been sufficiently studied.

How do the American Academy of Pediatrics (AAP) and your pediatric clinician decide which claim is really a study and which studies teach us useful information? There is a standard, reliable process for deciding whether a new treatment is effective. This process is called the *scientific method.* Through it, investigators can subject any treatment approach to a reliable series of tests or studies to evaluate its effectiveness. There is a great deal written these days about evidence-based medicine (EBM), which is a set of procedures, resources, and information tools for appraising the strength of the scientific evidence to assist practitioners in applying research findings to the care of individual patients. The medical community now expects treatments strongly recommended for ADHD to meet these EBM standards. Studies of treatments for ADHD conducted according to the scientific method make use of research tools, including structured observations, rating scales, and objective tests of the child's functioning, whenever possible. They are structured so that extraneous factors that might influence results are taken into account and designed so that they can be reproduced by other researchers to make sure similar results are achieved.

One of the tools that EBM has available is that of meta-analysis. *Meta-analysis* searches out all studies that have been done with rigorous methods, such as including placebos, following children as the study is proceeding (prospective), and where neither the investigator or the parents know if the treatment the child is receiving is the study treatment or the placebo (double-blind).

According to the scientific method and EBM, we can only rely on the results of studies relating to a particular treatment if the researchers have

- **Formulated a clear hypothesis.** The researchers must state what they want to determine through the study. For instance, they might state the hypothesis, "Because diet and nutrition are known to affect brain development, a diet fortified with extra vitamins will have a positive effect on ADHD symptoms." This, then will be proved or disproved by a well-conducted study.

- **Created a detailed plan to test the hypothesis.** The researchers must then define the nature of the treatment (eg, state which vitamins will be administered, at what dose, and how frequently), how it will be administered (eg, by parents, by a physician, by the children themselves), how it will be monitored (eg, by counting the number of pills left in the bottle at the end of the study), and how the effects will be measured (eg, through a daily dosage checklist, parents' reports, physicians' records, teacher observations, etc). In this way, the study results can be systematically explained (eg, perhaps it did not work because the children reported taking the vitamins but did not always do so), and other researchers can confirm the results by using the same methods with different sets of children.

If you become interested in using complementary and alternative treatments, be sure to discuss your plans first with your child's pediatric clinician.

- **Defined the group to be tested.** This is an important and sometimes difficult part of creating a reliable study. Can a child be allowed to participate in the study solely on the basis of whether he looks hyperactive to the researchers? Must he have been diagnosed by his pediatrician? Or have the researchers made their own diagnosis according to rigorous research criteria? The group under study must also be large enough for the treatment results to apply to the population as a whole; 1, 6, or even 100 children may not be enough, depending on the research question. The group receiving the treatment must be compared with a group not receiving the treatment and/or another group or groups receiving a different type of treatment for ADHD. The members of the groups under study should otherwise be as similar as possible, and children who might be affected by extraneous influences, such as coexisting conditions, high or low extremes in intelligence, and unusual family circumstances, are sometimes screened out. Depending on the question to be answered, the researchers must limit as many other variables as possible, aside from the treatment under study.

- **Eliminated the power of suggestion.** One way to test whether a treatment is effective is to compare the proposed treatment with a placebo treatment. People often tend to respond to placebos—inactive medications or treatments they believe may work—whether or not the treatment is actually effective in the long run. A person with a headache who is given a "sugar pill," believing it is pain medication, may report that the headache is gone a short time later. In many studies placebos can be shown to be somewhat or very effective. One way to test whether a treatment for ADHD is effective, for example, is to make sure that the subjects do not know whether they are really receiving the proposed treatment or a placebo treatment. In the vitamin treatment example, half the subjects in the study might receive actual megavitamins and the other half would receive an inactive, neutral, but identical-looking pill. Depending on the type of investigation, the study design may work even better if used in a double-blind experiment—that is, if the subject, his family, his teacher, and the researchers do not know whether the actual pill or a placebo was used in a particular patient until the study has ended. That way there is no danger that the researchers have inadvertently communicated this information to the subject, his family, or his teacher, or that the researchers misinterpreted the results because of what they knew. Of course, if the treatment has specific effects, such as an unusual taste difficult to mimic in the placebo, it may be impossible to keep everyone in the dark about which person got the experimental treatment. Placebo treatments are more difficult to create when the treatment involves a procedure, such as psychotherapy, rather than a pill. Still, researchers must make every effort to make the real treatment and the placebo treatment equally convincing to the subject. Having independent evaluators who are unaware of the treatment being used, called *blinded*, to whether the treatment is, for example, the megavitamin or the placebo preparation improves the accuracy of the study.

- **Monitored and reported adverse events.** Some treatments can be ineffective or, worse, harmful. It is important to know how the study monitors for adverse events and whether any participants dropped out of the treatment and why.

- **Provided a valid means of evaluating the results.** Some treatment results are easier to evaluate than others. As you've already read, in the case of ADHD, results can be difficult to judge because they cannot be measured through precise laboratory tests or other fully objective measures. Still, researchers can standardize test results through such techniques as counting specific behaviors (eg, having teachers report how many times per day a child interrupted a conversation, got out of his seat without permission, or failed to hear someone talking to him), using standard rating scales, comparing the study subjects' performance to that of the other groups in the study who received different treatments, and measuring changes in the behaviors being studied at predetermined intervals throughout the course of the investigation. Treatments can be evaluated by standardized tests (eg, performance on standardized math tests), as well as in terms of the child's performance in the real world (eg, measures of classroom behavior, improvements in family relationships). Rigorous statistical techniques are then used to find any significant differences in results among the groups in the study. The methods and results of any study are then reviewed by other experts in the field. This process, called *peer review*, is required before the study is published in a reputable scientific journal. If a treatment proves successful, it is also helpful to follow up with the children on the treatment for longer than the period that was studied to make sure that the beneficial results continue and do not cause any serious long-term side effects.

Which Treatments Have Been Shown to Work?

The treatments for ADHD supported by the strongest evidence are stimulant medications and behavior therapy techniques (eg, parent training in behavior management), often used together. These forms of treatment have been the most studied and validated by the types of rigorous scientific research described previously. For this reason, pediatric clinicians can feel secure in recommending these approaches as proven, safe, and effective—or, in other words, *evidence-based, first-line treatments* for ADHD.

Many other forms of treatment for ADHD have been tested in studies using the scientific method. Some, such as traditional psychotherapy and cognitive therapy, have been able to show through convincing research that they help in treating the condition's core symptoms. Another group of potential treatments for ADHD has been tested to a lesser extent so that the studies are too few in number or were conducted with some flaws in study designs, or the results were too ambiguous, to prove that the treatments work. Evidence of a treatment's effectiveness may be insufficient if the

- Studies involve too few subjects, so that results cannot be generalized to the ADHD population at large.
- "Proof" relies on anecdotal evidence, such as parents' testimonies or one pediatric clinician's experience with his or her own patients, rather than on a large group that has been part of a well-designed scientific study.
- Study results have not been subjected to the scrutiny of experts who would have reviewed the study prior to publication to identify any possible flaws in the study design or the results. This is called peer review, and it is an important indicator of quality.

In the following sections, you will find discussions of the evidence supporting or refuting the usefulness of a number of the most popular alternative approaches to treating ADHD and associated problems (Table 10.1). Some of these approaches have simply not been studied. Others are based on inaccurate assumptions about the nature of ADHD or its causes and are, therefore, unlikely ever to lead to an effective treatment. Still others may eventually be shown to have a significant positive effect, though the current supporting evidence is insufficient, and information about safety is limited.

In examining the facts behind the theories, you can not only learn more about these particular treatments but can also become more comfortable in critically assessing future proposed ADHD treatments on your own.

Table 10.1. A Parents' Guide to Medical Study and Evidence-Based Medicine		
Term	Definition	Comment
Study hypothesis	What question the study tries to answer	Beware of conclusions that were not part of the study hypothesis.
Placebo	An inactive treatment that looks like the medicine being studied	It needs to look and feel the same to the patient.
N	The number of subjects or patients in the study	The bigger the N, the better the study. Be cautious if the N is small.
Randomized controlled trial (RCT)	The patients studied are randomly assigned to receive drug or placebo.	RCTs with a large N are better able to prove a treatment's value.
Quality of evidence (QOE)	An assessment of how strong the value of the experimental data are	See the US Preventive Services Task Force QOE tables.
Proof of efficacy	Evidence for effectiveness and value	*These are proven treatments.*
Proof of harm	Evidence of danger	*These treatments should always be avoided.*
Insufficient evidence for recommendation	Studies either do not exist or cannot tell if a treatment has value.	*These treatments should be considered only if there is no other option and then be carefully considered.*

Your Child's Diet: A Cause and a Cure?

It is easy to understand the temptation to attribute ADHD-type behaviors to some dietary causes or to believe that particular changes in diet can diminish the symptoms related to the condition. Add to this a widespread concern about the effects of sugar, artificial additives, and other elements in children's diets and it is no wonder that special diets have become the most popular alternative to medication and behavior therapy treatment for

ADHD. Recent scientific research has, in fact, supported the belief that eating properly can lower the risk for heart disease and other chronic conditions.

Certainly, concerns about nutrition are valid for all children and should not be dismissed. It is also true that some forms of dietary management, and the addition of some trace elements through special supplements, may help with some specific health- or behavior-related problems and, thus, are a sensible complementary approach. However, as you will see, none of the special diets designed to treat the symptoms of ADHD have yet been conclusively shown to be effective for most children with the condition. The 2 dietary approaches most discussed for ADHD are adding to a child's diet nutritional supplements thought to be insufficient or missing from his diet and eliminating one or more foods from his diet.

Supplemental Diets

It stands to reason that an adequate diet is necessary for a child's healthy growth. Proper nutrition, including an array of vitamins, minerals, amino acids, and essential fatty acids, is particularly necessary in the first few years after birth to support brain development and prevent certain neurologic disorders. Even among older children, a lack of certain dietary components, such as protein, or an insufficient number of calories can negatively affect a child's learning and behavioral abilities, and vitamin or mineral deficiencies can certainly interfere with learning over the course of a school year. *After many years of consideration, there is no evidence that a poor diet causes ADHD or that dietary supplements can be used to successfully treat the condition.* Nonetheless, healthy eating and family meals are lifestyle choices generally supported by the AAP.

Megavitamin Therapy

In the 1950s Drs Abram Hoffer and Humphry Osmond began using megavitamins containing large amounts of vitamin B_3, vitamin C, and, later, pyridoxine (vitamin B_6) to treat schizophrenia. This treatment was based on the now disproven and discarded theory that schizophrenia and some other forms of mental illness are caused by a genetic abnormality that greatly increases the body's vitamin and mineral requirements. By providing patients with enormous doses (megadoses) of these substances, Hoffer and Osmond felt that psychiatrists could provide an "optimum molecular environment for the mind" in which the symptoms of mental illness would diminish or disappear.

In the 1960s the chemist and Nobel Laureate Linus Pauling put his support behind this theory, giving it the name *orthomolecular psychiatry* and greatly increasing its visibility among experts and the general public. In the 1970s Dr Allan Cott claimed that hyperactivity and learning disabilities were also the result of vitamin deficiencies and could be alleviated with megavitamins and large doses of minerals. Treating ADHD symptoms in children with nutritional supplements—supplements that contained at least 10 times the recommended daily allowance of vitamins, minerals, and other necessary elements—became an increasingly popular alternative to stimulant medication, particularly among families who considered megavitamins the more "natural" approach.

Research has failed, however, to reveal significant positive results from megavitamin therapy for children with ADHD. While some early studies resulted in improved classroom attention ratings for subjects taking megavitamins, these studies were marred by the fact that the children, their parents, their teachers, and the researchers were all aware that the child was being given this new form of treatment. When the studies were repeated using the double-blind method discussed earlier, so that no one knew whether a particular child was taking a megavitamin or a placebo, no behavioral improvement was shown. In fact, it was discovered that disruptive behavior increased in a significant number of the children given megavitamins. Studies have also suggested certain abnormalities in the way the liver functions among children on megavitamin therapy, signaling possible toxic effects of this high level of vitamin intake—a strong reminder that "natural" substances are not always safe, especially in the highly "unnatural" doses prescribed here. As a result, experts have concluded that megavitamin therapy for ADHD is of little benefit for nearly all children with the condition—and potentially harmful. In 1976 the AAP Committee on Nutrition issued a formal statement to that effect. No subsequent studies have provided evidence that would change this opinion. This is not to say that children with ADHD should not take any vitamins, just that vitamins at normal doses and even megadoses are not in any way an effective treatment for ADHD.

Other Vitamin and Mineral Supplements

In the wake of the enthusiasm for megavitamin therapy, a number of specific nutritional elements have been studied regarding their possible role in the development of ADHD and their potential for treating the condition. These elements include iron, magnesium, pyridoxine (vitamin B_6), and zinc.

All these substances are known to be necessary for optimal brain development and function. However, *no difference between children with or without ADHD has been shown for levels of zinc, iron, magnesium, or vitamin B_6, and no links between these low levels and ADHD-type behavior have been established to date.* No significant improvement in ADHD behaviors has been demonstrated when supplemental doses of these substances are provided. As with all children, any true nutritional deficiency should be corrected with a standard supplement or a change in daily diet. But supplementation should not exceed the daily recommended allowance because higher levels of some elements (zinc in particular) can prove toxic.

Additional Supplements to Improve Performance

A number of other dietary supplements have been proposed to replace the use of stimulants in treating ADHD. Principal among these are *nootropics, antioxidants,* and *herbs.* Nootropics, specifically a substance called piracetam, have been advocated as cognitive enhancers for children with Down syndrome, dyslexia, and ADHD. While there is no scientific proof of positive effects relating to Down syndrome, one convincing study did show improvement in reading ability and comprehension among children taking piracetam supplements. While there is a rational basis for theorizing that piracetam may also improve ADHD-type behaviors because it is believed to enhance the transmission of the same brain chemicals influenced by stimulant medication (dopamine and noradrenaline), no controlled studies have yet been published, so this treatment cannot be recommended.

Children with ADHD, as well as people who eat a modern American diet, may have low levels of certain essential fatty acids (including eicosapentaenoic acid [EPA] and docosahexaenoic acid [DHA]). In a study of nearly 100 boys, those with lower levels of omega-3 fatty acids had more learning and behavioral problems than boys with normal levels. Studies examining whether omega-3 fatty acids can help improve symptoms of ADHD have found mixed results. A few studies have found that omega-3 fatty acids helped improve behavioral symptoms, but most of these studies were not well designed. One study that looked at DHA in addition to stimulant therapy found no effect. More scientifically rigorous studies demonstrating beneficial effects clearly need to be found before omega-3 fatty acids can be recommended for children with ADHD. Deanol (DMAE), lecithin, and phosphatidylserine are other cognitive enhancers (nootropics) frequently found in over-the-counter ADHD remedies available in health food stores or on the internet. Lecithin, DMAE, and phosphatidylserine have not yet been sufficiently studied as treatments for this condition.

Antioxidants and herbs, used for many centuries in traditional medicine, have only recently come under scientific study. Some of the substances that have been marketed as treatments for ADHD include *pycnogenol,* an antioxidant derived from pine bark; *melatonin,* another antioxidant known to successfully treat sleep cycle disturbances in certain children; *gingko biloba extract,* often used in Europe to treat circulatory and memory disorders; and such herbs as *chamomile, valerian, lemon balm, kava, hops,* and *passion flower.* While melatonin can be useful in addressing sleep disturbances in a child with ADHD, and the herbs mentioned may also be useful as mild sleep aids, the reported positive effects of these antioxidants and herbs as treatments for ADHD core symptoms have been solely anecdotal so far, and there is insufficient scientific evidence to support their use.

If you do decide to administer any of these substances to your child, it is important to inform your child's pediatric clinician and then carefully monitor their use because some can lead to harmful effects if used in combination with other medications. Gingko biloba extract, for example, must not be taken with aspirin, anticoagulants, or antidepressants, and the herbs listed should not be used when taking sedative medications due to the danger of compounding the sedative's effects. It is necessary to keep in mind that these substances can vary considerably in potency from one preparation to another and that they are not standardized or regulated by the US Food and Drug Administration.

Elimination Diets

Other theories about the causes of, and treatment for, ADHD have evolved from the hypothesis that certain substances that are *present,* rather than absent, in a child's diet may lead to or worsen the condition. The suspected harmful substances include artificial food additives, preservatives, sugar, or other elements speculated to cause allergic responses or yeast infections that can lead to the development of ADHD. According to these theories, eliminating such elements may eliminate or diminish the symptoms of ADHD.

Feingold Diet

In the mid-1970s a groundswell of concern about the effects of food additives, artificial flavorings, and dyes in the American diet accounted for, in part at least, the huge popularity of the Feingold diet as a treatment for ADHD. Dr Benjamin Feingold, a practicing allergist, theorized that these food additives, as well as substances called *salicylates* (contained in many fruits and vegetables), were causing hyperactivity and learning disabilities in many children. In his book, *Why Your Child Is Hyperactive,* Dr Feingold claimed that when these children were given a special "elimination diet" that omitted these substances, half of them showed a dramatic improvement in behavior. When the elements were reintroduced into the children's diet, the symptoms returned. Most controlled studies do not support that elimination of these substances leads to better outcome for children with ADHD. Only about 2% of children with ADHD on the Feingold diet have shown consistent behavioral improvement when several specific food dyes were eliminated. However, reduction of processed foods that contain artificial dyes and substitution of healthy foods may, in general, promote better long-term health. Moreover, the parent training in behavior management strategies to change a child's eating behavior from frequent use of candies and processed foods to healthy choices are similar to the techniques that are used to improve concentration and increase work production. However, to change a child's eating habits without good behavior management techniques can lead to more conflicts and frustration not focused on improving a child's behavior challenges due to ADHD.

Diets Eliminating Sensitizing Food Substances

In the decades since the Feingold diet was introduced, studies of the effect of diet on behavioral disorders have become more sophisticated and reliable. Newer research has shown that behavioral improvement using elimination diets is more likely in children who have inhaled their food and have food allergies, a family history of migraines, and food reactivity. Younger children seem to be the most responsive. Whole foods like milk, nuts, wheat, fish, and soy have been implicated in addition to additives. Elimination diets can sometimes influence sleep and mood disturbances as well as ADHD symptoms. Sensitivities to substances in the environment—in medicines, clothes, water, our homes, the air, and so on—have also been studied as they relate to children's health and behavior. The results suggest a link between sensitizing foods and some health and behavior problems in a small percentage of children with ADHD. There is no evidence for this suggested link. In most cases, these children experience a variety of coexisting health and behavioral difficulties in addition to ADHD, particularly sleep-related and neurologic problems. They are also likely to have a family history of food sensitivities or migraine headaches.

Meanwhile, it is important to understand that for most children with ADHD who do not have food sensitivities (and for some who do), elimination diets are not effective treatments for ADHD itself. If your child is on a special diet, you will need to make sure it is not replacing a more effective treatment for ADHD symptoms. In most cases, stimulant medication, behavior therapy, and the other measures described in previous chapters will have a much clearer positive effect on your child's ADHD-related behaviors, while a well-balanced diet with few processed foods may improve his general health and attitude.

Sugar-Free Diets

Humans are naturally attracted to sugar because it tastes good and because our bodies rely on *glucose*—the form of sugar found in natural foods—for metabolic processes. Like many other children, those with ADHD often have strong sugar cravings, and this has contributed to the belief that sugar and candy consumption can cause hyperactive behavior. A great deal of objective evidence, however, has shown that this assumption is untrue for most children with or without ADHD. While one early study did reveal a link between high sugar consumption and hyperactive behavior, there was no evidence that one caused the other or that the behavior problems were not due to different parenting styles or other factors. A number of subsequent scientifically rigorous studies could not demonstrate any adverse effects of sugar on the behavior of children. As for children with ADHD, sugar consumption has not been shown to cause or enhance ADHD-related behavior.

Of course, allowing sugar only in moderation makes sense for any child. Again, assuming leadership within the family, making healthy choices about what is offered to the child, and using parent training in behavior management to educate children to reduce sugar and processed food may have general benefits. If your child shows an uncontrollable craving for sugar and carbohydrates, discuss this with his pediatric clinician. Aside from issues relating to general health, particularly its contribution to obesity and dental caries, a sugar-free diet is not considered a useful tool in treating ADHD. Researchers have found again and again that the simple elimination of sugar or candy, with few exceptions, does not help children with ADHD.

Sugar consumption has NOT been shown to cause or enhance ADHD-related behavior. Of course, allowing sugar only in moderation makes sense for any child.

Aspartame-Free Diet

Aspartame, an artificial sweetener that became available in the early 1980s, consists of amino acids that cross from the bloodstream into the brain to affect brain function. (Interestingly, it was used as the placebo in some of the studies of sugar's effects on behavior.) It was believed that among individuals susceptible to this substance, aspartame might lead to seizures or ADHD-type behaviors. No such effects have been demonstrated, however, and elimination of aspartame for children with ADHD is not considered an effective treatment except for children with phenylketonuria, a chemical disorder that prevents some people from being able to break down or metabolize aspartame.

Caffeine and Energy Drinks

Caffeine, which is present in coffee, tea, soft drinks, and energy drinks, is also a stimulant and has some similar effects as stimulant medications to treat ADHD. However, it is much less potent, and as the amount is increased it frequently causes jitteriness, usually making it ineffective in treating ADHD symptoms. It occurs in the highest concentration in energy drinks and coffee, less in tea, and the smallest amount in soft drinks. The high sugar and calorie content of these drinks are further reason to not consider them for your child.

Vision, Inner Ear, Auditory Integration, and Sensory Integration Problems

An entire class of theories about the causes of ADHD and effective treatments for it centers on the workings of the senses. Problems relating to sight, hearing, balance controlled by the inner ear, sensory integration, and so on have been proposed as underlying conditions that lead to ADHD and accompanying problems and disorders. Each theory is linked to a treatment approach, and each form of treatment is supported by a large number of vocal enthusiasts. The theory behind sensory integration therapy, done by occupational therapists, is that through structured and constant movement, a child's brain can learn to integrate and better react to sensory messages. There is, as yet, no evidence that it helps children with ADHD. One of the tools that EBM has available is that of *meta-analysis*. Meta-analyses of several disabling conditions have not found sensory integration to be significantly helpful. These studies did not include children with ADHD, and there is no evidence-based support at this time for its use with children who have been diagnosed with ADHD.

Optometric Training

Optometric training, a kind of eye training for children with learning disabilities, is based on the theory that faulty eye movements and problems in visual perception can cause dyslexia, language disorders, and other learning problems that frequently accompany ADHD. Named behavioral optometry by the optometrists who developed and support this form of therapy, the treatment consists of teaching children specific visual skills as a way of improving learning. These skills include tracking moving objects, fixating on or locating objects quickly and accurately, encouraging both eyes to work together successfully, and changing focus efficiently. The skills are taught through the use of eye exercises and special colored or prismatic lenses. Optometric training is often supplemented with training in academic skills, nutrition, and personal relationships. This treatment is frequently quite expensive.

Little research has supported the theory that dyslexia or other learning disabilities are caused by vision defects or problems; thus, vision training is an ineffective approach to reading and learning disabilities. Initially in 1984 and with subsequent updates, the AAP, along with the American Association for Pediatric Ophthalmology and Strabismus and the American Academy of Ophthalmology, issued a policy statement affirming that no known scientific evidence "supports the claims for improving the academic abilities of dyslexic or learning-disabled children with treatment based on visual training, including muscle exercises, ocular pursuit or tracking exercises, or glasses (with or without bifocals or prisms)."

Because vision training is not only ineffective but may delay more effective treatment for coexisting learning disabilities, it is not recommended. There have been no studies on optometric training for children with ADHD, despite its widespread use.

Interactive Metronome

Difficulties with auditory integration—that is, organizing, attending to, and making sense out of information while listening—have also been suspected as a cause of ADHD. One recent approach has been to use interactive metronome training.

The interactive metronome is a computerized version of the metronomes used by musicians to help train them to keep time at a constant rate. It produces a rhythmic beat that users attempt to match by tapping their hand or foot. The program gives children feedback on their accuracy. The theory behind this is that children will gain motor planning and timing skills. These skills have been found suboptimal in many children with ADHD. Incoordination is a frequent accompaniment to ADHD because children with ADHD often act motorically before thinking (ie, they are impulsive). Fine motor skills are sometimes helped considerably with stimulant medication. There is no evidence for effectiveness of this therapy improving or reducing hip-hop dancing skills in children with ADHD or their matched controls.

Neurofeedback, Hypnotherapy, and Guided Imagery

A number of proposed treatments for ADHD, including hypnotherapy, self-hypnosis, guided imagery, neurofeedback, and relaxation training, are aimed at helping a child begin to regulate his own behavior and psychological state. The fact that these techniques can be used quite successfully for children in other areas of self-regulation (eg, headache management, bowel control) increases their appeal as a form of treatment.

Hypnotherapy has not been shown to significantly improve the core symptoms of ADHD, though it may improve such accompanying problems as sleep difficulties and tics when used as part of an integrated treatment approach. One difference between the use of hypnotherapy for headaches versus ADHD is that children learn to institute the self-hypnosis at the early signs of a headache. There is no comparable "trigger" with ADHD, and children cannot do self-hypnosis all day long.

Neurofeedback treatment involves placing electrodes on a child's head to monitor brain activity. Children are asked, for example, to change the aspects of a video game (eg, "making the sun set with your mind"), which happens when their brain waves are of a desired frequency. The theory is that learning to do this increases their arousal levels, improves their attention, and results in reductions in hyperactive/impulsive behaviors. This is based on findings that many children with ADHD show low levels of arousal in frontal brain areas, with excess of theta (daydreamy) waves and deficit of beta waves (indicators of a highly focused mind), thereby reducing ADHD. The studies on the use of neurofeedback to date have been criticized for lacking a control or comparison and not having random assignment of children to the treatment or placebo treatment groups. It should also be pointed out that neurofeedback is an expensive approach to treating ADHD.

Homeopathy

Homeopathy, a therapeutic approach developed in the 1800s that is especially popular in Europe, springs from the concept that illness results from a disorder of "vital energies," and that these energies must be restored if a patient is to recover. Vital energies can be restored through the use of diluted animal, plant, or mineral extracts designed to treat specific symptoms. Homeopathic treatment for ADHD is increasingly widespread in the United States as individual accounts of success have spread. It cannot be recommended as a proven therapy at this time. If you do become interested in using this approach, be sure to discuss your plans first with your child's pediatric clinician. Some extracts can interact negatively with medications your child may be taking.

Chiropractic

Chiropractic is a system based on the theory that disease and disorders are caused by a misalignment of the bones, especially in the spine, that obstructs proper nerve functions and that adjustments and spinal manipulations can restore health. Some chiropractors believe that ADHD can be treated with spinal adjustments as well as sensory stimulation, including various frequencies of light and sound. Others believe that realigning the sphenoid bone at the base of the skull and the temporal bones on the side of the head can address the symptoms of ADHD and learning disabilities. The theory is that when these bones are misaligned, an unequal pressure is created in different brain areas. These treatments are not compatible with present views of the causes of ADHD and learning disorders, and there is no evidence for effectiveness of these approaches.

Using the Internet

An excellent source of medical information and valuable advice, the internet can also be the source of a great deal of dubious health-related theories, "facts," and testimonials. In searching the internet for information about a proposed ADHD treatment, or for any other information about ADHD and related conditions, it is always a good idea to start with the most reliable general information websites and expand from there.

A good way to quickly ascertain the reliability of an internet resource is to look at the suffix of its website address. Government information website addresses end in ".gov." These include sites such as the National Institutes of Health and the National Institute of Mental Health that have a wealth of health-related teaching materials for the general public. Professional, nonprofit, and advocacy organizations such as the AAP (www.aap.org) and CHADD: The National Resource on ADHD (www.chadd.org) have websites ending in ".org"; however, not all organizations put out materials as reliable as the materials from these 2 organizations. Academic websites have ".edu" suffixes on their internet addresses, and many of these have evidence-based educational materials geared toward parents. Websites with the suffixes ".com" generally are commercial websites that are not necessarily affiliated with an educational entity or a source of reliable information.

Take some time to look at these sites—and be sure to explore any website first before having your child follow its recommendations. Consult Table 10.1. Does the website you are looking at give you recommendations based on studies or stories? If studies, are they randomized controlled trials, and what is the N (the number of subjects or patients in the study)? Remember, randomized controlled trials with larger Ns are more trustworthy and perhaps deserve your attention.

On the other hand, does the website under consideration base its claims on stories, referred to as *anecdotes?* These are often called "testimonials," "parent experience," or another sometimes vague description of a patient's story. The teller of the story might passionately believe in his or her personal experience. But, as one pediatric EBM expert correctly commented, "The sum of anecdotes is not data!" By this she meant that even several convincing stories should be confirmed by study. Beware of testimonials used to promote any product; such testimonials may not always be real and factual.

New Remedies for ADHD: You Be the Judge

Claims about a new treatment can be difficult to resist. Who wouldn't love to find a "miraculous" new treatment that would completely eradicate the symptoms of ADHD and involve only healthy, "natural" substances that appear in our ordinary diet? Yet the very terms that tap into your longing to use them to conquer this condition—terms such as *cutting edge, amazing,* and *revolutionary*—should also serve as signals that it is time to take a hard look at the evidence that backs such claims up. Many of the proponents of these cures carry impressive initials after their names—many are "doctors" or "professors" of some kind. Many are sincere in their belief that they have found a major treatment or even a cure for this complex and often baffling disorder. Yet sincerity—even passionate belief—is not enough to render a treatment effective.

In reviewing the summaries of the popular ADHD-related theories and treatments described previously, you have seen how important it is to go beyond proponents' claims—no matter how convincing or intuitively "right" they may seem—to examine the scientific research backing up those assertions. As you encounter news of new proposed treatments for ADHD, ask yourself the following questions, provided by CHADD (see fact sheets at www.chadd.org):

Will it work for my child?

Suspect an unproven remedy if it

- Claims it will work for everyone with ADHD and other health problems
- Uses only case histories or testimonials as proof
- Cites only one study as proof
- Cites a study without a control (comparison) group

How safe is it?

Suspect an unproven remedy if it

- Comes without directions for proper use.
- Does not list contents.
- Has no information or warnings about side effects.
- Is described as harmless or natural. Remember, most medication is developed from natural sources, but "natural" treatments may still be ineffective or harmful. Remember As, atomic number 33, from your high school chemistry class: arsenic is a natural ingredient.

How is it promoted?

Suspect an unproven remedy if it

- Claims it is based on a secret formula
- Claims that it will work immediately and permanently for everyone with ADHD
- Is described as "astonishing," "miraculous," or an "amazing breakthrough"
- Claims it cures ADHD
- Is available from only one source
- Is promoted only through infomercials or self-promoting books, or by mail order
- Claims that treatment is being suppressed or unfairly attacked by the medical establishment

Even when an alternative treatment has been shown to be potentially useful for specific symptoms or behaviors that have been targeted for your child, it is important to consider, and to discuss with your child's pediatric clinician, whether it is more effective than already proven treatments, whether it may involve any uncomfortable or dangerous side effects or health hazards, how expensive it is, and how difficult it is for your family to implement. If your child's pediatric clinician is not knowledgeable about the approach in question, you will need to do much of the research yourself through the avenues discussed previously.

Keep in mind that the first and most important step in choosing the best treatment for your child is obtaining a full and accurate diagnosis of his ADHD and any coexisting problems or conditions. A standard medical evaluation is also necessary to learn whether your child could benefit from special treatment for any nutritional, vision, hearing, or other problem. Standard treatments, such as stimulant medication and behavioral therapy, should always be considered as first-line approaches for ADHD. If you, your child, and his treatment team prefer an alternative treatment, the scientific validity of the treatment and its appropriateness for your child need to be carefully reviewed, analyzed, and discussed.

Pediatric clinicians, like parents, have many different views of the role of complementary and alternative treatments for children diagnosed with ADHD. Physicians can play a constructive role in helping families make these kinds of treatment choices by reviewing the stated goals or effects claimed for a given treatment, the state of evidence to support or discourage use of the treatment, and a review of known or potential side effects. As you've seen from the material in this chapter, there are many categories of complementary and alternative treatments: those that have been found to be effective, those that have not been proven to be effective, those that have been shown to be ineffective, and those that can have dangerous effects or side effects. Common sense would lead to the approach of considering the use of proven treatments as the foundation of a sound plan, and then to consider treatments that are unproven, while avoiding treatments that can be dangerous. Parents may find themselves using treatments that have been shown to be ineffective from time to time and feel that they might be working but remain unsure.

If you choose to use some of these complementary treatments, it can be very helpful to introduce only one new treatment at a time in a systematic way. One suggestion for introducing the treatment is, before you start the treatment, to make a list of changes that you hope to see if it is effective. Make the items on your list countable (as suggested in other parts of this book); for example, "James will go from 40% missing assignments per week (his present baseline) to 25%." Also commit to the time frame in which you expect to see the change. For supplements and dietary manipulations you should be able to see differences within a month or two. For expensive treatments you may need to specify the funds you are willing to commit and then calculate the time frame based on that funding. After the designated amount of time, if these goals are achieved, stop the treatment and see if the number of missing assignments returns to the baseline number. If the problem reoccurs, start the treatment again and see if it improves again. Make sure that your own behavior remains neutral in this personal experiment so that your expectations do not alter the outcomes. Many of these complementary and alternative treatments can add structure, commitment, and hope to families' lives even if they are not totally healing.

CHAPTER 11

ADHD in Adolescence

For every teen, with or without attention-deficit/hyperactivity disorder (ADHD), adolescence is a time of important change—a time of transitioning from depending on and identifying with her family toward a separate, independent adult self. Research indicates that ADHD persists into adolescence and adulthood for at least 65% of children diagnosed with the condition. As the parent of a teenager with ADHD, you will need to understand and prepare for the many ways in which the typical developmental process can affect your teen's academic (school) and social performance and her relationship with you, as well as how ADHD may affect her overall development. In some cases, ADHD symptoms tend to become subtler during the teenage years, so treatment plans will need to be reviewed carefully and regularly.

Adolescence may seem to bring on a wider gap between the teenagers with ADHD and their peers. Studies of adolescents with ADHD have shown a significant lag in brain maturity, particularly in the prefrontal cortex. This is the area that is responsible for paying attention, planning motor activities like writing, and impulse control. This prefrontal cortex also provides the systems that temporarily store and manage the information required to carry out complex tasks such as learning, reasoning, and comprehension. It is absolutely important to respect your teenager's need to become progressively independent, but her independent successes may be slowed compared to her peers while she waits for her prefrontal cortex to fully develop.

Your teenager's medication plan will need regular review as her activities expand. Her willingness to take medication may waver if she feels this makes her "different" from her peers. The increasing demands of middle school and high school may require more attention to planning and staying organized, and changes in her educational plan should reflect this.

At home, your teenager may now respond negatively to parenting techniques you once found effective. Increased conflict is to be expected, as is true for all adolescents. The presence of ADHD may be accompanied by delays in the development of skills necessary to support an increasingly independent life.

Remember that your teen is a teenager first and foremost. Be careful not to overthink what part of her behavior is from "being a teenager" and what part is connected to ADHD. Teenagers are growing and developing daily, weekly, and monthly, in small and often imperceptible ways. Almost all will be responsible adults. Like other parents of adolescents, offer support, deal with the challenges along the way, provide love and praise, and wait while watching the process of maturation unfold. Remember that people with ADHD have to work hard, probably harder than those without it. If, as younger children, they learned that challenges of ADHD can be viewed as obstacles to overcome, rather than debilitating things that happen to them, they are better equipped to overcome future challenges.

Adolescence may, at times, be challenging for your entire family. But it is a time of great promise as your teenager begins to explore her potential as a unique human being, one who has a great deal to offer the world. Finding the ideal balance between protecting your teen and allowing her to become independent will be your task as you parent, yet there is nothing more exciting than watching your teenager start to fully accept, manage, and master her own situation. Your earlier efforts to help your child take control of her own progress will pay off as she enters early adulthood.

This chapter will outline the additional steps useful to

- Help your teenager meet new academic challenges.
- Help her manage new social and emotional pressures.
- Help you parent more effectively.
- Learn to take care of yourself as your teenager works on becoming more independent.

ADHD and Your Teenager's Development

Every teenager's developmental task is to begin the process of becoming an individual and creating a sense of self, which is separate from her identity with her family. A child's sense of her own uniqueness begins early in life, of course, but kicks into high gear at around age 11 or 12 years. An early step in this individuation process is for her to establish as clearly as possible the ways in which she is not like you. Her differences or boundaries from her family must be securely defined in a process described as *separation*. Separation and individuation will occupy much of your child's energy for the next few years. And as she masters these tasks, by later adolescence she begins to understand who she is.

Establishing a separate sense of self is not easy for the younger teenager. Even she may not always understand why she so frequently tunes you out, slams her bedroom door when she is angry, or hides her journal, and her own behavior may confuse or upset her at times. Our current understanding of brain development explains this. In the early teen years, the temporal lobes of the brain are developing, along with the strong feelings associated with temporal lobe function. But it is still a few years before the frontal or higher-thinking lobes come on line, bringing thoughtful modulation of stronger temporal lobe–generated feelings.

Now we can understand how your child's personal identity can be so fragile that even a minor threat, such as a parent's criticism or a sibling's teasing, may lead to extremely defensive behavior. At the same time, her developing sense of who she is can leave her vulnerable to peer pressure and other potentially negative outside influences. And with her ADHD-related behavior, she needs to be reminded that she is not bad or stupid but, rather, impulsive. She needs help in learning to stop and think. It sometimes helps to remind her of her friends and peers with asthma, diabetes, or other medical conditions who, like her, need to take steps to manage their condition.

While your teenager continues to mature, the typical adolescent's developmental tasks— her need to separate from her parents, define herself, fit in with her peers—put her at greater risk than in earlier childhood for academic failure; experimentation with tobacco or inhaled nicotine from vaping or Juuling, drugs, or alcohol; early sexual activity; and all the other possible adolescent behaviors that keep parents up at night. Most teenagers develop new strengths during these years that help them with decision-making on their own as their parents' influence starts to fade. They improve their ability to think long term, resist momentary impulses, and regulate their own behavior. Teenagers with ADHD experience the same need for independence as their peers, yet often lag in these areas.

Attention-deficit/hyperactivity disorder–related behaviors may actually increase the risk that your teen will impulsively engage in some of the self-defeating activities that other teenagers may be able to avoid. In part, this is because teenagers with ADHD can lack insight about their own functioning and may be less able to realistically assess their abilities than their peers. This makes self-management more difficult. Unfortunately, this occurs at exactly the time that they need to assume greater control of their lives.

The manner in which ADHD manifests during adolescence depends on its severity, subtype (predominantly hyperactive-impulsive–, inattentive-, or combined-type ADHD), and your teenager's particular profile of strengths and weaknesses. Her ADHD-related behavior is also strongly affected by her stage of development, her risk-taking behaviors, and the presence of any coexisting conditions, such as depression, learning disabilities, or anxiety disorder. The quality of her home and school environment can make an enormous difference in how well she functions in her daily life.

Teenagers with ADHD tend to behave in varying ways. A teenager who has participated in her ADHD treatment all along and experienced successes may show marked improvement at school and with friends as she grows able to help manage her own medication and take greater control of her areas of strength and weakness. A teenager with good verbal and language skills may have managed to keep up her grades and go undiagnosed for ADHD in elementary and middle school, but she may start to fail her high school courses as the demands for a high level of work production expose her organizational weaknesses. On the other hand, a teenager with hyperactive-impulsive–type ADHD and a coexisting disruptive behavior disorder may get into fights constantly at school and be suspended several times each semester, while another with inattentive-type ADHD and depression may fall behind in school, lose self-esteem, and escape special notice until she starts "self-medicating" with marijuana or alcohol.

Studies of boys and girls with ADHD have shown differences in their teenaged experience with their condition. Both girls and boys can and will do well, but they may have very different adolescent experiences. Compared with boys with ADHD, girls with ADHD report more anxiety, distress, and difficulty taking charge of their own problems. Compared with other girls, girls with ADHD are more likely to experience depression, anxiety, distress, poor teacher relationships, feelings that they cannot control their own fate, and more struggles with academics.

Each subtype of ADHD can present its own challenges during adolescence. By educating yourself about these issues and how they come into play in different ways for different teenagers, you can better support your teen as she proceeds through this new developmental stage.

Poor Impulse Control

Most adolescents often act impulsively, and teenagers are known for favoring short-term pleasures over long-term benefits. Teenagers with hyperactive-impulsive– or combined-type ADHD, however, can have more difficulty than their friends in regulating their impulses. Just like when she was younger, your teen may still act first and think later. But now the stakes are higher, and impulsiveness can potentially lead to substance use, aggressive behavior, unprotected sex, reckless driving, or other high-risk situations. Minor impulsive behaviors, like interrupting others or fidgeting at her desk, may cause academic or social problems for your teenager as others may not be aware of her ADHD and expect more mature behavior.

Is It Adolescence or ADHD?

When faced with a disruptive 14-year-old, a 10th-grader with a sudden drop in grades, or a high school junior who regularly ignores the curfews you impose, it is difficult to tell whether such behavior is part of normal adolescent development or an aspect of your teen's attention-deficit/hyperactivity disorder (ADHD). As was the case earlier in childhood, behaviors related to ADHD resemble those of teenagers without ADHD but can be more extreme and are likely to continue for months or years after they have diminished in peers who do not have ADHD.

Is it really important to know whether a particular behavior is or is not ADHD related? Your response in either case should be the same. Unacceptable behaviors need to be met with consistent limits and appropriate consequences. Your teenager's potentially greater difficulties with impulse control, focusing, and organizing and long-term planning may require extra consistency, structure, and thought on your part, but that is no different with or without ADHD.

It is important for you and your teenager to understand that behaving impulsively is not a failure on her part but an aspect of her ADHD that she will need to work on and that she may need help with. Your adolescent will benefit from learning about ways to minimize this problem behavior. Later in this chapter, you will find suggestions that may help with managing impulsiveness in your teenager's personal, academic, and social life.

Difficulty Focusing and Organizing

Teenagers with predominantly inattentive- or combined-type ADHD generally do not concentrate or sustain their attention as well as their classmates. At times they can find it almost impossible to focus on a class lecture, take good notes, or complete homework or other tasks. Others may characterize them as flighty, lazy, or a daydreamer, but these behaviors are aspects of ADHD, not willful behaviors or personality traits.

Such difficulties can get in the way of your teenager's desire to take greater control of her own academic success. She may start the school year determined to bring home excellent grades and then have no idea why she is struggling with her grades so much more than her peers. Difficulty with focus can also require increased effort to succeed socially or at a job. Help your teenager understand that extra support can be made available to help her achieve the higher demands of adolescence. Help her realize that this temporary support is a necessary step along the road toward independence.

Problems With Long-term Planning

The adolescent surge toward independence is accompanied by a burst of maturation. This helps most teenagers achieve their eventual goal of individuation. They become their own person. This development centers on what are called *executive functions*— the ability to plan ahead, conceptualize, and prioritize the steps necessary to reach a goal, and move systematically and non-impulsively toward that goal until it has been achieved. Teenagers with ADHD, however, often lag in this form of maturation. Executive function is developing in adolescents with ADHD but often 12 to 18 months slower than their peers.

As a result, while your teenager may be as determined as her peers to control her own destiny—wanting to get a job or apply to colleges all on her own—she may often need extra support in achieving these goals. Discuss ahead of time how you and others can help and support her to take the steps she needs to succeed. Help her understand that a key to being a truly self-sufficient person includes knowing when and how to seek assistance. Whether that involves scheduling a meeting with her teacher, asking a counselor for special guidance, or using a coach to help her organize and plan her homework, everyone from time to time will wisely ask for help.

Low Self-esteem

Teenagers with ADHD might experience a good deal of difficulty in academic, social, or personal areas. Even with your support and empathy, such experiences can decrease your teen's confidence and self-esteem. Low self-esteem may lead her to refuse medication, avoid special educational activities, or do anything else that might make her appear or feel different from her peers. Lack of confidence may also leave teenagers with ADHD more vulnerable to peer pressure regarding drug use or other dangerous behaviors as they try to prove they are just like anyone else.

Low self-esteem may also be a sign of depression. Depression affects many adolescents, and the risk is higher for those with ADHD. If low self-esteem appears to be associated with sadness lasting more than a few days or with social withdrawal, contact your teen's school guidance counselor or pediatric clinician. "Watch and wait" can be a dangerous approach to depression.

This is an age when teens need to be able to follow their passions and identify islands of competence. It is important to support these passions even if you have concerns about them. Not all our passions need to be work related for us to gain skills from them. Success in activities that interest them can help teenagers see that they are competent and can learn anything by applying the same persistence to school, or music, or whatever else interests them.

Independence Issues

All adolescents expect to attend parties, get a driver's license, and generally enjoy increasing amounts of privacy and independence with each passing year. Yet it is important for you and your teenager to understand that having ADHD can potentially

Make it clear that you support your teenager. It will mean a lot to your teenager to know that you will always be in her corner.

make some activities riskier, and these may need to be monitored more closely than for her peers without ADHD.

A teenager dealing with significant inattention problems, for example, may need to agree to drive only while her stimulant medication is in effect. If your teen's problems completing homework have led to poor or failing grades, she may need help with reviewing her work each night to be sure she has met her goals. Most teens resent and resist some of these potentially helpful measures because they want to be independent and in charge. But your teen relies on you to set and enforce necessary limits. You can make it easier for her to accept this continued dependence by problem-solving *with* her. In this manner you respect her needs by making sure that she is invited to help create the rules and routines that will help her achieve her own goals.

The increase in the use of social media and video games has added an additional challenge for teenagers with ADHD. Excessive use of social media and videogames beyond 2 hours a day can worsen a teen's attention span, increase her risk for obesity and depression, and worsen her sleep patterns.

Your Teenager's Treatment Plan

The best strategy for preparing your child to successfully manage any challenges of ADHD in adolescence begins in her preteen years when you invite her to be actively engaged in all elements of her treatment plan.

A Parent's Story

Feeling Involved

"We've always made it a point to have Seth be part of his school conferences and medical visits. When he was in grade school he dreaded his visits to his pediatrician to discuss his treatment.

"He would tell us, 'She always asks me the same questions about school and about my medicine and always tells me the same things about how my medicine works.' Then when he was about 11 she started meeting with him alone for part of our visits, and he would usually come out with a list of 3 or 4 things that he was going to work on. Eventually we began to notice that Seth was beginning to take more responsibility on his own for making sure that his homework got into his backpack before he left for school, and he would remind us if we forgot to put out his medication in the morning. By the time he was in 11th grade he had pretty much taken over the responsibility for his medication and even asked us if we could get him a coach/tutor to help him organize one of his long-term projects. We feel like we did something right by keeping him involved in his own treatment."

Joyce, Chicago, IL

Predictors of Success During Adolescence

Some of the most important factors in teenagers with attention-deficit/
hyperactivity disorder (ADHD) who do the best during adolescence include

- Parents and educators anticipate and address special needs.
- Self-understanding and acceptance of problems and issues.
- A supportive family.
- An understanding and developmentally attuned school system.
- An appropriate Individualized Education Program or Section 504 plan, if
  indicated.
- A willingness to engage in appropriate counseling, mentoring relationships, and
  "coaching" surrounding production and completion of work.

Some of the highest-risk factors leading to negative outcomes for teenagers with
ADHD include

- Delayed identification of difficulty, diagnosis, treatment, or adjustments
  in treatment
- An ongoing cycle of failure
- Serious behavior problems in school
- Substance use
- Medication refusal
- Damaged self-esteem resulting from failures or from problems being viewed as
  character flaws rather than ADHD-related behaviors
- Giving up or lack of motivation

Changing Treatment Needs

Throughout this book, you have been encouraged to continue addressing your child's
functioning problems and to meet regularly with her treatment team to reassess her
needs. This case management function becomes especially important as your child

enters adolescence and academic, social, and emotional pressures start to increase. As the parent of a teenager with ADHD, it will be important to have an agreed-on system to keep track of homework production and grades and also to arrange with teachers for regular, brief contact about progress. Weekly home-school report cards and other monitoring tools (see Chapter 7) used with younger teenagers can help reveal any academic or behavioral concerns before they become problems. Some of these efforts have been made easier through email and web-based communications among you, your teen, and her teacher on a regular basis. Often helpful changes in treatment or education programs can be easily applied. Chances are your teenager may object at some point to this level of scrutiny, which is more than her peers without ADHD probably receive; attention to her privacy is vital. And make sure that you provide ample opportunities for her to assert her autonomy in as many appropriate situations as possible and encourage her to direct as much of the monitoring system as is developmentally appropriate.

Aside from changing academic needs, many teenagers may experience greater social conflict and increased emotional stress during middle school and high school. You may hear about some of these problems—particularly disruptive behavioral issues—from school personnel. However, important changes may remain virtually invisible to you as a parent, such as depression and anxiety, increasing social rejection, or plunging self-esteem. As your child begins the typical adolescent process of separating from you described previously, she is less likely to confide in you about these types of problems. For this reason, it is important to have regular follow-up visits with her pediatric clinician, nurse practitioner, or other clinician or therapist. Be sure to allow time for your teen to meet privately with her pediatric clinician during every treatment review session to ensure that she receives a careful screening and discussion about these symptoms and additional diagnostic work or help if needed.

Keep in mind that the older your child gets, the more aware she is of the special attention she is receiving, and the more sensitive she will be to what this says about who she is and what her capabilities are. Help her take charge of her care and build on the strengths that she already has demonstrated. Successful athletes or actors learn to improve their skills. The more you can present monitoring techniques as skill-building tools for her own self-empowerment, the more positive your teen's attitude toward her treatment is likely to be. This does not limit her personal growth—it strengthens it!

Medication Management

If your child has been successfully treated with medication in the past, her medication management plan should be carefully reviewed as adolescence begins. There is no hard-and-fast rule about the changing medication needs of teenagers. With increasing body size the dose may or may not change. Children do not "outgrow" ADHD sometime in their teenage years. Hyperactivity often becomes less of a problem, but impulsive behavior and inattention usually persist. The medications have been found to provide continued benefits for most teenagers with ADHD and are effective in both teenaged boys and girls.

Here is a useful way to think about ADHD: as your child matures, she acquires more skills and abilities to compensate for her weaknesses due to her ADHD. Some individuals compensate well enough that they no longer require any specific treatments. On the other hand, while your child is developing these abilities, her environment is changing and frequently becoming more demanding. As a prominent example, she goes from elementary school, with 1 or 2 teachers for the school year, to middle school, with around 5 teachers, and then to high school, with more teachers and shorter class periods. She also goes from daily to weekly or longer assignments. If she goes on to college, her class days and assignments are more varied. The extent to which she requires treatment and accommodations is dependent on the balance of the demands on her and how well she can compensate.

The dose for your adolescent may need to be increased or lowered on the basis of her function academically, behaviorally, and socially. Medication dosing needs sometimes change because of increased homework demands or complex schedules. If your teenager leaves for school at 7:30 in the morning, has soccer practice after school, and does not get to her homework until 8:00 pm, even long-acting, 12-hour stimulant medication will have worn off by that time. Your daughter's pediatric clinician will be able to suggest helpful approaches. It's important to note that accommodations at school can take into consideration your teen's medication schedule; for example, scheduling challenging classes that require greater attention in the morning when her medication is at its peak.

Your teenager craves independence, but it is likely that both of you realize that ADHD means she will probably need extra structure and support from you. She may resist taking her ADHD medication, or she might argue about following the guidelines for managing her medication. Be honest with her about your concerns and ask for her help in designing a medication routine that will best address her concerns.

If conflicts arise over the balance between limits and freedom, ask your teenager's pediatrician or pediatric clinician, psychologist, or school counselor to contribute ideas or mediate a solution. Some teenagers dislike taking medication, stating that they don't feel like "themselves." This is a side effect, and your teen's pediatric clinician will need to work to try to adjust the dose of medication to minimize this effect. Individual time with your teen's pediatric clinician gives her power and input over her medication. When she refuses to take medication or wants a trial off medication, her pediatric clinician, nurse practitioner, or physician assistant will view this as a positive, and take her seriously. Her input is valuable and a sign that she is taking interest in and control of her ADHD. If your teenager feels that she can succeed without medication, encourage her to set up an alternative plan that works. Going back on medication may become the default option. Remember, you don't *want* your teen to take medications; you want her to succeed whether she is on or off medication. It is common for any child with a chronic condition to not want to or to refuse to take needed medication.

Your pediatric clinician may suggest a "trial" on and off medication. Conducting such a trial will also respect your teen's need to participate in decision-making about treatment. Careful teacher observations of relevant academic, behavioral, or social concerns for a specified period will be sought, as teachers' observations offer important information. These observation requests are best not implemented during test-taking times or at the beginning of the term. The teacher may be asked to make these observations without knowing which period is off and which is on. Your teen should be encouraged to keep a careful diary of her own observations. These observations can be reviewed after the trial for any significant differences in homework completion, grades, and other factors on and off medication. Now your teenager can be helped to make a better-informed decision about whether to continue medication as a part of her treatment plan.

This type of trial can be particularly effective for skeptical teenagers who prefer to see before they believe. Medical professionals can also provide your teenager with written or other media information about ADHD treatment, or refer her to ADHD support groups that can help her understand how others have learned to manage their ADHD.

A Teenager's Story

Feelings About Medication

A high school student recently wrote, "I don't want to take my medication because I don't like the way it makes me feel and it makes me lose weight, which hurts me in football. My friends and family have their own advice for me. My good friend Dylan said I should stay on the medication. He thinks that I am more relaxed and that I am more focused on topics when I'm taking medication. My other friend Jacob thinks that I should stop taking the medication. In his opinion I am more of a loner when I am on the medication and I avoid people. It's true. I liked it better when we used to hang out more. My mom thinks that the medication is great for me. She feels that I am more organized with my homework in school and that I write a lot neater. She also noticed that I memorize faster and that she doesn't need to study with me as much. Since I started taking medication, I have proved anyone who thought I was stupid is wrong. Now I am working to pick out a college to attend. I am sure that I would slip up if I did not take my pills and then lose my chance at college."

Adapted with permission from Heimerl J. ADD drugs? Not easy to take. *Twin Cities Daily Planet.* https://www.tcdailyplanet.net/add-drugs-not-easy-take. Published December 1, 2009. Copyright © Three Sixty Journalism.

Sticking to a Medication Schedule

Teenagers who are more likely to adhere to the prescribed use of stimulant medications are more likely to have

- A positive self-concept
- Family stability
- Confidence in their ability to solve problems
- Simplified medication schedules
- The absence of side effects from medications
- A positive relationship with their doctor

Derived with permission from Reiff MI. Case report: an adolescent who no longer wants to take medication. *Consultant for Pediatricians*. August 2007;(suppl):12.

Abuse of Stimulant Medication

Adolescents who are doing well on a treatment plan that may include taking stimulant medications are *less* likely to abuse stimulants and other drugs than those who are not taking medication. Those without a treatment plan, and perhaps medications, are more likely to experience low self-esteem, more impulsiveness, and poor judgement about taking risks.

Stimulants are classified as schedule II drugs by the US Drug Enforcement Administration, meaning they are closely regulated in an attempt to prevent diversion to street use. Sooner or later patients with ADHD who take stimulant medication become aware of its street value. Your teen may be tempted at some point to give or sell her medication to others or to take more than the prescribed dose herself.

It is a fact of life that most teenagers experiment with some form of high-risk behavior, such as a single episode of alcohol or drug experimentation. It is especially important for you and your teen's pediatric clinician to discuss the dangers of drug abuse with her. Attention-deficit/hyperactivity disorder medication use should be monitored.

If your teen has a coexisting behavioral disorder or has abused or sold medication in the past, develop a system that reduces these possibilities to the greatest extent possible. This may include choosing an alternative non-stimulant medication that doesn't have abuse potential.

Meeting New Academic Challenges

Any young person can quickly become overwhelmed by the increasing academic demands of middle school and high school. Some students with ADHD—particularly those with milder symptoms, good parental support, and strong abilities and verbal skills—may manage the shorter assignments and the less complex concepts of elementary school. The upper grades may bring academic difficulties from the *quantity* (longer assignments, more homework) and *quality* of work expected (increasingly abstract language, more complex ideas). In addition, there are greater expectations for increasing independent study.

Adolescents with ADHD frequently procrastinate, heeding Mark Twain's advice to "never put off until tomorrow what you can do the day after tomorrow." They may do poorly on tests, be careless when doing their schoolwork, and have trouble tracking and turning in their assignments on time. Because they have more classrooms and teachers in middle school and high school, there is a greater need for organizational skills. A treatment plan with specially targeted academic support at home and in the classroom is essential. Proper medication treatment can go a long way in supporting your child's academic efforts.

Certain higher-level academic tasks, like those requiring doing 2 or more things at the same time, may develop more slowly in your teenager with ADHD. This is not to say that your teen will not do as well academically as her peers, but it does mean that she will probably have to work harder with structured and individualized systems, strategies, and supports. Because there is no routine one-size-fits-all formula for these aids, your adolescent may also need to rely on professional advice in designing the best routines and your own support, patience, and commitment. This structure is often best put into place with a Section 504 plan.

A Student's Story

Feeling Overwhelmed

"Last Thursday I forgot to take my pill. As the day progressed, I became increasingly distracted. By eighth period I could, for the first time, hear the low electrical buzz in the chemistry lab. I noticed the dripping of one of the faucets and the curled corner of a piece of paper peeling off its poster-board backing. I saw the faint streaks that lingered on the whiteboard that hung on the classroom wall. As a classmate's wisps of breath lightly touched my hair, I could feel the strands' small movements. Occasionally, I could discern fragments of conversation coming from the hall outside. As my head whirred with this overload of sensations the air seemed to congeal; grow slow. I felt heavy and lethargic; my senses seemed to have thickened and blurred. When class ended, I realized I had neglected to write down any of the directions for the next day's experiment.

"I would often sit down and start my homework with the best of intentions. Two hours later I would look up and discover, to my surprise, that I had spent the whole time reading a 'few' chapters of a novel or staring out the window. I couldn't understand how I had lost that time!"

Sharon, Topeka, KS

As students mature, they are expected to be able to carry out more complex learning tasks. These include

- **More consistent and sustained attention** to classroom lectures and desk work
- **More efficient processing of information** encountered through reading or classroom lectures
- **Mature visual-spatial skills** that help interpret and reason
- **Complex thinking** that allows for advanced problem-solving and the ability to handle abstract concepts

- **Higher-level language abilities** required for a greater emphasis on abstract language and fluency in written language, as well as for studying a second language in school
- **Fine motor skills** needed for efficient note-taking, keyboard use, and speed writing
- **Better self-organization** needed to complete schoolwork each day and turn it in on time
- **Improved sequencing skills** to schedule enough time for schoolwork every day, plan the steps necessary to complete long-term assignments, prioritize work assignments, and keep up with school demands

This is a heavy menu of new demands for any student, and some of these tasks may prove especially challenging for your adolescent with ADHD. Delayed development of any of these skills can lead to poorer academic functioning. As your child moves through adolescence, pay special attention to how well she is managing these types of challenges. Help her put support systems into place if and when they become necessary.

Reviewing Your Teenager's Education Program

Overseeing your teen's academic career during adolescence is easier in some ways and more difficult in others. As your teen matures, she is better able to communicate her school-related problems to you. But, as a teenager, she may be reluctant to do so. The fact that she attends multiple classes with a number of different teachers might allow you to compare her performance among classes and, therefore, more accurately identify problems and needs. However, teachers who now see her for just one period a day are less likely to know your teen well and may not be able to provide insight into her strengths or challenges. Finally, while the chances are greater that, by now, you and your teen have been able to create structures and strategies that have worked for her over time, occasionally problems may have been made worse by earlier failures, a decrease in self-esteem, the development of behavioral or emotional disorders, or an academic or social reputation that may be difficult to overcome.

Focus on your teen's strengths; these will allow her to begin to tackle weaknesses. If you have not met with her principal or special education coordinator, or if your teen is changing to a new school, meet with either of them soon to discuss your teenager's diagnosis and any classroom accommodations that might be available. If your teenager is having significant school problems and you have not already worked with school personnel to create an education program that meets her needs, consider seeking additional help for her under the Individuals With Disabilities Education Act (IDEA) or Section 504. Refer to Chapter 7 for information on how to implement these important supports. If you feel that you need more support in this, meet with your teen's pediatric clinician and ask the clinician to contact your teen's school directly. Review Chapter 7 for ideas on other options.

Request a meeting with your teen's educational team to help you prepare for each coming academic year. Emphasize from the start that you are there to support the teachers' efforts to help your teenager and not to second-guess the teachers or tell them what to do.

At this meeting find out when regular parent-teacher conferences are scheduled, and plan additional regular meetings, phone conversations, or other communication if you and the teachers agree that these would be helpful. Decide together how to communicate about any issues that arise. Discuss how any special educational services or accommodations will be implemented. If you have decided to use weekly report cards, find out if these will be online or written. It is also a good idea to understand each teacher's philosophy concerning ADHD and to have a tactful conversation about any broad misconceptions. If no meeting can be scheduled, try to arrange for early conversations with as many of your teen's teachers as possible once the school year has begun.

After 2 or 3 months have passed, you, your teen, and her teachers will have accumulated enough information about her performance to review a list of academic goals and make any necessary changes to her education program. Pay attention to the special skills she needs to develop to handle her increased workload, including

- Completing homework and turning it in on time
- Breaking down long-term assignments into manageable chunks and prioritizing daily assignments
- Comprehending and recalling what she reads

- Listening in class and taking adequate notes
- Memorizing facts
- Managing her time
- Organizing her study area, backpack, and class folders
- Writing legibly and quickly, or typing efficiently on a computer keyboard

Behavioral issues in the classroom should also be discussed because they can strongly affect your teenager's ability to learn. Teenagers with inattentive-type ADHD may especially need help in participating in class discussions or seeking extra help when they need it. Those with hyperactive-impulsive–type ADHD or a behavioral disorder are more likely to have problems with disrupting the class, arguing with teachers, getting into fights with classmates, or skipping class.

Once you have identified any functioning problems that your teen is experiencing, prioritize them in order of importance. Start with the most important problem and try to pinpoint exact targets for improvement. For example, does she have trouble memorizing facts because she tries to memorize too many in a single session? Does her disruptive behavior occur when quiet desk work has gone on for longer than her patience allows or when school pressures and test-taking make her anxious? What happens if she has forgotten to take her medication?

Comparing your teen's functioning in one classroom with another may add insight into precisely where a problem lies.

- If she is making As in math and Ds in history, for example, is it because her math teacher has a knack for keeping her attention or limiting her disruptive behavior? Perhaps the math teacher would be willing to share thoughts and experiences with others who teach your teen.

- Is it because special accommodations, such as untimed tests or shorter homework assignments, are provided in math class but not in history? Could the accommodations be available in every class?

- Might your teen have an undiagnosed reading-related learning disability that is affecting her performance in history? Ask her special educator to check to see how she reads her assignments.

- Or is your teen simply passionate about math and less interested in history? Encourage her passions and address her insecurity in other classes.

- Does her schoolwork worsen in the late afternoon, and does this have anything to do with her medication beginning to wear off? Discuss this with her prescribing pediatric clinician.

Remember that adolescents with more intense needs may qualify for Individualized Education Programs under IDEA or Section 504 of the Rehabilitation Act, as discussed in Chapter 7.

Specific Schoolwork Strategies

One of the best ways to teach your teenager the skills she will need to succeed in school is to break complex processes down into a series of simpler steps. Often teenagers with ADHD fail to succeed at school just because they do not know how to study effectively. Preparing for tests, keeping school notebooks organized, or planning for more complex assignments are processes that we call *executive functions*. These techniques are not always easy to develop naturally.

You might share with your teenager the strategies that you use, but remember that what works for you will not necessarily work for her. You could ask your teen's teachers or school counselor to refer you to a tutor who can problem-solve with your teenager to help her find her own most effective ways to memorize material, more fully comprehend what she reads, study for tests, organize her backpack, manage her homework assignments, or accomplish whatever other school-related tasks you have identified. Your teen's teacher or guidance counselor may also be able to contribute valuable ideas. Some teenagers with ADHD also find peer tutoring programs and study-skills classes very helpful, and these are usually available in their school. Study and time management tips are also available at www.chadd.org. In most cases, such instruction requires only a few brief sessions. You can then follow up on this instruction at home with your teen.

Good Habits for Academic Success

Helping your teenager to discover the tools and motivation to organize his life can make an immense difference in his academic progress and, in turn, his self-esteem. Remember, study habits need to be individualized, and what works well for one person may not for another. Here are some tips that he might choose to try.

- **Keep organization simple.** Consider keeping one folder for all work that is completed, another folder for all work that still needs to be done, and a third folder for graded work and notes from the teacher to the parents. When your student gets home, he can pull out one folder containing all the assignments he needs to complete. At the end of the evening, all these assignments will have been placed in the completed work folder. At the end of the next school day the completed work folder should be empty, because all the work has been turned in.
- **Use a paper or electronic daily planner** to record school assignments, doctor's appointments, and other meetings, and to schedule work on long-term projects. Keep it simple; elaborate systems may be more detailed but more frustrating to use.
- **Use a backpack as the location for all schoolwork and supplies.** Supplies can be kept in the side pockets, his assignment planner in a separate outside pocket, and his notebook in the main body of the pack. All schoolwork goes into the backpack.
- **Make lists** of tasks to be accomplished, ideas to be included in a written essay, people to call about a project, etc. The more short-term information a teenager has on paper, the less he has to hold in his head. Keep the lists in a designated place (eg, a computer, a backpack, a "note box" at home). Lists scattered throughout the house can be harder to find than remembering the information they contain.
- **Use an outline or flowchart format to take notes.** An outline or flowchart can help a teenager understand the structure underlying the information he hears and can save him from having to write down every word.

- **Preview.** If there are questions in the back of a chapter in a textbook, reading these questions first can help your teen know ahead of time what he should take away from the chapter.
- **Break up large tasks into a series of small steps.** Study for tests in a series of relatively brief periods over a number of days instead of cramming the night before. Good study habits can include surveying the topics to be tested; creating questions about the material, then rereading the material to answer his questions; formulating answers in his head or discussing them with you, a tutor, or a "study buddy"; and practicing writing down answers to questions that seem likely to be on the test. He could plan a writing assignment by doing the research one day, thinking about it the next, writing a first draft on the third day, and revising it on the fourth.
- **Set aside a routine time and place for doing homework.** Most teenagers with ADHD can benefit from a routine, non-distracting environment for completing work. This usually means no television or Internet access unless it is required for an assignment.
- **Take advantage of his learning style.** A teenager should pay attention to how he learns best. Is it easier for him to memorize by using abbreviations or acronyms (making a word from the first letter of each memorized term), looking at lists or charts, reviewing facts verbally with a partner, or testing and retesting himself on paper? Does he work better in short bursts or for longer periods? Alone or with others present? In his room or at the dining table?
- **Create bypass strategies.** Teenagers with uneven learning styles can benefit from developing *bypass strategies*—strategies designed to help work around a particular problem. For example, if a student gets overwhelmed by a long-term assignment because of extreme difficulty with handwriting, a bypass strategy would be to use a computer. If a student has extreme difficulty multitasking (eg, writing while thinking) and, because of this, loses track of his thoughts, it may be helpful to first dictate several ideas into a computer or recorder and then

write them down, separating the 2 tasks and making each one more doable. Consider that all the suggestions in this box are not one size fits all. Some may be successful and others not. Some of them can be easily used as stated; others may have to be adapted to your adolescent's learning style to be helpful.

Social and Emotional Challenges in Adolescence

All teenagers have concerns about being accepted by their peers. Unfortunately, some teens with ADHD have come to expect some social rejection if they have had trouble controlling their behavior and understanding others' social signals. Social issues encountered in childhood can be even greater challenges in adolescence. Rejection and bullying are worse and feel worse during the teenage years. This rejection can hurt academic performance and emotional health and can be more troubling to an adolescent than poor grades in school. A teen with ADHD who appears emotionally immature compared with her classmates will often be more comfortable interacting with younger peers or with adults who show greater acceptance of her immature actions. She may also find better acceptance by playing the role of the class clown.

Difficulties with social interaction can be helped by having adolescents learn specific social skills. Chapters 5 and 6 discussed a number of ways to teach younger children how to interact positively with others, including role modeling, role-playing, analyzing interaction, and practicing new techniques. As a new adolescent, advice about social issues is now more often sought from peers than from parents. Your teen is likely to experience new motivation to improve her social life, and you can help too.

Friendships

Teenagers with ADHD can certainly have the close friendships that are important for happiness and self-esteem. Your teenager can learn to improve her social understanding of others and to also monitor her social interactions. Support her developing friendships by allowing her friends to hang out in your home. By helping to provide the kind of supportive environment that facilitates all friendships, you are teaching your teen essential friendship skills. Observe how friends relate to one another. You can provide feedback tactfully after her friends have left—if you feel that it will be received in a positive and constructive manner. Find a good time to have this conversation when no one is tired, upset, in a hurry, or hungry. When giving feedback and suggesting changes to how she acts, timing really is everything! Teenagers with ADHD need to be increasingly aware that friendships take organizational skills too—returning texts or calls, arriving at meeting places on time, and following through on plans.

Conflict Resolution

It is important for your teenager to learn how to resolve conflict without anger or resorting to physical fights and how to avoid becoming the target of others' aggression. Resolving conflict can be a difficult task if ADHD impulsiveness causes her to quickly get upset. Can you help her to identify her own anger cues? Together can you brainstorm about positive actions and solutions she can apply to future conflicts.

If this is an issue for your teenager, discussions with you and trusted peers, post-conflict analysis, and sessions with a counselor, therapist, or social-skills instructor can be very successful. Your teen might learn to talk herself down when she finds herself frustrated: "I'm going to take 3 deep breaths and think about my best choice in this situation before I say anything." She can learn conflict-prevention techniques, such as providing an alternative: "How about if we go bowling first and then see a movie?" Another solution might be to add provisions to an agreement: "OK, you can drive, but then I get to decide on the restaurant." Changing the subject is always easy if food is involved and very often it works: "I'm starving. You want to get some pizza?"

Once your teen has learned a few of these, she will probably be surprised at how effectively she can now avoid the crises that used to ruin her social life! If you are seeking counseling in this area, the most proven approach is known as cognitive behavior therapy (CBT). This is a type of talk therapy that views behavioral issues as related to the interaction of thoughts, behaviors, and emotions. In CBT, the therapist and adolescent will work on identifying and directly changing behaviors that are problematic.

Working on Social Skills

Help your adolescent hone her social skills and interactions with others by

- Developing a list of specific target behaviors that together you decide need to be addressed

- Outlining a step-by-step plan to address each one

- Having her teacher and peers provide consistent, tactful feedback

- Teaching techniques to identify cues that set off her anger

- Scheduling counseling and training to improve social skills and manage anger (This can be individual treatment or group therapy.)

- Addressing any coexisting conditions that may affect her social interaction (See Chapter 9.)

- Giving positive feedback for improvement in targeted social skills

- Encouraging continued involvement in rewarding prosocial activities such as club or team membership

Many people with ADHD may continue to have trouble with certain social interactions throughout adolescence and into adulthood. Overcoming social rejection can be very difficult. Keep in mind that even teenagers who are socially unhappy in high school can still go on to find rewarding friendships in college or work situations. It will mean a lot to your teenager to know that you will always be in her corner and that you support her no matter what.

Your Teenager's Emotional Development

Academic, social, and family strains can create a heavy emotional burden for adolescents with ADHD. Low self-esteem caused by academic failure and social rejection can lead to depression, defensiveness, pessimism about the future, hostility, and physical aggression. Combined with ADHD-related impulsiveness, it can pave the way for unsafe sexual activity; alcohol, tobacco, or drug abuse; and other high-risk behavior.

Take a moment to consider your teenager's emotional state. Does she seem sad or irritable nearly all the time? Does she spend nearly all her time alone in her room? Is her anger starting to get out of hand? Has she been suspended from school this year,

Teenagers with ADHD certainly can have the close friendships that are important for their happiness and self-esteem.

or are you receiving reports of inappropriate behavior? If so, discuss these issues with your adolescent and seek help from her therapist or pediatric clinician.

Anxiety and depressive disorders (see Chapter 9) are common conditions also seen in teenagers with ADHD. They must be considered anytime an adolescent's social, academic, or behavioral functioning starts to deteriorate without an obvious explanation. In the teenage years, depression and anxiety increase significantly in all youth, and especially in those with ADHD. The sooner an adolescent's depression, anxiety, anger, substance use, or other problem behavior is recognized, the greater the chances that the situation can be effectively addressed.

Risk-taking

Adolescence is a time when all teenagers are prone to testing limits and engaging in risk-taking. Adolescents with ADHD and impulsivity are more prone to taking risks. Surveys have shown that teenagers with ADHD can have an earlier age of first intercourse, more partners, less use of effective birth control, and more sexually transmitted infections and teenage pregnancy than their peers. Education about these issues in the preteen years and continuing guidance is important.

Driving can be a particular area of concern. Teenaged drivers with ADHD have been reported to be 8 times more likely to lose their license, 4 times more likely to be involved in a collision, 3 times more likely to sustain a serious injury, and 2 to 4 times more likely to receive a moving violation. As a parent, consider this information carefully. Make sure that your adolescent is at a maturity level appropriate for driving and set appropriate limits with her. Many states now issue only graduated licensing for new teenaged drivers, which limits the number of passengers and nighttime driving for a period, to allow new drivers to acquire skills and experience without distractions. Distractions from cell phones or other electronics are now addressed in state laws. These restrictions are not in place in every state, but parents can also restrict the time of day when their adolescent with ADHD can drive and make driving contingent on responsible driving behavior.

Discuss safe driving at home. More importantly, teach by example and be a safe driver! Parents who fail to wear their seat belt and require passengers to wear theirs, who text and drive, who operate a motor vehicle under the influence of alcohol or marijuana, or who drive aggressively and angrily place their adolescent with ADHD and her passengers at even greater risk of harm.

When medication is found helpful in cutting down on impulsivity, it makes sense to consider driving times. Teenagers who respond well to medication have been shown to be better drivers when on their medication. (Driving risk will likely be higher in the times when medications are not taken or have worn off.) Finally, even if use of alcohol or drugs is never condoned by parents, develop a clear understanding that it is always safe for your teenager to call you and ask you for a ride home if she is even minimally impaired from these substances. It is most effective to agree that if she calls for help, you will not impose punishment for that episode of substance use.

Effective Parenting of Teenagers With ADHD

In chapters 5 and 6, you learned of a number of parenting techniques aimed at helping you interact positively with your younger child. These parent behavior management training techniques can still provide a basis for healthy family relationships. As your teenager grows more independent, you will need to deal with more complex family issues that may require new approaches. A number of these issues are discussed in this section, along with some effective techniques you can use to address them. Remember too that just as when your child was younger, you are likely to benefit enormously from sound parenting education information specially designed for families of teenagers with ADHD, or from the counseling of a therapist trained in these techniques.

Helping Your Teenager Become More Independent

Again, achieving independence is the primary developmental goal for every adolescent. Your teenager will experience this urge as strongly as her peers who do not have ADHD, but her impulsivity, inattention, and aspects of delayed maturation mean that she may need to move more slowly toward full self-supervision. Sensitive monitoring of your adolescent's behavior and reasonable limit setting will be critical as your teenager works her way toward mature self-management and autonomy. Parents play an essential support role in this maturation by

- Working harder at consciously modeling your own responsible behavior
- Breaking down tasks and responsibilities into smaller steps and rewarding your teen systematically for accomplishing them
- Developing a plan for transferring responsibilities over to your teenager as she works on her own independence

Remove limits and grant privileges at a rapid a pace as is possible, once your adolescent shows that she can handle responsibility. Long-standing loss of privileges harbors resentment and has little teaching value.

For example, what about curfews? Any adolescent would resent a 10:00 pm curfew if her friends are allowed to stay out until midnight. You may be concerned that parties tend to get wilder after about 10:00 pm, a time where you have observed that her impulsivity usually increases, or that driving is potentially riskier late at night because her medication will have worn off by then. You can address your concerns directly with your adolescent. Share with her the reasons you worry about her staying out later. Of course, the best time to do this is when you both are calm and probably not as she is going out the door.

If she counters that she is ready to take responsibility for staying out later, and you believe that this may be true, talk together about how she can be safe for the later hour.

Is she aware that her medication will have worn off and no longer be helping her? What will she do if there are drugs or alcohol at the party? How about if others suggest or start risky behaviors? How will she keep herself safe? Who will be driving home? Will she call you for a ride if that is the safest way home?

If she arrives home on time with no evidence of high-risk activity, praise her and reward her with a continued later curfew. Frank discussions help your adolescent to continue to systematically build on her successes while giving her the chance to extend the boundaries of her independence. Such triumphs in mutual trust and respect are vital for a teenager's self-esteem and positive attitude.

Providing Structure and Support

During your child's earlier years, you were encouraged to actively monitor her behavior in the classroom and at home, providing frequent rewards and, when necessary, consequences. Now that your teenager is growing more independent, you may feel it is time to stop this type of monitoring. However, many teenagers with ADHD continue to need parental monitoring and structure more than their peers without ADHD.

Some adolescents with ADHD may need continued monitoring to see that they are completing their work and turning it in on time, but they realize that their friends who do not have ADHD are now allowed to manage their own academic work. While other parents may grow more lax about knowing where their older teenagers are every minute, you may have reason to continue monitoring where your teenager is, with whom, what she is doing, and when she will be home, particularly when you sense that she might find herself in a high-risk situation that may be difficult for her to manage.

But since you are encouraging your adolescent's independence, won't your continued help be a problem? Ongoing parental oversight is most effective if done in a manner respectful of your teenager and her developmental needs. Talk together about her goals, your concerns, and how you might work together.

Establishing and Enforcing Rules

Teenagers with ADHD may have an argumentative style. Every teenager's resistance to continued monitoring will lead to testing, negotiating, and rebellion. All families will have a few *nonnegotiable* rules considered essential. These absolute rules should be reserved for critical issues of safety or family functioning. You may decide, for example, that use of illegal drugs of any kind, including marijuana, alcohol, vaping, Juuling, and cigarettes, will not be tolerated in your house. Some families require that driving only be done at times when stimulant medication still has an active effect.

When you have arrived at these few essential rules, write them down and have a prepared and calm discussion about them with your teenager. Share your list and solicit her input. Explain that compliance with these few important rules for safety and family well-being will build trust important to discussing other freedoms she craves. Negotiate together the rewards for compliance, like extended privileges in other areas, and the consequences for breaking these rules, such as loss of other privileges. By making your opinion clear and discussing compliance, you are now prepared to enforce these rules consistently.

Negotiating With Your Adolescent

Once you and your teenager have agreed on these few essential rules, you are both now likely to feel more at ease when negotiating other issues. Together you have established ground rules for effective discussions, and they have worked! As the parent of an adolescent with ADHD, you are becoming adept at using negotiation to shape behavior and to resolve conflicts while respecting her need for independence. Successful negotiation trains your adolescent to take a more active role in creating the rules by which she lives. If you wish to gradually lead her toward a thoughtful independence in managing her behavior, it is important to establish the fact that right now, as her parent, you assume the final responsibility for rules and consequences.

A good way to negotiate rules or solutions to family conflicts is to use a technique called *problem-solving training.* This technique consists of the following steps:

1. Define the problem and its effect.

2. Come up with a variety of possible solutions to the problem.

3. Choose the best solution.

4. Plan how to implement the solution.

5. Renegotiate a new solution if necessary.

Commonly conflicts arise over media use. Your teenager may resent the fact that you limit television and other media on school nights. To resolve this conflict, you could hold a family meeting to discuss the issue. First, you would *define the problem* and allow her to explain why it upsets her: "Stacy, you want to watch 3 to 4 hours of TV on weeknights like you say all your friends are doing, but I see that when you watch that long that you usually only get about half of your homework finished."

Stacy might respond, "Everybody talks about what they watched the night before, and I never have anything to say. It makes me feel left out and like a loser." This is a great start. Now that both of you know what each other needs, you can work together to address those needs.

Next you, your partner, and your teenager will each *contribute ideas to resolve this problem.* Usually 6 to 8 ideas are sufficient. Each family member should contribute whatever solution comes to mind, even if it seems somewhat unusual or impractical—taking turns, if necessary, to allow each person to contribute his or her share. At this point in your discussion, it is important and useful to *not* express judgment or respond to any of the suggestions in any way, positively or negatively. Your adolescent or you should write down each potential solution until all suggestions have been recorded.

Next, each family member may take a turn *evaluating* each solution in order. The family member should consider whether a particular solution would work for him or her

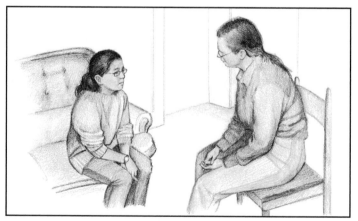

As a parent of an adolescent with ADHD you will need to become skilled at using negotiation to shape your teen's behavior and resolve conflicts as they occur.

and whether it would work for others in the family, and then assign it a plus (+) or a minus (-). As the family works down the list of solutions in this way, each solution will accumulate a series of plus and minus ratings that can be used to choose the best idea.

To choose a solution, you and your family can select any idea that has received all pluses and discuss its benefits and weaknesses. If more than one solution has received all pluses, you might be able to pick the one that seems most reasonable to your adolescent.

If none of the suggested solutions has received unanimous approval, choose the one that was best liked and discuss how you might make it acceptable. Or you may choose to brainstorm again to find an even better solution that is acceptable to everyone. For a solution to work well, it needs to create a win-win situation—it needs to make sense to everyone. In this way, you will end up with a solution that you can all live with, even if none of you consider it perfect.

Now you have agreed on the best solution. Next you will need to agree on *how it will be implemented.* Who will be responsible for seeing that rules are followed? Who will remind your teenager to comply with the rules when necessary? What are the rewards for complying and the consequences for breaking the rules? The clearer you all are at this part of the agreement, the less time and energy you will spend arguing about the rules later. The entire agreement might even be written down and all might choose to sign it.

For example, if you have agreed that your teen can watch television for 1 hour each school night once she has completed her homework, you must jointly decide how late at night she can watch television. If needed, who will be responsible for reminding her that her homework needs to be finished first? Will you check to make sure it is done? She can help in these decisions and be proud of her part.

It is best to start problem-solving in this way with issues that are important but not emotionally intense for your teenager or for you. Once you have practiced these new techniques with one or more easier topics, you can move toward resolving what may be more volatile conflicts. Eventually you may become so adept at this rational form of problem-solving that you and your teenager will be able to resolve arguments on the spot, in most cases, using informal versions of this technique.

Providing Appropriate Consequences

Remember, the most powerful tool that any parent has to change a child's or adolescent's behavior is to pay attention to what you want and ignore what you don't want. Throughout this book, we have emphasized the importance of providing positive reinforcement whenever possible, ignoring negative behaviors that are not dangerous or destructive, and providing reasonable consequences for only the few intolerable behaviors on which you and your child are currently focusing. This practice should continue throughout adolescence, and don't forget that the more positive feedback you can offer your teen during these difficult years, the more competent she is likely to feel. Catch her doing a good job! And tell her. Save consequences or other negative feedback for the times when you really need them. Constant criticism or punishment will desensitize your teen to your reactions, so that she may be less likely to respond when you try to address significant concerns.

Consistency is essential in enforcing the rules and procedures on which you have all already agreed. This is true for rewards and consequences. If enforcement becomes necessary, consequences are best announced in a calm voice, using as few words as is possible, and soon after the behavior has occurred. Measures such as time-outs are no longer age appropriate for adolescents. More appropriate consequences include pre–agreed-on losses of privileges, such as temporarily losing car privileges for coming home late. Your already negotiated and agreed-on consequences are so much more valuable and effective than argument, recrimination, yelling, or nitpicking. Keeping the conflicts and emotions out of it, and simply providing the appropriate response, has not only been studied and shown to be more effective but is also a way to keep family life relatively pleasant and upbeat.

Fostering a Positive Attitude and Giving Each Other Breaks

Research shows that the presence of at least one fully supportive adult in the life of a child with ADHD is one of the key factors in determining that child's future success. Your support and sensitive parenting can make all the difference to your adolescent, who may meet with rejection, frustration, or even failure at school. Provide as much quality time for your teenager as you are able and make it fun and rewarding for both of you. Sometimes, when things get too tough at home, it is a good idea to take a break from one another. Parents need support too! It's OK to take a break when you need it and there is another family member or trusted adult who can provide you with a break.

Together You'll Succeed!

Adolescence is an exciting period. It is a time of exploration and emerging independence, the transition from childhood to adulthood. This can be a highly rewarding journey, even if it takes occasional tumultuous turns. As any teenager explores newly accessible choices, she will inevitably make good and bad decisions. This is a normal and important part of becoming a responsible adult.

As your family negotiates this developmental stage, it pays to keep in mind that your adolescent is a teenager first, and a teenager with ADHD second. Allowing your adolescent's exploration of independence is a critical element to her becoming a capable, responsible adult.

Q & A

Q: *When our son was first diagnosed with ADHD at age 9, my husband and I worked hard to put a consistent system of rewards and consequences in place to help him manage his behavior. Now that he's 13, however, he's gotten very good at circumventing one parent's rules by getting the other to agree to concessions, and even just ignoring the limits we've set. For the first time this year, he was suspended from school for behavior issues, and we're afraid things might be getting worse. Are we doing something wrong?*

A: First, it is important to remember that nearly all adolescents test behavioral limits and experiment with how best to circumvent parental rules.

That said, it is especially important during these years that you remain as consistent as possible when discussing, setting, and enforcing a behavioral bottom line. Have a serious conversation with your teenager, as described in this chapter, about the reasons why he needs to follow certain rules. It becomes more and more important at this age to make sure that he agrees that the consequences and rewards are fair to him—but negotiate these beforehand and not in the heat of battle. Make sure you and your partner are presenting him with a united front; allowing him to play one of you against another is one

of the easiest traps that parents fall into. If you feel that he believes there may be no consequences to his behavior, consider creating a written contract for all of you to sign, stipulat-
ing the rules to be followed and related rewards and punishments.

Keep in mind that teenagers with ADHD can be impulsive, and many find that it is
difficult to keep their behavior within tolerable limits. However, where impulsive behaviors
in grade school may have included pushing in line and blurting out answers before the
teacher finished asking the question, impulsivity in teenagers can include high-risk
behaviors leading to drug use, unsafe sex, teenage pregnancy, serious conduct problems,
and school dropout. This makes it particularly important to develop a parenting style that
includes your adolescent in the decision-making, leads to good self-esteem, and includes
setting reasonable, sensitive, and fair limits when appropriate.

Q: *Our 14-year-old daughter, who has inattentive-type ADHD, has changed completely over the
past 6 months. Her grades, which used to be Bs and Cs, were nearly all Ds and Fs this past
semester, and she spends almost all her free time locked in her room. We've met with her and
her teachers about the grades and she's promised to work to get them up, but I haven't seen
her changing her behavior much at all since then. Is this a normal part of being a teenager, or
should we be concerned?*

A: An abrupt change in behavior and declining grades are 2 warning signs that any teenager,
and especially an adolescent with ADHD, needs help. The behaviors you describe could
be signs of depression, anxiety, substance use, or a serious decline in self-esteem caused
by social or other problems. Any sudden and persisting changes in behavior that lead to a
decline in functioning should be considered red flags and be evaluated as soon as possible.

Because adolescents are so concerned with independence, your daughter may not be
able to ask you for help directly. She actually may be expecting you to interpret her behavior
of locking herself in her room as a cry for help. Reach out to her and pursue your concerns.
And get help from her pediatric clinician, school social worker or guidance counsellor, or
therapist, if she has one. In this way you convey a powerful message of support for her.

CHAPTER 12

A Look at Your Child's Future

All children and teenagers find the elementary school and high school years difficult in one way or another. New and special challenges may emerge as your teen with attention-deficit/hyperactivity disorder (ADHD) reaches the end of adolescence and looks forward to a more independent life. Whether going straight from high school into a job, getting vocational training, or attending college, your teen will need to continue to self-monitor his ADHD, advocate effectively for his needs, and structure his life in ways that will bring success.

Between one-half to two-thirds of children with ADHD will continue to have some significant symptoms as adults. To help your teen with the transition to more independent living you will need to assume new roles to assist in the acquisition of self-care skills. In this chapter, you will find helpful information on

- How to help your teen research and apply to trade schools, colleges, and universities that match both his interests and needs
- How to best create a smooth transition to life as a young adult in college or in a job
- Determining what the health and safety issues of special importance are to adults with ADHD
- Identifying relationship challenges and family responsibilities that your grown child may need to learn to manage
- Identifying current and future research that may help your child live more successfully with ADHD in the years ahead

After High School: College and Work

Your teenager can best prepare for this giant step toward independence by thinking about what sort of adult life interests him. Whether choosing vocational training, college, or work, he will need to continue to develop life-management skills (often described by health care professionals as *executive function*). These include the abilities to organize, plan, prioritize, and stick to plans rather than act on impulses, as well as to learn how to know when plans might need to be altered. These skills are necessary to live on your own, and developing these skills may be harder if you have ADHD. But executive function does mature during the young adult years, and those who work on these skills during high school—money management, time management, planning, and daily life maintenance skills—will continue to develop these skills in the workplace or college.

Has your teenager with ADHD been frustrated by the work demands of the high school environment? Is he looking forward to when he will be able to be more independent? Does he have a special passion or talent that is engaging and motivating? Are higher

Talk frequently with your teenager about his special passion, talent, or interest. This can help him think about what sort of adult life he hopes to have.

education and professional job prospects important? This may be the time to explore those interests more deeply through an internship, apprenticeship, or entry-level job. If he is considering attending college explore the programs each school provides to help students with ADHD.

Of course, no high school student can be expected to come up with a definitive answer to all these questions right away, but it is important to at least start to consider them before jumping into a first job or higher-education experience. Frequent job and career changes are one reason why some adults with ADHD lag behind their peers in career success. Thinking things out carefully and resisting the impulse to "act first and think later" may save time and effort in the long run.

High school is also the time to work on the skills needed to be successful at college and in life. Is your teen able to self-manage daily living needs such as

- Getting up in the morning
- Getting to bed at night at a reasonable hour
- Managing laundry and other personal needs
- Taking responsibility for medication and treatment programs by
  - Making appointments at the doctor
  - Calling for prescriptions to be filled and refilled
  - Taking his medications on a regular basis
- Organization and time-management skills, like
  - Creating a schedule for all assignments
  - Planning and scheduling after-class activities
  - Paying attention to time spent gaming and using social or other media

Take this opportunity to look at your role in your teen's development. Now is an excellent time for you to step back and allow your teen to try out self-management while still at home by setting up a program that allows your teen to grow and take on more responsibilities.

Once your teen has begun working on the various skills needed for a successful launch into adulthood, the next step is thinking about the path that best suits his needs at this time. High school counselors can be a valuable resource in this process. A good counselor can provide an objective picture of the school and learning profile and discuss the match between interests and further schooling or perhaps different jobs and occupations. If your student has had an ongoing Individualized Education Program (IEP), the counselor can also help see that the types of post–secondary school transition steps mandated by the Individuals With Disabilities Education Act (IDEA) (see the "Transition Plans: Preparing for the Future" box) are being carried out effectively. Your teen should also discuss plans for the future with his pediatric clinician, psychologist, psychiatrist, or other medical advisor, particularly in terms of how his ADHD symptoms may affect experiences in various colleges, jobs, and professions and how to continue to effectively monitor and self-manage those symptoms. There is help from those who have helped him in the past as he determines a satisfying path toward potential career goals.

Thinking About College

Choosing their best school is a complicated process that may be even trickier for students with ADHD. Not only must they find a college that suits their academic, social, and geographical preferences, but they also must decide whether the education format and the special services provided by the institution will be sufficient to support unique needs. Like his peers, your adolescent needs to ask, "Is this the right fit for me?"

Teens often are unaware of how different college is from high school in academic as well as other areas. No one will be there to make sure classes are attended, assignments are completed on time and turned in, or services are accessed. In addition, while many of the services students are accustomed to receiving in high school will be available at college, college students have to seek them out. Self-knowledge and a good transition plan are important to ensure success at the college level.

Transition Plans: Preparing for the Future

The Individuals With Disabilities Education Act stipulates that, from about age 14 years, when a youth with attention-deficit/hyperactivity disorder (ADHD) enters high school, the Individualized Education Program (IEP) team should start to discuss and consider goals for post-school transition to adult life. By age 16 years or even earlier, if appropriate, the IEP must include a statement of the transition services your teen will need; that is, services that will facilitate progress toward career, academic, or other aspirations. Such services may include preparation for the SAT, the ACT, or other proficiency tests necessary when applying for college admission, as well as training in self-advocacy and self-sufficiency skills.

During your teen's junior and senior years of high school, a reassessment for specific executive functioning problems related to ADHD, learning disabilities, and any other coexisting conditions should occur. This is valuable for plans to attend college and to enter the workforce. Your student will need to provide detailed documentation of these disabilities to qualify for untimed or other special college-entry testing accommodations and for special support services at college. The IEP alone, or a general diagnosis of ADHD, may not be sufficient to obtain these services.

Once your teen graduates from high school, your local school system will no longer provide services. However, if your teen has been receiving services, such as counseling and vocational evaluation and assessment, as part of the transition plan, those services may continue to be received. An Individualized Written Rehabilitation Plan (IWRP) will be created to allow your teen to take advantage of such services.

Not every student with ADHD will need a formal transition plan, an IEP, or an IWRP. However, a well-thought-out plan that touches on the same themes will still be important. For more information on this and other aspects of preparing for life after graduation, consult your son or daughter's school guidance counselor or pediatric clinician.

What to Look for in Postsecondary Education

Location, size, and academic offerings are 3 important elements for all prospective students to consider when choosing among the many colleges available to them. Questions to consider include

- Would it be preferable to attend school near home, which would allow taking advantage of familiar resources, or farther away, with the opportunity for increased independence?
- What supports are needed to successfully get into college?
- What supports can come from home and what may be needed in new medical and support services at a new school?
- Which is better for your student?
  - A small college, where personal attention may be easier to obtain
  - A large university with possibly better funding and more options for support services
- Are specific services available and tailored to the needs of students with ADHD?
- Will the institution's academic demands and supports match your student's learning style and needs?

Because the transition to a self-structured life outside the home can be especially challenging for teenagers with ADHD, it is critical that your teen be well-prepared for independent living. He will need to know and explain to others his various strengths and weaknesses as well as be willing to access services on his own. While the presence and effectiveness of a college's ADHD support program is a prime consideration, your teen must be mature enough to know that he needs to access the program.

A few colleges specialize in educating students with learning disabilities. Others offer comprehensive support systems with trained, experienced staff and many specialized services for students with ADHD. Most offer limited specialized services and accommodations for students with ADHD, while some provide only a single learning center serving all students with disabilities and students who need temporary tutoring. *The quality of support services offered by a college or university may outweigh considerations and preferences in other areas.* Family discussions, for example, may conclude that a large or geographically distant university may work as a first choice if its support services are stronger than those of a college closer to home.

College Support Services and Accommodations

Before choosing an appropriate college, your teenager will need to consider—ideally with you and her guidance counselor, teachers, pediatrician or other health care professional, or psychologist—which services or accommodations may be needed to succeed as an undergraduate. Services and accommodations for college students with attention-deficit/hyperactivity disorder (ADHD) may include

- **Special orientation programs** to introduce students to the institution's academic structure and available services
- **Specialized academic advisors or counselors** to help students identify the classes, professors, class load, and even the major best suited to their interests and needs
- **Priority scheduling** to allow students to sign up for the most appropriate classes at the most appropriate times of day
- **Reduced course loads,** which prevents students with ADHD from becoming overwhelmed (A reduced course load may mean that the student will have to make up credits during summer school or a fifth year.)
- **A private dormitory room** for students who may find the presence of a roommate too distracting or disruptive
- **Math laboratories, writing workshops, computer laboratories, and reading courses** to supplement and improve basic academic skills
- **Specialized tutoring** for students with ADHD, emphasizing organizational and planning skills and effective study techniques, as well as help with specific coursework and examination preparation
- **A "personal coach"** to check in with the student each day, reviewing the daily schedule and the work expected to be accomplished
- **Classroom technology,** such as laptop computers and other recording aids, to facilitate students' ability to retain and review the information in classroom lectures
- **Academic aides,** including in-class note-takers and homework editors
- **Special testing arrangements,** such as untimed examinations or testing in a separate, quiet room

- **Advocates** to help communicate a student's diagnosis and needs to professors when appropriate and to help obtain needed services
- **Support groups** or contact with other students with ADHD who can provide companionship, emotional support, and information
- **Career guidance and mentoring** for students with ADHD

Once your son or daughter has identified the services that are high priority, the search can begin for colleges and universities that provide those services. Support services are not always described in college catalogs and brochures, so you and he may need to do some extra research to find out exactly what is available at each institution. The first step for your daughter is to call or visit the special services office of each institution being considered, to determine which services may be available at that college or university. He may wish that you join him for this visit. The actual name of the services office tends to vary by institution. It may be listed as "student disability services," "learning support services," or something similar. Early contact and familiarization with the student support office is important because this office is most often responsible for notifying professors about any classroom accommodations to which a student is entitled. Once enrolled at the college, students must register with the office and provide documentation of their disability to receive special services.

Some students, however, may choose to start college without ever disclosing their ADHD diagnosis, or they may decide to disclose it to the special services office only when they feel they would benefit from the types of services described previously. The choice of whether and when to disclose this information is highly individual but deserves thought and discussion as your adolescent begins his college search. There is certainly no right or wrong approach, but students with obvious and ongoing support needs in high school might strongly consider exploring support services at the time that they begin thinking about college.

Following is a list of general questions that your son may want to present to the representative of each college's special services office. Of course, the questions will need to be tailored to apply to your student's particular anticipated needs. More helpful information may be obtained by also providing the representative with a list of the accommodations or services being requested along with documentation supporting the diagnosis of ADHD and the need for particular aids. Here are some great questions.

- What services or accommodations does the university or college routinely provide for students with ADHD? For example, are specialized academic advising, early registration, a private dormitory room, untimed testing, or any of the other services listed previously provided? Is there an extra charge for any of these services? If the college does not provide them, are they conveniently available off campus?

- How long has the support services office existed? How many, if any, staff members are specially trained to work with students who have ADHD?

- How many students with ADHD does the office serve?

- Does the university provide other services for all students that may especially benefit students with ADHD, such as web-based services that provide lecture notes or videos online, small seminars to review material covered in classroom lectures, and a willingness to work with new instructional techniques or technology?

- Are academic counselors or therapists available on an ongoing basis to help students with ADHD adjust to college life and help with any problems that arise?

- Do counselors help connect students with faculty members who are knowledgeable and supportive regarding the needs of students with ADHD? Is there a program in place to educate faculty members about ADHD?

- Do support groups for students with ADHD exist on campus? Can the office provide your teen with the names of other students with ADHD who are willing to be contacted?

- Does the college track how many students with ADHD graduate?

Another consideration is that some youth with ADHD are slower to mature than others, so that starting at a local community college with your teen living at home may provide a more gradual opportunity to adjust to the college environment. Then, in a year or two, he may be better able to adjust to the challenges of attending college away from home. On the other hand, some students who have started college may find a need to return to the family nest. Your teen might let you know that he is struggling to develop the life-management skills that independent living requires, particularly in the context of the freedom of college. These are options to consider that may provide your teen the opportunity to further build his skills as well as his self-esteem. In the future, he can be in a better position to reenter and be more successful in college academic and social life.

How to Apply

Once your adolescent has created a short list of colleges that best suit his individual interests and needs, the application process can begin.

Most colleges and universities require applicants to take the SAT or ACT examination, although a newer trend is for some colleges to not require this testing. A student with ADHD can apply to take these tests under extended time conditions or with other special accommodations. To do this, a written diagnosis of the condition signed by a qualified, appropriate professional must be presented. The diagnosis must have been confirmed or updated within the past 3 years, and evidence of early impairment, current impairment, and specific problems may also be required. In addition, a copy of the student's IEP or Section 504 plan will be needed as proof that testing accommodations at school are similar to those being requested. Because further documentation and possibly testing by a psychologist may be required, and specific dates are reserved for special testing, your family should view the website of The College Board (https://www.collegeboard.org), the organization that administers the SAT, before registering to take either test.

Your family should not have to be concerned that revealing your adolescent's ADHD diagnosis will negatively affect his chances for admission. The Americans With Disabilities Act bars discrimination against students with disabilities in the college application process, and admissions committees cannot legally discriminate against students with ADHD. *Having a diagnosis of ADHD is much less important than a student's demonstrated ability to manage schoolwork sufficiently to meet the school's academic standards.* If your child believes his high school academic record does not accurately represent his potential, a personal interview with a college admissions officer can provide a key format for discussing the reasons for past difficulties and plans for addressing them in the future. Meanwhile, an open attitude toward his strengths and academic successes, as well as his academic weaknesses and support needs, may help him start his new life with a healthy attitude and an opportunity for greater success.

A student's acceptance into a college or university is an important landmark in the challenging process of transitioning from adolescence to independent adult life. To help smooth the way, some colleges offer summer programs prior to the beginning of freshman year. These programs can be especially helpful for students with ADHD. Your adolescent can further prepare for his freshman year by exploring his future college's library facilities, social opportunities, academic services, and other offerings. He might also contact his future roommate or talk with older students who can explain more about the school. Talking with you and older siblings or family members about the challenges and joys likely to be encountered the next school year is certainly important as well.

Your College Student's Rights

Attention-deficit/hyperactivity disorder (ADHD), when it substantially limits a major life activity (eg, learning), is legally categorized as a disability under Section 504 of the Rehabilitation Act of 1973 and the Americans With Disabilities Act (ADA). Section 504, which applies to all colleges that receive federal funds (all public and most private colleges do), prohibits discrimination against students with this type of disability and requires colleges to provide the academic accommodations and services necessary to make courses, examinations, and activities accessible to these students.

The ADA provisions apply generally to public and private colleges, whether or not they receive federal funds. This act prohibits discrimination against otherwise qualified students with ADHD-related problems that substantially limit their learning and requires those students to be provided with reasonable accommodations.

A student with ADHD may or may not choose to disclose his diagnosis when applying to college. If he does not want special accommodations during the SAT, ACT, or other testing, or during other aspects of the application process, he may decide to disclose his disability only after admission. Disclosure after admission, and registration with the college's special services office, is necessary to receive services and accommodations to meet his ADHD-related needs.

Adjusting to College Life

Social Life

From move-in day to the college dormitory room, a student with ADHD will be confronted with an array of choices that can challenge any freshman. A most immediate concern may involve finding his place socially. In some cases, the effort to fit in at social gatherings and to form new friendships may lead to misuse of alcohol or drugs. This is now a risk for every student. However, students with ADHD may be more likely to use drugs and alcohol impulsively or to consider using marijuana or substances to ease their social discomfort, or "numb" their ADHD-related symptoms. Marijuana use has been associated with short-term memory loss, a particular concern to anyone with an attention problem. It is important to note that the use of stimulant medication as prescribed should not increase the risk of drug and alcohol misuse and may, in fact, diminish it, as it helps to decrease impulsive behavior.

Before leaving for college, it can help to have a frank discussion about the high risk of alcohol or drug misuse and its consequences. Acknowledge the fact that growing up involves a great deal of experimentation and that the temptation to go along with what others are doing will be great. At the same time, lack of sleep, poor diet, prolonged social media use and gaming, and constant partying can throw any student off-balance. Self-care of ADHD requires rest, regular exercise, and a reasonable diet, as well as attending to studies. Poor self-care intensifies any anxiety or other ADHD-related vulnerabilities, so your student may be tempted to "self-medicate" with alcohol or drugs.

Certainly, everyone makes mistakes during the difficult transition from adolescence to adulthood. The important thing for students is to maintain awareness of how well they are doing in all areas of functioning and to get help early if they find themselves in trouble. This is not the time to take a wait-and-see approach or to try to solve such problems on their own.

If a student will be taking medication or will need to make use of counseling services, it may be necessary to get a referral to an appropriate physician or psychologist in or out of the student health service before classes begin. It helps to have the names, phone numbers, and email addresses of key personnel in an appropriate place. Email encryption should be used, if available, to increase privacy.

If your teen is taking medication for ADHD or other mental health conditions, he should bring a letter from the treating physician stating the diagnosis and treatment prescribed. Transferring refills of these medications to someone on or near campus to facilitate the process of obtaining refills may be convenient but is generally difficult to arrange. If the need arises for treatment of other issues, the sooner your teen seeks help from a psychologist, counselor, residential advisor, or other university support person with whom he has familiarized himself when applying to the school, the sooner he can maintain control over his life and the fewer academic, social, and emotional setbacks will be experienced.

Medication Diversion

Discuss strategies to discourage misuse of prescription drugs. Some colleges require students to sign contracts stating they will not misuse pills or share them with classmates. Students prescribed controlled substances need a secure way to store them, such as a medicine cabinet lockbox, so they will not be stolen. Some students will appropriately choose to keep their ADHD medication use a secret from peers, to avoid classmates begging, offering to purchase, or stealing stimulants. Review what steps your teen will take to safeguard his medications. If your teen is on stimulant medication, he is going to need a local prescribing physician if his college is out of state. It may be worthwhile to try switching from a stimulant medication to a non-stimulant medication. Non-stimulant medications are not controlled medications and, therefore, have less restrictions.

Emotional Changes

Some students with ADHD welcome college life as a chance to "start over" in a place where no one knows that they have any special needs. However, if they neglect to carefully plan for and follow through with their study time, fail to take their medication, or do not attend counseling sessions, problems that they may have been able to overcome in high school may start to resurface or increase. This experience can be extremely demoralizing to a young adult just beginning an independent life. The college students most able to avoid these setbacks are those who consciously plan to balance their activities, study habits, sleep patterns, and social lives and limit their drug and alcohol use within the framework imposed by their ADHD-related needs and limitations. Obtaining support in this area, such as joining a college support group for students with ADHD, may help them with this type of healthy self-monitoring and encourage them in their efforts to integrate ADHD interventions into their adult life. However, for many students with ADHD this approach may not be enough, and they may need to seek out support services to ensure success.

Academic Concerns

While social and emotional concerns may take center stage when a college freshman first arrives on campus, academic issues may soon follow. Well-prepared students arrive at college with a good idea of their academic strengths and weaknesses and some tested strategies for dealing with them. If they have already presented the documentation necessary to register with the college's special services office, they will have had the opportunity to learn about available services and accommodations and meet members of the services staff. Through early registration, online research, appointments with professors, and conversations with older students, a student with ADHD can start to learn which professors and classes may be most appropriate for him. Some college students with ADHD have trouble advocating for themselves (eg, requesting early registration, asking a professor to allow them to take tests untimed or in a private room if that has proved helpful in the past, getting permission to use assistive technology or a support person or aide to take notes in class). Counselors in the special services office are usually available to help students obtain the services or accommodations they need. It is important to request such modifications in advance, rather than expecting a professor to agree to an accommodation on the day of the test or lecture.

College students with ADHD may find it useful to arrange for a "personal coach" (see Chapter 7) who serves as a daily monitor—someone who is available for brief daily check-ins, asks what the most important tasks are for that day and what the specific plans are to accomplish them, and provides positive feedback and support for working toward those goals. While such coaches can help younger children with ADHD learn healthy habits of self-awareness and self-monitoring, they can be especially useful in helping college students bridge the gap between parental monitoring and full independence. Some special service offices at colleges and universities are beginning to provide such coaches, or references to off-campus coaching services, to students with ADHD. There is almost always an extra charge for this service. However, for a student who is struggling to stay on track while adjusting to college life, a "coach" can make a critical difference.

Again, your child should be strongly encouraged and reminded to seek help early if problems are encountered with schoolwork, testing, or other academic issues. (See Chapter 11 for academic strategies that may improve college performance.) In addition, academic and special supports available on campus are likely to include a freshman orientation, freshman experience course, residential advisor, freshman advisor, tutoring network, writing center, computer laboratory, counseling center, career counselor, health center, and fitness center. All these services are paid for as part of the tuition, so they are readily available—and the sooner and more frequently your student takes full advantage of them, the more on-track and successful the college experience is likely to be.

Employment and the Workplace

People with ADHD can have successful and fulfilling work experiences, and those who are especially successful have learned to make adjustments for or "work around" their attention differences. Life in the workplace is an important adjustment for a young adult with ADHD. Arriving at work on time may be more stressful than expected, as well as managing paperwork or other detail-oriented work, attending frequent meetings, meeting deadlines, and otherwise conforming to what can often be a noisy, stressful, and, in some cases, physically inactive environment. Not only is your young adult exposed to the same social and emotional pressures as his peers on college campuses, but he must also perform in a work environment that typically provides few or no supportive services and where no one may know he has ADHD. As a group, adults with ADHD often switch jobs and earn less money than their colleagues.

Young adults with ADHD will be more likely to start off on the right foot by spending time during high school considering what types of jobs might best suit someone with their particular interests, strengths, and weaknesses. Working to develop time-management and self-care skills are important. Career counseling services are often available through the high school guidance office and may be mandated under IDEA. Any job can be made more "ADHD friendly" if the employee with ADHD knows how to alter the environment to better suit his individual needs and to advocate effectively for appropriate accommodations.

Coping With the Workplace

A teenager or young adult with ADHD who joins the workforce but finds a job too difficult can be encouraged to get help in analyzing where the job-related challenges lie. Is he overwhelmed by paperwork? Does he get in trouble for arriving late on too many days? Does he put off tasks and, thus, fail to complete them? Does he forget his employer's instructions? Does he find it impossible to concentrate with all the noise around him? Is it hard for him to get along with coworkers or his boss?

Once he has identified his problem areas, he can brainstorm on his own or with coworkers, a job coach who has knowledge and training in ADHD, a counselor or a psychologist, a family member, or members of the treatment team about ways to address them. He may decide to use a daily planner or computer software to manage daily tasks and appointments. A watch with alarms or a timer can help to keep track of work arrival time or deadlines, and any number of apps can be used to record tasks to be accomplished. It may be helpful to carpool with a coworker to help get to work on time. Taking regular, brief "exercise breaks" helps work off excess energy and has been shown to increase the ability to focus. Remember, there is no one-size-fits-all approach to these problems. Suggestions that work for one person with ADHD may not work for someone else. Each brain is unique!

Asking an Employer for Help

If these self-help techniques prove insufficient for your young adult with ADHD, he should consider asking employers or managers about accommodations that could help to increase work performance. To do so, he must feel comfortable and safe disclosing some of the functional issues related to his ADHD. If the workplace has a human resources office, this might be a good starting point. Many, if not most, employers will welcome the opportunity to help an employee be more efficient and effective in the workplace. Good business practice dictates supporting employees to do their best work.

Accommodations might include a less distracting office or workspace, a daily review each morning of work to be done, help with breaking complex jobs into smaller tasks, or even flextime or a transfer from a heavily detail-oriented, time-pressured job to one that better matches his strengths. It may be difficult to work up the courage to ask for such help at first, but chances are that the employer will make a real effort to be helpful. Challenges at work may have puzzled or displeased his supervisor if she did not previously understand the source of her employee's difficulty, and she will probably appreciate and respect her employee's effort to improve his performance. As is the case in any aspect of life, people are likely to meet with greater success on the job when encouraged to focus on their strengths rather than their weaknesses.

Adults with ADHD are often among the most creative, imaginative, energetic members of society. Empowerment, self-esteem, and the ability to effectively be a self-advocate in any present or future job comes from understanding how ADHD affects work. The more successfully people can understand and communicate to their employer their talents and strengths, as well as their needs, the harder their employer may work to help them. It is important to remember, however, that ADHD symptoms are not an excuse but an explanation of why difficulty is being experienced.

As was pointed out earlier in this chapter, an adolescent may be entitled to continue counseling services and assessment under an IDEA-mandated Individualized Written Rehabilitation Plan. If this is not the case, however, he will need to be extra-vigilant about any ADHD-related concerns that are beginning to get out of hand, because routine accommodations are rarely provided by an employer. Make sure that your young adult has the names and phone numbers of physicians, job counselors, therapists, and other community resources who can help with a variety of potential difficulties. The most helpful parent may include providing nonjudgmental help or "reality checks" if you are approached about these issues. Parents should remember that their role is not to enable or provide excuses but, rather, to empower their adult child.

If the employer offers a health insurance plan, it is important to review its coverages, along with other job-related benefits, to learn what counseling or other support services can be obtained. It may also be beneficial to consider using a credentialed ADHD coach to help with some of the transitions from adolescence to adult life. A thorough understanding of an individual's ADHD-related strengths and weaknesses, coupled with a determination to monitor and manage the symptoms, is the best way for your growing adolescent to join the ranks of other young adults with ADHD who enjoy stimulating, fulfilling, and successful careers.

Health and Safety

A growing number of studies have shown that adults with ADHD may be at greater risk for health- and safety-related problems than their peers without ADHD. Their greater risk-taking behaviors and frequently erratic driving practices, such as an inability to follow driving rules or inconsistent operations of a vehicle, increase the chances of injuries. During adolescence and young adulthood, their impulsivity may lead to more unprotected sex with a greater number of partners than those without ADHD and, therefore, a greater risk for acquired sexually transmitted infections.

It is important that your child be informed as early as the preteen and early teen years about these areas of increased risk. A healthy and proactive stance for young adults with ADHD includes monitoring their risk-taking behaviors closely. In general, the more fully your child understands that his health and safety are his own responsibility and that monitoring his risk-taking behavior will always be an important part of his life, the better prepared he will be to meet these challenges. Switching to long-acting stimulant preparations or making sure symptoms are under control when driving or well into the evening hours may also help with critical decision-making and problem-solving skills affected by uncontrolled ADHD symptoms.

A Brief Look Forward: Adults With ADHD

While adulthood has its challenges for all of us, it can be particularly challenging for individuals with ADHD. Their ADHD-related symptoms, such as impulsiveness, inattention, and lack of organization, can interfere with their family functioning. It can make long-term personal relationships and parenting more challenging. Frequent job challenges and the highs and lows of entrepreneurial life can also take their toll on family life. However, there are many adults with ADHD who have been able to overcome these challenges, in part through the efforts and help that their parents provided as they grew up. Every family's and health care professional's goal is that when your child with ADHD reaches adulthood, he will find increasing success in family life and parenting. Your careful evaluation, treatment, and monitoring throughout childhood and adolescence teaches sound principles of behavior management as adults.

Just like in academic life and on the job, a gentle, direct, and straightforward approach is often best when trying to minimize any effects of ADHD on personal relationships. Partners of an adult with ADHD are far more likely to accept and try to work around the lack of attention to their feelings and ideas if they understand where these concerns are coming from in the context of ADHD.

Some common complaints of family members—that the person with ADHD is selfish, unperceptive, disorganized, and forgetful and takes too many risks—are all aspects of ADHD, and not a personality defect or an indication that he does not love them. Efforts to communicate this fully to his partner and, later, to his children can go a long way toward putting his family life on the right track. A counselor or family therapist may be especially helpful with this important task. Once the entire family understands how ADHD can affect behavior and influence personal interactions, they can begin to identify problem areas in their daily lives and experiment with the best ways to address them. Loving family members come to understand that the parent's or spouse's inattention or impulsiveness is not his "fault" and that they can often help. Typical relationship-enhancing approaches include

- **Understanding the need for structure.** Because adults with ADHD often lack structure in their inner lives, they may need more external structure if they are to function well. Partners of adults with ADHD often find that life goes more smoothly when family members routinely make lists of tasks to be done, maintain a family calendar to which everyone can refer, clarify which family member is responsible for which chores, and remind the person with ADHD, if necessary, of time constraints.

- **Breaking down tasks into manageable steps.** It may be possible to get through a mortgage application together or to plan a daughter's wedding without major setbacks—when partners agree to take it one step at a time.

- **Playing to each other's strengths.** If one partner is a more organized bill payer and the other can commit to driving the kids to their after-school activities, there is no reason why these tasks cannot be divided in the most acceptable and effective way. Taking on too much responsibility for daily chores is a major complaint of partners of adults with ADHD, so it is important to make sure that, even if the adult with ADHD is better off not being assigned deadline-oriented duties, he makes up for it by taking on other chores that are viewed by his partner as having an equal payoff value.

- **Learning how to communicate effectively.** Despite the best efforts by an adult with ADHD, ADHD-related behaviors can still cause resentment in family members. Rather than expressing anger in nonproductive ways or risk intensifying the resentment by trying to talk about the issue with an inattentive partner, it may be better to agree ahead of time on a more effective way to communicate. This may be over the phone, via email, or by using a timer to ensure that each person has a chance to speak. In times of major conflict, agreeing to take a time-out allows each partner to cool off and can be very effective. Families might also seek the help of a family or couples therapist who has knowledge and experience with ADHD behaviors.

- **Maintaining realistic expectations.** Just as all adults have areas of strength and weakness, some adults with ADHD may never be able to handle the family's finances as well as their partner. If their partner is also unwilling or unable to take over responsibilities, it may be better to hire outside help than to blame a partner for his inadequacies.

- **Understanding that relationships are a 2-way street.** Couples and families need to take care that the entire burden to solve ADHD-related problems is not placed on the person with ADHD. Just as adults with ADHD must work to manage personal challenges with organization or impulse control, their partners should try to support and facilitate those efforts. Mutual respect will help motivate all family members to continue doing their best.

- **Celebrating the joys of the partnership.** Adults with ADHD typically bring a great jolt of energy, spontaneity, inspiration, and excitement to marriage and family life. Couples should remember to take breaks from problem-solving to remember why they got together in the first place, and to appreciate what they have accomplished together and who they have become.

Specific techniques for addressing problems as they arise can be adapted from the earlier education and treatment experiences of the adult with ADHD, or both partners may be able to create new ones together and on their own.

Successful Arrival at Young Adulthood

Adults with ADHD are much more likely to enjoy successful and satisfying lives if they are helped during their childhood and adolescence to learn to monitor and manage their symptoms on their own. Throughout this book, you have been encouraged as a parent to give your child the gift of *self-empowerment*—to include your child in the process of understanding his symptoms, all decisions relating to his evaluation and treatment, discussions of the ways in which ADHD is affecting and may later affect his daily life, and planning for his future as a student, a family member, and a productive member of the adult world. By parenting to your child's strengths, continually building his knowledge base, taking care to applaud his efforts, and otherwise nurturing his self-esteem through childhood and adolescence, you have taught your child to think of himself not as an "ADHD adult" but as an "adult who has ADHD."

Now as your adolescent enters adulthood, armed with the knowledge, experience, and practiced ability to manage his ADHD-related symptoms, the benefit will be an independent life in a stronger position than that of previous generations. Of course, every young adult with ADHD is different, and no individual outcome can be predicted. But by incorporating the guidelines presented in this book and empowering your child to use this information as you watch him transition from childhood, through adolescence, to young adulthood, you will have helped your child take advantage of his unique strengths and take charge of his vulnerabilities as he begins adult life.

Index